Pawnee Bill

Pawnee Bill

A BIOGRAPHY OF MAJOR GORDON W. LILLIE

by Glenn Shirley

UNIVERSITY OF NEW MEXICO PRESS, ALBUQUERQUE, 1958

COMPOSED, PRINTED AND BOUND
AT THE UNIVERSITY OF NEW MEXICO PRINTING PLANT
ALBUQUERQUE, NEW MEXICO, U. S. A.
Library of Congress Catalog Card No. 58-6870

TO HIS SISTERS — LENA AND EFFIE

Contents

TEXT ILLUSTRATIONS

HALFTONE ILLUSTRATIONS

Following page 72

Foreword

MAJOR GORDON W. LILLIE—"Pawnee Bill" to thousands of
Americans—was the last of the hardy band of heroes in buckskin
who opened up the West. A son of Illinois, he early was attracted
by the free outdoor life of the great Western plains and, before he
came of age, he had joined other famous characters of the time in
various enterprises, including the lucrative business of shooting
buffalo for their hides and trapping the varied and plentiful fur-
bearing animals whose skins brought fancy prices in the Eastern
markets and in London.

Widely known as a showman, a teacher and friend of the Indian
and finally as a colonizer in Oklahoma and builder of his state, he
toured the country and the world, first alone, then in partnership
with Colonel William F. (Buffalo Bill) Cody, with a Wild West
show that had no equal. Its wild Indians were terrifying, its horsemen were death-defying, and not the least of its attractions was
Pawnee Bill, wearing long, flowing hair and buckskin, who, from
horseback, plugged glass balls in mid-air with six-shooter and
Winchester.

A successful businessman with a keen sense of values, he was able
to retire at an early age on his large ranch near Pawnee as a bank
vice-president, with heavy investments in cattle, real estate and oil.
But his genuine sentimental attachment to the day of the buffalo
and the roaming Indian disrupted any dreams he had of living out
his years in leisure and peaceful contemplation.

He fought to save the American bison from extinction and maintained what is said to have been the largest privately owned herd
in America. He surrounded himself with priceless Indian relics and
souvenirs of the vigorous life of which he was an integral part, and
served as a sort of oracle to the many historians of the period who

journeyed to Blue Hawk Peak, his spacious ranch house overlooking the scene of many of his early adventures.

He built highways half across the United States, served as envoy to Old Mexico, became active in national politics and chaperoned a tribe of Indians to the nation's capital to take part in the inaugural ceremony when Senator Charles Curtis, himself an Indian, was made Vice-President. Though he hob-nobbed with millionaires and men of affairs, he was never at home in a tuxedo. The only time he ever bowed to the conventions was on the opening night of the "Two Bills" show in Madison Square Garden. That night he wore a long-tailed coat with a boiled shirt and standup collar, but a pair of brilliantly shined cowboy boots adorned his feet and a wide-brimmed hat took the place of the shiny tile. And New York society liked it.

He lived, in his eighty-two years, a life not only colorful but of material aid in the development of the West. His was a story book existence come true, and he will long remain a small boy's hero in fact and legend.

GLENN SHIRLEY

Stillwater, Oklahoma

Acknowledgments

WHILE much of the material for this work came from the author's private collection, I wish to express my sincere thanks to the staffs of the Kansas State Historical Society, Topeka, and the Oklahoma State Historical Society, Oklahoma City, for assisting me in locating certain old records and giving me entry to certain collections containing material on Major Gordon W. Lillie.

My especial appreciation goes to the staff of the Division of Manuscripts, University of Oklahoma Library, Norman, Oklahoma, for their generosity in granting me full use of the Gordon W. Lillie Collection, and permission to reproduce many of the photographs used to illustrate this volume.

Further, the life of Major Gordon W. Lillie, as presented in this book, is officially endorsed by Mr. Allan Rock, by special arrangement of the author with Mr. Rock, founder of The Pawnee Bill Archives in New York City, to whom Major Lillie personally presented firsthand his complete biography with all property rights for its use, including all commercial rights to the name "Pawnee Bill."

THE AUTHOR.

1.

Call of the Frontier

GORDON WILLIAM LILLIE always credited the exploits of William F. (Buffalo Bill) Cody as the chief reason for his early wanderings and exciting experiences on the Western frontier.

He often said:

> When I was a small boy, my mother would read stories of him in *The Saturday Magazine,* a publication similar to the *Saturday Evening Post* of today. As I grew older, Ned Buntline (E. Z. C. Judson) became my favorite author.

Buntline's stories of adventure in the Seminole, Mexican and Civil wars, and later, of the Western plainsman whose life seemed made up of one thrilling escapade after another, made life in the rural Illinois town of Bloomington, where Gordon was born the first of four children on February 14, 1860, seem unbearably monotonous:

> Everybody had the itch to go West in those days, and I was no exception.

In 1860 Illinois was still considered a Western state. It had been a member of the Union only forty-two years. Less than thirty years before, the Black Hawk War had broken out, resulting in several massacres and the removal of the Sac and Fox tribes into Iowa and Nebraska. Hostility to the Mormons had led to the mob slaying of the founders, Hiram and Joseph Smith, in 1844, and the subsequent emigration of the sect to Utah. In 1847, a new constitution had been framed, but the final one of 1870 was yet to be written.

Bloomington was the seat of McLean County, on three important railroads, a little more than a hundred miles southeast of Chicago. Despite its population of 15,000 and its rapid growth as a center of coal-mining, pork-packing, vegetable canning, flour-milling, as well as harness, agricultural machinery, furnace stone and brick manufacturing, Bloomington was still thought of as a Western city.

A remnant of the Oldtown Indians lived only twenty miles from Bloomington. Each fall Gordon, his younger brother Albert, and two sisters, Effie and Paulina, would make a trip to the Indian reservation to pick wild blackberries, which grew there in abundance. They would build a campfire over which Mrs. Lillie cooked their food. They made their beds on the ground under a huge oak tree, and Gordon would stare through the branches at the twinkling stars. It reminded him of the wondrous tales that his cousins, the Evans boys, told him.

The Evans boys—George, Oscar and Ira—had settled in newly organized Sumner County, in south-central Kansas, bordering the Indian Territory. From them came intriguing stories of great buffalo herds and semi-wild Indians dressed in buckskin, beads, and bright-colored blankets, who carried tomahawks and bows and arrows. They were nothing like the Oldtown Indians, who dressed in overalls and eked out a miserable existence.

They told Gordon of the wide open spaces and long distances, where you could travel all day without seeing any sign of human habitation; where the freight was hauled by long strings of oxen driven by a long-haired, long-whiskered, whip-throwing "bullwhacker"; where springs of pure sparkling water flowed out of the mountains, through the foothills and across the plains into the Arkansas, Canadian and Cimarron, winding southeastward into the great vacuum to the south—the Cherokee Outlet, a vast no man's land of luxuriant grasses that made it a mecca for every species of wild game and fowl migrating north in the summer and south in the winter.

In one season they had seen countless millions of buffalo, some of the herds so large as to halt army convoys for days until they passed, covering the earth from viewpoint to horizon. On a single trip by wagon down the Chikaskia they had killed seven deer, fifty

wild turkeys, dozens of prairie chickens and quail, and one mountain lion.

In the late summer of 1869, Ned Buntline had sought out Buffalo Bill on the plains of Nebraska. The fight at Summit Springs,
in which a band of Sioux and Cheyenne under Chief Tall Bull had
been pursued and routed by General Eugene A. Carr of the Fifth
Cavalry, aided by Major Frank North and his Pawnee Scouts, filled
the newspapers, and Buntline was eager to put the hero of this
battle in his next novel.

Major North and his brother, Luther, with their Pawnees and
some United States troops, had come upon their quarry lolling in
the shade of their tepees in the hot July afternoon. The village was
captured in the charge, and many of the hostiles killed. Others fled,
or concealed themselves in ravines that seamed the prairie. The
Pawnees were spread out in little parties, killing them where they
were concealed, when Major North and his brother came riding
out from the Indian village. They had approached within fifty yards
of a steep-walled ravine when an Indian raised his head above the
bank and fired. Frank fell from the saddle as if hit. He ordered
Luther to gallop away with the two horses. As he had anticipated,
the hidden Indian peeped over the bank again to see if he had
killed the rider. Frank drew bead and fired. Then he quickly re-
loaded and ordered his brother to bring up the horses. When they
reached the ravine, Tall Bull lay dead with his warriors.

When Buntline approached the Major for an interview, North
made it plain that he had no use for writers and a lot less desire to
become a dime novel hero, and referred him to young William F.
Cody, who was asleep under a wagon. Cody knew all the details,
Frank North said, and Buntline found the young scout very co-
operative. He spent the next few weeks on the Platte with Cody,
and in December, 1869, Street and Smith advertised a new serial in
their *New York Weekly* entitled "Buffalo Bill, the King of the Border Men—The Wildest and Truest Story I Ever Wrote."

And at the age of ten, Gordon Lillie gasped at the first full account of how Cody himself had slain Tall Bull, gallantly riding
into the jaws of death at the head of a charge that wiped out the
entire camp just as the renegade chief was raising his tomahawk to
strike down the white heroine held captive by the Sioux.

As weeks passed, other adventures of Cody came to young Lillie in installments, describing his horse "Powder Face," his associate "Wild Bill Hitchcock" (Hickok) and the "M'Kandlas" (McCanles) gang he had slain single-handed in a knife and gun battle in a stage station at Rock Creek, Nebraska. Fictitious heroines and numerous other characters shared in Buffalo Bill's hairbreadth escapes, while Buntline wrote for his ever-widening circle of readers.

These exploits and the adventures of the Evans boys fired Gordon's imagination to the wildest fancies, tempered only by the encouragement of his Irish mother to prepare himself for a good position before going out in the world. Susan Ann Conant Lillie, a favorite child of the noted Boston banking family, was well-educated and intelligent. She was always deeply concerned about the education of her children. She wanted Gordon to become a teacher. It is noted that he was not an exceptional student, but he showed plenty of grit and energy, and never appeared in his classes that he was not fully prepared to answer any question or tackle any problem placed before him, though he burned much midnight oil to do it.

His father, who had been born in Three Rivers, Quebec, was of Scottish parentage and a true pioneer in every sense of the word, and part of Gordon's heritage was the Scotchman's stubborn fearlessness, characterized by caution rather than recklessness or truculence. Newton Wesley Lillie had migrated to Bloomington from Canada, working a while for the city. He operated a flour mill, was well-respected and considered prosperous.

Gordon said, years later:

> Teaching school was all right with father. But he already owned the town's largest steam mill. He would expand, and one day I would succeed to the business. By the time I was thirteen, I was working in the mill of evenings and Saturdays, earning my first money and learning the business from the ground up.

Though small in physique, Gordon had developed an amazing strength for a youngster his age, and a proficiency in all outdoor and athletic sports. The intense energy and relentless determination displayed in all his activities and interests of childhood and youth were to characterize him in later years.

There was enough work in the mill and enough home school work to make the yarns in Street and Smith's *New York Weekly*, Beadle and Adams, and other favorites of the day, holiday relaxation. Gordon recalled:

I read them in the bins at my father's mill, or sprawled in the shade of the trees and Soldiers' Monument in Franklin Park.

It is doubtful that young Lillie could have escaped his "attack of Western fever" even if those old pirated editions of Buntline's and other authors had never reached Illinois. By his later admissions, he aspired not to emulate any of the characters nor, like Major North, himself become the subject of a paperback novel. Rather these tales of the Far West inspired his fanciful dreams of easily gotten wealth in this unknown land and it was in quest of that rather than a bloodthirsty desire to scalp Indians that gave impetus to everything he did. Working in the mill, mastering high school to become a teacher—both offered means of earning money, an accumulation of which was the first step in freeing himself from the narrow confines of Illinois.

He neglected no opportunity to be around when the Evans boys would "pay a visit to the home folks back East," to hear their thrilling tales of Indians and cowboys and hunting wild game and buffalo.

When he had enough money and got a little older, he told them, he would join them in the West. On one visit, they offered to take Gordon back to Kansas, but his parents "spiked the idea at once." They got him a job teaching school the next fall and winter, and in the spring and summer he kept books at the mill.

Gordon was only delayed, not halted. He saved his money, determined to go West eventually.

Meanwhile, Buffalo Bill's fame had spread. He had escorted James Gordon Bennett of the New York *Herald* and his party of wealthy friends on a lavish Western expedition as guests of General Phil Sheridan, where he taught them to shoot buffalo from the back

of a racing pony and that the delightful Western custom of taking a
shot of bourbon before breakfast was "more refreshing than brush-
ing the teeth." In the fall of 1871, he guided the Grand Duke Alexis
of Russia and his royal party, who were touring the United States,
on a camping trip and buffalo hunt, for which the Grand Duke
rewarded him with a Russian fur coat, a set of jeweled cuff links
and studs. Wearing these, and with $500 sent him by Bennett, Cody
headed for New York.

His serial by Buntline in the New York *Weekly* had been rewrit-
ten as a play by Fred Meador, and Cody witnessed its first successful
run, with his counterpart, in an imitation buckskin shirt, drawing
loud applause. The drama was simple, full of action, blood and
thunder, and easily understood.

Acting looked easy. Buntline convinced Cody they could make
more money and achieve even greater popularity if he played his
own part, and on December 16, 1872, Buntline and Cody, with an
ex-scout from Jeb Stuart's Confederate cavalry, "Texas Jack"
Omohundro, opened at the amphitheatre in Chicago with their
stage play "The Scouts of the Plains." Box office receipts disclosed
the show's real popularity, and they moved to St. Louis for their
next performance in the Grand Opera House on December 23.

The audience cheered. The "utter absence of anything like stage
art" convinced them they were seeing real scouts, not play actors.
Huge crowds appeared in Cincinnati at Pike's Opera House, at
Albany and Boston. In New York City, to the consternation of serious drama critics, their show drew "the only satisfactory receipts of
the week," while back in Bloomington, young Gordon Lillie avidly
devoured the contents of Buntline's new novels: "Buffalo Bill's
Last Victory; or Dove Eye, the Lodge Queen"; "Dashing Charlie,
the Texas Whirlwind"; "Buffalo Bill's Best Shot; or the Heart of
Spotted Tail"; and "Texas Jack, the White King of the Pawnees."

In May, the Scouts moved to Philadelphia. At Harrisburg, they
disbanded for the summer. The show had grossed $200,000 of which
Buffalo Bill received only $6000 for his share. He and Texas Jack
decided to continue the show without Ned. They employed Wild
Bill Hickok, a genuine gunman, to take Ned's place the next season,
and this brought about the next event which prepared Gordon for
departure:

One day after school, I went on an errand in downtown Bloomington. As I passed along Main Street looking west, I saw a large crowd in front of the St. Nicholas Hotel, which was then the best and most popular hotel in town.

Thinking it was a fight, boylike, I hurried to the spot as fast as I could run. But the thrill I got was the greatest I ever had in my life, for there in the center of this immense crowd sat three frontiersmen, clad in big sombreroes, with long hair falling to their shoulders and wearing buffalo robe coats.

They were relating their experiences of the plains to each other. These men were Buffalo Bill, Wild Bill and Texas Jack Omohundro. They appeared that night at Schroeder's Opera House in a play called "The Scouts of the Plains."

When Gordon left the show that night, he knew that he had to escape from the routine of mill work and city life. He was going West!

He made preparations. His parents knew that to protest this time was futile—they would let him go.

But they didn't have to. The Lillie mill caught fire a few nights later and burned. Disheartened by the loss of most all his property, Newton Lillie salvaged what machinery he could and faced the task of making a new start.

The Evanses wrote him to try his luck out West and "grow up with the country." The cowboy era in Kansas was at its height. The Kansas Pacific Railroad, completed to Abilene in 1867, and now extended to Newton, Ellsworth and Wichita, had opened a vast Northern market for Texas' three and a half million cattle, and investors were making millions of dollars. One railroad had reached the Pacific. Two others were building in that direction. Hundreds of thousands of immigrants already had claimed homesteads on the plains.

Sumner County was offering the greatest inducement with its "magnificent" climate and soil. There were no less than 8,000 settlers within the county limits, and a half-dozen towns. Wellington had won the fight for supremacy as the county seat, while the others looked to local and transient trade and natural advantages for their future greatness. Caldwell, situated on the southern border, where the Chisholm Trail entered Kansas, thrived on the trade by men with herds of Texas cattle, and was becoming a "red-hot" town.

An unprecedented demand for industry loomed. There was real need for a flour mill on the Kansas frontier. Opportunity for expansion was unlimited.

But young Gordon did more than anyone else to get the Lillie household goods in the great covered wagon on the long trek through Missouri to Kansas. The mill equipment went to Wichita by rail and had to be freighted down to Wellington.

Here Newton Lillie left his family with the Evanses while he searched for a place to call home. The Evanses lived west of town, and there was a claim joining them on the north. But Newton Lillie was not satisfied with it. The family continued to live with the Evans' until fall, when he finally got a choice piece of land thirteen miles southeast between Slate Creek and the Ninnescah.

Then began their vicissitudes, not unlike those of the hardy pioneers who had preceded them. With a team and an ax and a few tools they built a one-room shanty with a dirt floor. It was not at all what they had been used to in Illinois. They cooked, ate and slept in the same room.

It was a happy home. The new country supplied their simple wants. They had milk and honey, and Gordon, hunting with his cousins, augmented the family larder with the wild game and turkey that abounded along the river. The country fascinated him. Out here beyond civilization, he no longer enjoyed the sights of forests. The only trees were scattered along the banks of the streams. Looking north, south, east and west, he could scan as far as the eye could see an ever-changing panorama, and it stirred him with a strange excitement and freedom.

Newton Lillie was delighted with the soil. It was a deep black loam, gravel and clay, through which the surface water passed to the subsoil rapidly. Soon he had the hundred and sixty acres under cultivation, the mill under construction and a kitchen added in an ell at the side of their shanty.

Farmers from the surrounding country brought their wheat and corn to be ground into flour and meal, or brought grain to be exchanged for flour and meal already ground. As homesteaders grew thicker, Lillie opened a small store so they could do their trading when they brought their grain to the mill.

Mrs. Lillie busied herself with household duties, and spent hours on the early education of the three younger children. Common schools had been provided for in Kansas in 1855, but territorial conditions were so unsettled that only a few towns and practically none of the country communities maintained them. Not until after the Civil War had the people been able to turn their attention to the needs of their communities, and schoolhouses built of logs or sod were springing up everywhere.

The minimum term was three months and usually ran during the winter when children could be spared from the farms. The work in the schools consisted chiefly of the three R's, "readin', 'ritin' and 'rithmetic." There was no such thing as graduating. The pupils started each year at the beginning of their books and worked as far as they could, continuing winter after winter until they were eighteen to twenty-one years of age, or older.

There were almost no high schools, so few received more than a common school education, and most of the teachers had no more than that. Young Gordon coached his brother and sisters at home. They made rapid advances in their studies and became star pupils:

> Mother encouraged me to take a school that winter, but I became so seriously affected with the chills and fever that I might have died had not a butcher in Wellington put in his suggestion.
>
> "Tell Gordon to come down here when we slaughter and drink warm blood," the butcher told my father, "that'll build him up."
>
> So I took my quota of beef blood on slaughtering days. I am confident this was all that saved my life.

While he regained his health, he taught school part of a term. He could have got a school the next year, but the desire for prairie life was strong upon him.

Beyond, for hundreds of miles, lay the wilds of the Indian and buffalo, the trapper, the trader and United States Army. The railroad had extended west from Wichita, and up the Chisholm Trail came the first longhorns bound for Dodge. Friendly Indians hung around Wellington. Since the advent of the railroad, Wichita had been the supply point for freighters transporting provisions into the Indian Territory for delivery to the several Indian agencies. The government, to save the expense of hiring white men, had made a deal with the Indians to haul their own freight. The Indians had large herds of ponies and the government furnished them harness and wagons. As they traveled to and from Wichita, they would usually camp outside the towns or near farm houses. The creek a half mile from the Lillie homestead was a favorite stopping point.

Stray bands of Indians from the various tribes already in the Territory were migrating from Kansas and Nebraska. The Pawnee had given up their lands on the Platte and the Niobrara in 1873, driven by the bloody massacre of their tribesmen by their ancient enemies, the Sioux, and trekked southward. Uncertain where they were to be located, they had kept to the west where the buffalo were still plentiful on the plains, living as they could among the little tribes along the valleys of the Cimarron and Canadian. In the spring of 1874, they had reached Anadarko and the Wichita Indians who had come down earlier. That summer they were notified by the government to go to their reservation at the confluence of the Arkansas and the Cimarron rivers. In 1875, their relatives and old people, who had been left behind, started for Pawnee Agency.

These straggling bands often camped near the Lillie home, to Gordon's advantage, for he was seldom idle. Sometimes he visited the cow camps of the Texas drovers, who grazed their herds on the trail along the Ninnescah. One day he decided to visit the Indians:

Mother was afraid to let me go. There had been a Cheyenne outbreak at Fort Reno in the Territory the summer before. Two freighters had been murdered, and a third burned alive a few miles south of the Kansas line, and Agent Miles and his family had fled to Caldwell for their lives.

The settlers all along the border had organized for an attack, but the trouble was soon put down at the reservation. There had been other scares, which later proved false, but the people were still uneasy by the presence of the Indian.

I told mother they were no different than the Oldtown Indians back in Illinois, and I finally got her consent to go into the camp.

One of the Indians could speak enough English for Gordon to understand what he meant. His name was Blue Hawk.

He told me I was a fine looking young man, and traded me a fine bow and some arrows for my knife. Then he took me through the camp, and all the Indian boys came out to see me. No one hurt me, and after I had stayed a while, I went home to tell mother all about it.

Afterwards, the thought of Indians ever doing him harm never entered his head. He visited them every day for a week. The Indians liked him because he was friendly, and Gordon liked them. Blue Hawk taught him how to shoot his bow and arrows, at which he became quite expert. He learned some of their language, and promised Blue Hawk to visit him some day on their new reservation.

This peaceful interlude in his life passed with regret, but he soon met Bob Gray, a Texas lad about his age, who had been up the Chisholm Trail twice. He told Gordon glowing tales of these end-of-the-track towns and offered to show him Wichita. Later they would ride south and join some cattle outfit and drive to Dodge. Older now, considering himself able to cope with the roughs and privations of the frontier, Gordon made his choice:

The day before we got ready to start, I took what money I had saved and bought a suit made of buckskin. This was the hide of a deer which had been tanned by an Indian. I also bought a pair of high-topped boots and a pair of big cowboy spurs.

Then I went to a horse dealer to buy a pony. He showed me one that he said was very gentle and I paid him what he asked and took the horse. Then, dressed in my buckskin outfit, I climbed into the saddle to ride home. I thought I would make a fine picture riding in on my horse, and that mother would be surprised and delighted.

But the moment I sat down on the back of that nice, gentle horse, he tossed me clear over his head. I climbed on again and we had a tussle. But, in spite of all his bucking and jumping and twisting, he didn't throw me this time. All the people downtown in Wellington were watching me, laughing and yelling and whooping. Then the horse threw his head around and busted my nose.

That was enough for me. I got off and led him home. My new buckskin suit was covered with dirt, my face grimy and my nose battered and bleeding. Instead of presenting a handsome picture to my mother, I was a sight indeed.

It was not in Gordon to leave home without his mother's consent. She wasn't surprised that he had made up his mind. She knew he would never be satisfied until he had carved for himself a life on the plains.

His worst trouble was getting away the next morning. His mother and sisters shed tears, but his father, stern and unbending, gave his benediction:

"Gordon William, you are the first to leave our roof, but my blessing goes with you. I left home before I was your age—and I knew you were bound to, sooner or later."

All stood at the gate as he climbed into the saddle and rode away, with a lump in his throat, unable to say good bye.

2.

Wichita

GORDON LILLIE had seen Texas herds passing up the Chisholm Trail as early as April, 1875. By June, most of the spring drives had reached Wichita, where they were held on the grazing grounds until shipped in the late summer or fall.

It was the high point of the season and the state already was overflowing with cattle. At least seventy thousand covered the country, east and west, and south to the Cowskin and the Ninnescah. The year before Ellsworth had dropped out of the picture and Wichita had become the king of the cowtowns.

At noon Gordon and Bob Gray reached the Ninnescah. They crossed the river and rode past a trader's station that kept for sale such articles and supplies as fitted the needs of travelers and the drovers and their crews. Enterprising merchants operated several of these stations along the Chisholm Trail. One of the best known was the old Pond Creek Ranch and Store in the Indian Territory, owned by a government post trader.

The Ninnescah River Station was one of the chief stopping places in Kansas. There were two stores here, which kept on hand at least two barrels of cheap whiskey. At the station, the roads to the various grazing grounds branched off from the main trail.

They rode past the forks of the trail and stopped to rest and graze their horses and eat some dinner. The large number of cattle grazing along the trail had left the grass short, so they stayed in camp until mid-afternoon before they saddled up and rode on.

The cattle thickened as they headed north. The trail was filled with herds of longhorns, each with its cowboys, garnished with belt knives and six-shooters, darting about like maniacs, cursing and yelling and cutting right and left with coiled riatas. Working their way around these herds would be a slow process, so they cut off across the rolling prairies dotted with cow camps and down hills and valleys almost black with cattle. They crossed the Cowskin near another trader's station late in the afternoon, and just before dark, reached Wichita.

They rode past the stockyards along the Santa Fe tracks on the west side of the river. All along the railroad, huge piles of buffalo and cattle bones which had been gathered on the plains awaited shipment to the carbon factories. A large sign at the side of the trail bore the legend: "Carrying concealed weapons strictly forbidden." They crossed the Arkansas on a ramshackle wooden bridge, and Gordon got his first view of the place Bob Gray had described as "the rip-roaringest town in the whole West."

Douglas Avenue was the leading business street and the noisiest. It was built up with several false-fronted wooden buildings and a few brick and stone structures. North Main Street boasted two and a half blocks of business houses, and there was a sprinkling of buildings on South Main. Beyond were the livery stables and corrals and a hastily constructed residential section. Hitching posts and rails lined the rutted streets and board sidewalks.

The intersection of Douglas and Main was the most important spot in town. On the northwest corner stood the famous Keno Hall —named for the fascinating game it had made a specialty—with its proprietor, W. W. "Whitey" Rupp, also presiding over chuck-a-luck, faro, monte, roulette and poker. As Gordon and Bob Gray rode past they could hear the shout of "Keno!" And up in the balcony a brass band struck up a popular melody.

Keno Hall advertised the "finest bar in Wichita." Next door was Pryor's Saloon, and in every direction other signs indicated such bars, gambling rooms, honky-tonks and dancehalls as the Empire and the Southern.

Across the street east, the New York Store outfitted the drovers with everything from new spurs to six-shooters, and Jake Karatofsky's clothing and dry goods store did a good business with the widest show windows in town. In the second block up Douglas from Keno Hall stood the Douglas Avenue Hotel, and diagonally across Douglas on Water Street was the Texas House.

But the buildings devoted to amusement and refreshment of one kind or another far outnumbered all other enterprises, and every

one of the two or three thousand transients that the cattle season
had brought to Wichita—the cowboys, gamblers, dancehall girls,
badmen and bad women, and land-seekers—seemed to be trying to
keep up the town's reputation.

The corner east of the Texas House was a popular place where
horses were sold at auction. The country itself provided every opportunity for stealing horses—plenty of grass on the prairies for
stock, and a thief with a stolen horse could travel hundreds of miles
without being seen. Many a settler's animal had "strayed" and
never been found. So many of the mounts sold at the auction place
were believed to be stolen that it was called "Horsethief Corner."

The Texas House had been occupied by the drovers. Gordon
and Bob Gray found a room at the Douglas. After a supper of
warmed-over longhorn steak, soggy bread and black coffee, they
relaxed in some dilapidated chairs in the lobby.

A talkative, thickset man with a gray mustache and dirt-stained
plug hat occupied a three-legged stool across the room by the stove.
He identified himself as a real estate broker, and had engaged in
conversation an Eastern party that had stopped off the train earlier
en route from a buffalo hunt west of Dodge. He entertained himself with laudatory remarks about his own prominent role in the
development of the townsites of Abilene, Newton, Ellsworth, and
finally Wichita. He had not only obtained a part of the land in
most cases, but had sold much of it off in town lots, greatly in-
creasing his financial status, and in his own opinion, was himself a
most important personage on the Kansas plains.

When a member of the party remarked that Dodge was booming
and might even excel Wichita in its wildness as a cattle center, he
exploded with a tirade of stories that held Gordon spellbound for
almost an hour.

"Wild! You should've seen the Delano district here when it was
runnin' wide open in '73. There was just two dancehalls and a
bunch of shacks down by the river, but it was the toughest spot in
America. These two dancehalls stood side by side, and each claimed
it was wilder than the other. One was run by Rowdy Joe Lowe and
his wife Kate, the other by Red Beard.

"Rowdy Joe was a rough character, short and stocky. He had
killed Jim Sweet in a gun fight up at Newton in '71.

"Red Beard was a big fellow, well-educated, and respectable back in his home state of Illinois. Nobody ever learned what brought him out here. He never come up on Douglas Avenue without carrying a double-barreled shotgun. When he sat down in a saloon, he kept it between his knees.

"Well, Rowdy Joe got to braggin' that his saloon was the swiftest joint in Kansas. One night Red and his friends got drunk and went over to Joe's to settle the argument. For a few minutes the pistol bullets and buckshot flew thick and fast. Rowdy Joe downed Red, but in the course of the killin', a dancehall girl was wounded and an innocent bystander blinded in both eyes by buckshot. Rowdy Joe was arrested, but never prosecuted, and went right on runnin' his dancehall."

This was only the beginning. He told of at least six killings and named five other men who were wounded in gun fights that year, when the police were lax in enforcement of the ordinance against carrying firearms.

"Yes, sir! Shooting, stabbing and fist-fights were as common as cattle. In 1874, it was even worse. All the roughs from Abilene, Newton and Ellsworth flocked here. Ben Thompson was around most of the season. And Hurricane Bill Martin and his Texas gang rode up and down the streets shootin' and yellin' while citizens fled for their lives and the police were afraid to venture out against their guns. One night one of the gang shot down a colored man in cold blood, and the rest held Marshal Bill Smith at bay with their six-shooters while the murderer escaped.

"Things got so tough the citizens organized a Vigilante Committee. Everybody kept a loaded shotgun, or Henry rifle, or pistol inside their door. A big triangle of bar steel hung outside the police court and jail in the basement of the courthouse up at First and Main street. A policeman sounded the alarm when serious trouble occurred.

"One afternoon Policeman Sam Botts arrested one of the Texas crowd for disorderly conduct and carrying concealed weapons. Hurricane Bill and the others put their pistols on him and were about to take the prisoner when the alarm sounded. Lawyer Tucker was up in his office jawin' with District Judge Campbell. He snatched up his shotgun and ran into the street ready for action.

"Bill and his bunch had gone west to the Texas House. The Vigilantes met them on the opposite side of the street. Marshal Smith asked the citizens to disperse before the affair ended in a wholesale killin'. But Tucker stepped up and said:

" 'This makes three times I've been out on this kind of call, and nobody's ever been arrested. I don't like trouble, but I'm used to it. Show me the man you want arrested, and I'll arrest him, kill or get killed.'

" 'All right,' replied Smith, 'arrest Hurricane Bill.'

"It got so quiet in the street you could hear a pin drop. Then Tucker stepped into the road, his shotgun levelled at Hurricane Bill and both barrels cocked.

" 'William,' he said softly, 'you are under arrest.'

"The Texan started to lift his pistols. The lawyer shouted: 'Drop them guns!'

" 'All right,' Bill replied, and pitched them in the street.

"The rest got so panicky at the disarming of their leader, they dropped their weapons. Then the citizens lined them up, fifteen or twenty of them, and marched them down to the station where Police Judge Jewett fined them $600 and sentenced Hurricane Bill to jail."

This was the end of concerted and open defiance of the law in Wichita, according to the real estate broker. Drunken brawls, murders and robberies continued as everyday occurrences until Wyatt Earp became marshal.

"He took them as they came, big and small. I'll never forget the day Shanghai Pierce, the Texas cattle king, got drunk and started raisin' Cain and braggin' he'd kill the first marshal who laid hands on him.

"Wyatt came up the sidewalk, snatched away Shang's gun, and tossed him through the doors of Collins' saloon. Twenty cowboys rode in to get their boss and went lookin' for Wyatt. The marshal slipped down an alley, met them in the street with his shotgun and marched the whole caboodle off to Judge Jewett, who fined them $100, and Shang paid all their fines.

"Wyatt kept the judge busy the first six months he run Wichita. His next big fight was with the Clements boys—"

The broker went on to relate the exploits of the marshal whose name already was becoming a legend in the Southwest. Gordon and Bob Gray left the hotel and strode about town.

The business of the day had ended and another class of business had begun. The saloons and gambling halls blazed with lights. Inside, billiard tables were uncovered and the click of balls punctuated the drone of conversation as the back rooms filled with others bent on more solid amusements of monte, faro and poker. Others found places where they might sit and drink and watch the show that began on a stage at one end of the room at eight o'clock and continued until after midnight.

From the second floor of Keno Hall, the man's voice calling out numbers in the game echoed loudly on the still night air. Going up there, Gordon saw a large room swarming with two to three hundred players, at least fifty sporting women and about two hundred men—gamblers, con men and other parasites who had followed the cattle business from Ellsworth. All around the room, on a sort of mezzanine above, ran a row of private booths from which the click and clatter of poker chips, balls, cards, dice, wheels and other devices mingled with the medley of crisp phrases: "Place your bets, folks!" "Thirty-five on the colors." "Are you all down? Up she rises!" "Keno!"

About nine o'clock the band from the beer garden struck up, and wandering down there, Gordon saw another huge crowd of men and women dancing to the music that blared out into the night.

The only rival this place seemed to have was the variety theater down the street where scantily clad cuties sang and danced, and comedians and actors with a taste for the dramatic performed. There were several street shows, including everything from magicians to freak men, women, animals and children, and a man with a hand organ who ground out popular tunes to draw a crowd.

Gordon felt strangely drawn to these carnival-like attractions, and he hung around them most of the evening, absorbing every detail.

About ten o'clock the regular public entertainment began. Several pugilistic encounters started in dancehalls, but all were of

short duration with the parties suffering damage of small consequence. Despite the signs posted at the entrances to the city, a few
had failed to dispose of their weapons, and there was one skirmish
with pistols in which both parties luckily came out with their lives.
Gordon had heard enough about gun-fights in Wichita to keep
clear of the streets as much as possible lest he encounter a stray
bullet.

After he had retired to his hotel at midnight, his attempts at
slumber were futile for fear a pistol ball might find its way through
the thin walls of his room. For the most part he suffered only from
crudely fashioned epithets and frontier vulgarities inspired by oft-
repeated doses of cheap whiskey to the boisterous crowds along the
streets.

The various stage performances being over, dancing began. All
night he listened to the call of figures for the old-time square dances
—"All balance left! Swing that lady on your right! Alamon right!"
—and the shout at regular twenty minute intervals: "Balance to the
bar! Everybody drink!" He finally dozed off at 4 a.m., but was
awake again at daybreak.

In the days that followed Gordon loitered among the motley
throng of the border town as suited his fancy. The people he saw,
the things he experienced, interested him; everything was raw,
new, far from the rut of home life. He realized more than ever that
he had to rely on his own resources. His genial good nature got
him friends quickly. Among these was Marshall M. "Marsh"
Murdock of the *City Eagle*.

"Hello, son, you look lonesome," Murdock said to him one
morning while making his rounds, picking up news of activities
from the night before. Gordon engaged him in conversation immediately. When Murdock learned what had brought him West, he
asked Gordon to call at his office.

At that moment Gordon Lillie had no idea he had struck up a
friendship with one of the most important men in Kansas.

Murdock, too, had come West to get a taste of the frontier. He
had arrived at Topeka in 1856, at the height of the border troubles,
in time to assist in cutting the ice over the Kaw River for John
Brown, who was making his last trip north over the Lane Trail

with a wagonload of escaped slaves. He had cast his first vote
against the Lecompton Constitution, and as corporal in a company
of free-staters had marched to Lecompton to participate in the
inauguration of the first free-state legislature.

He had aided in a tour and inspection of southern Kansas, south
of the Neosho and Cottonwood rivers, establishing a town on the
Verdigris in territory forming Greenwood County; played the
"squatter-sovereign," pre-empting a claim six miles east of Em-
poria; and freighted to the Pike's Peak gold mines of Colorado
before the outbreak of the Southern Rebellion. At the time of
Quantrill's raid, he was in Lawrence working with John Speer on
the *Republican,* and barely escaped death by ducking into a cellar
in the midst of the terrible massacre of the people. Commissioned
lieutenant colonel by Governor Carney, he had organized the Santa
Fe Battalion, afterward commanded it, and fought in the battles of
Westport and Little Blue.

Back from the war, he had plunged into politics, serving as secretary of the state Republican convention in 1864, docket clerk of
the Senate that winter, secretary of the state convention in 1865,
and county clerk of Osage County in 1866-67, holding several
minor offices meanwhile. In 1868, he had been almost unanimously
elected State Senator from Coffey and Osage counties, and re-nomi-
nated and re-elected in 1870 by overwhelming majorities. In 1871,
he sold the newspaper he had run for nine years and established one
in Wichita. The *City Eagle* made its appearance in the spring of
1872.

That fall he had been elected State Senator from the twenty-six
southwestern counties, which included the entire territory in the
Canna, Walnut and Arkansas valleys, and in 1874, received sixty-
five votes in the Republican state convention for lieutenant governor, a position he was not even seeking. He had been appointed
postmaster of Wichita the same year and still held this position and
edited the *City Eagle.*

Gordon found him earnest, though conservative. Although a
poor public speaker, possessing only moderate oratorical powers,
his loyalty to the interests of the people never wavered, and his
friends numbered in the thousands. He took a liking to Gordon,
and called him "Bill." As "Bill" Lillie, he introduced him to a

young man with a pleasant face and well-tailored clothes, who wore
his hat at a rakish angle and two big, worn-handled pistols in a
heavy belt.

"This is our marshal, Mr. Earp," Murdock said. "But just call
him Wyatt."

It was Gordon's only formal meeting with the famous marshal,
though he had seen him on the streets several times. For one who
had curried as many wild cowboys and gunmen as Earp, Gordon
thought he was the mildest, best-mannered man in Wichita.

Another man in Wichita was attracting almost as much attention
as Earp. People called him "Oklahoma Dave." David L. Payne had
come to Kansas from Indiana in 1858, pre-empted a body of land
in Doniphan County and set up a sawmill. It had proved a poor
venture. Doniphan County at the time was the grazing ground for
vast herds of buffalo, deer, antelope and other wild animals, and
Payne became a hunter. He had penetrated the mountains of New
Mexico, explored the course of the Cimarron through the Indian
Territory, and become so familiar with the topography of the
Southwest that he was soon being engaged as a scout by private
parties and the Government and becoming intimate with Kit Carson, Wild Bill, Buffalo Bill and California Joe.

He had served with the Fourth Regiment of Kansas Volunteers
in the Civil War, and served in the Kansas Legislature in the session
of 1864-65. In 1866 he had returned to his occupation of plainsman,
hunting and guarding caravan trains. Congenial, commanding of
figure and ways, he held the respect of the wild Indians of the
plains, and earned himself the title of Cimarron Scout. During the
Indian outbreaks in western Kansas, he had raised a company and
was commissioned by Governor Crawford as Captain of Company
D, Eighteenth Kansas Cavalry. His regiment was sent to Camp Supply in the Indian Territory, attached to the command of General
Custer and participated in the campaign against the hostiles in the
western part of the Indian Territory and in the Texas Panhandle.
In this and other expeditions he had gathered extensive informa-
tion about the country included in the boundaries of the Indian
Territory, and at once realized the resources and possibilities of this
great domain as a basis on which to found a new American
commonwealth.

In 1870, Captain Payne moved to Sedgwick County, near Wichita. In 1871, Sedgwick County elected him to the legislature as a Democrat, although the county was largely Republican. In 1872, he was nominated for State Senator, but defeated. He decided to move to Newton and turn over a new leaf. He was well liked and respected by Newton citizens, and for a couple of years his hopes were high, but Payne was always careless in money matters. Through a hocus-pocus of loans and mortgages, he lost all his properties, and returned to his old home in Indiana. While there, his father died, and the family estate, divided among the surviving heirs, again gave Payne sufficient funds to plan a new life.

In 1875 he turned his eyes toward Washington, and was now in Wichita securing testimonials and recommendations from powerful politicians like General Tom Ewing, John J. Ingalls, and Preston B. Plumb for a position as an officer in the United States House of Representatives.

Murdock introduced Gordon to leading merchants and other important people about town. They were building churches and schools and teachers would be needed, Murdock said. But Gordon wanted to look around some more on the frontier. He didn't know then how closely his life was to be bound with the editor of the *City Eagle*.

He and Bob Gray had been in town ten days. Bob had found a job for them with an outfit on the Cowskin that was getting ready to start back to Texas. But regular hours at teaching school or punching cows irked Gordon's roving spirit. The West he had dreamed about still lay out there where the sun went down. It was not here in Wichita or on a Texas cattle ranch. Out there were the greatest ranges in the world where rich boys and poor boys alike were making a good living killing big game. British lords, American millionaires and army officers were doing it for sport. Gordon was determined, too, that he should go on a great expedition. He decided to talk to Marshal Earp. Earp had had considerable experience on the buffalo plains before coming to Wichita.

Gordon started down Douglas Avenue late in the afternoon to seek out the marshal when he noticed a group of men in the street. There was a flurry of scuffling in the center of the crowd, rough voices, then raucous laughter. As Gordon walked up, he saw that some idlers were having fun with a drunken Indian.

Although federal law prohibited the sale of whiskey to Indians, the aborigines still craved their "firewater," and any unscrupulous white could buy whiskey from a saloon and furnish it to the redman at a profit. The Indian was staggering and waving his arms wildly. His tormentor, a rough, unshaven drover about Gordon's size and build, held a cheap watch in his hand. Each time the Indian reached for it, he would jerk it away, shove his other hand into the Indian's face and send him sprawling in the dust.

"Come on, Injun," he taunted. "If you reach it, it's your'n."

The Indian scrambled to his feet and staggered toward the watch. Again the cowboy shoved him in the face and sent him sprawling on the ground. Words of bitter protest poured from the redman's lips in his own tongue, which none of the crowd understood, and all guffawed.

Taking the part of an Indian wasn't exactly the thing to do in Wichita. Indians were constantly coming into town and getting drunk. On one occasion a small party of them had "tanked up on bad booze," killed a farmer a few miles west and plundered his ranch. Redmen in Kansas, like the buffalo, were "on the sunset trail," growing fewer and degenerating—those that hadn't been shoved onto reservations in the Indian Territory.

When Gordon saw the Indian floundering in the street, he decided to help him. As the redman rose to his feet, reaching for the watch being dangled before him, young Lillie felt more sorry for him than ever.

Gordon edged into the circle. "Whose watch is it?" he asked.

"The Injun's," the man next to him answered. "Braden's just havin' some fun."

"At the expense of a helpless Indian?" Gordon said bitterly.

"Better not interfere," the other warned.

Gordon turned abruptly and stepped up to Braden, who was holding out the timepiece for the fourth time. The cowboy was unaware of his presence until Gordon's hand closed over the watch and snatched it from his fingers.

"Hate to break up your little party," said Gordon calmly, "but I don't like to see anybody picked on who can't help himself."

He turned his back to the surprised cowboy, placed the watch in the Indian's eager grasp, whereupon the Indian thanked him volubly and staggered away. The next instant, Braden's fist crashed into the back of Gordon's head, sending him sprawling to the street.

"Maybe you like it better down in the dirt with your Injun friend!" the cowboy's voice crackled as he stood over Gordon with fists doubled, waiting to knock him down again the moment he tried to rise.

Gordon came up quickly, diving for the cowboy's stomach, trying to grapple him. Braden stepped back to safety with a confident grin and swung an uppercut to Gordon's mouth.

Gordon reeled back, catching himself on the hitch rail. He shook his head to clear his brain, steadied himself. Blood streamed from his broken lips.

Braden came in a bull-like rush, mouthing curses and swinging his fists, determined to finish the fight quickly.

Gordon's legs were unsteady as he braced himself for the onslaught. He lashed out with his right arm, blindly, desperately, and felt his fist smash solidly against bone and flesh. And in that moment he discarded defense for attack.

He leaped upon his opponent like a wild panther, swinging both fists in a surprising, relentless fury born of passion. Braden tried to retreat, but Gordon sprang in swiftly. Again his slugging right landed on Braden's jaw, and the cowboy, caught off balance, slumped to the ground senseless.

Gordon stepped back, panting, wiping blood from his lips.

"Holy smoke, kid, he'll kill you," said a man in the crowd.

"I think not," Gordon replied quietly, adjusting his coat.

"Then you better get out of Wichita 'fore he comes to."

"I'm in no hurry," Gordon said.

"Got a gun?"

"No."

"Then you better get one. You're game, boy; but you're up against a tough bucko. This man is *Trigger Jim* Braden."

"Never heard of him." Gordon walked on down the street.

He went back to his hotel room, bathed his face in cold water. He was weak and trembling from the ordeal, and had had little rest since coming to Wichita. He took off his coat and boots, lay down and was soon asleep.

He awakened with Bob Gray shaking him. "Gordon, get up. You've got to get out of here."

"What's wrong?"

"Trigger Jim's been drinkin' up a storm all night—swears he'll get even. He's on his way to the hotel."

"He's bluffing," Gordon said. "I licked him in a fair fight—he don't want anymore."

"It's not fists this time—he's going to kill you!"

Angry voices broke downstairs. "It's him or me—I'll shoot on sight!" It was Braden's voice, and there was no mistaking his intentions. Gordon slipped on his boots and snatched up his coat.

"Take my gun," Bob said. "Go down the back way. I'll meet you around front with the horses. Get goin'."

"Thanks, Bob." Gordon let himself out into the hallway and went down the back stairs. "By thunder," he said to himself, "things are moving lively for me. Only ten days on the frontier—and already somebody's wanting to decorate a grave with my body."

Quickly examining the revolver and testing it, he turned the corner of the hotel, gun in hand, his coat in the other. He heard the alley door slam, and someone curse. Again Braden's voice rose in the darkness.

"That damned kid is yellow. He's runnin'."

Gordon stopped and turned back. A heavy blackness covered the alley and the side of the hotel. It was difficult to see a dozen paces ahead.

"Braden!" his voice rang cold and clear in the night. "I'm coming back. I want a fair fight—out in the open."

"I'm waitin', kid!" shouted Braden.

Gordon moved toward the corner of the hotel, keen-eyed, ears alert. A head popped around the corner and jerked back. A pistol hammer clicked.

Then a dead silence.

Gordon stopped. He could hear the cowboy breathing. Braden was waiting for him to appear in the alley.

Gordon made a quick decision. A half-dozen steps from the corner he coughed suddenly and threw his coat straight ahead. It passed the corner where Braden waited in ambush.

A flash of flame spurted from the cowboy's pistol.

The ruse had worked.

"Take that you damned pup!" yelled Braden, jumping into the open as he saw the coat fall.

Too late he realized his error and whirled to fire point-blank at Gordon. Two shots roared simultaneously. Braden pitched headlong to the ground. Gordon wiped a trickle of blood from his left ear that had been nicked by the cowboy's bullet.

A coroner's jury acquitted him before daylight. He went to the hotel and packed his things. He realized he had only been a youngster and a tenderfoot. It hadn't taken long for Wichita to open his eyes. Tenderfeet were undesirables, and men who couldn't handle a gun and handle it quick were not much use on the frontier.

Bob Gray wanted him to ride back to Texas with the outfit on the Cowskin, but Gordon had had all the experience he wanted with Texas cowboys. He still had $300 in his clothes. He stopped at the New York Store and picked up a single-action Colt and a Winchester rifle. A few minutes later, he rode out of Wichita.

Avoiding the cattle outfits on the Cowskin and Ninnescah, he headed southeast along the Arkansas. He had decided to visit his Indian friends at the Pawnee Agency in the Indian Territory.

Unfamiliar with the country, he kept to the bottoms, following generally a course parallel to the river. That night he camped far east of the cattle trails, between the Arkansas and the Walnut.

Building a fire, getting supper, and with coffee boiled and his tin cup filled, he felt as much alone as if he had been a thousand miles from anybody. He might have gone back to Wellington and to school teaching, but he put his loneliness down as another experience a tenderfoot had to overcome before he could pass as a frontiersman.

3.   Among the Pawnee

GORDON slept little that night. The pony he had bought in Wellington was a good one, and he thought that his horse, if anybody's, would bring top prices on the auction block at Horsethief Corner. These reflections, together with the fact that being caught in this country without a mount might be disastrous, caused him to keep his pistol and rifle handy and doze at short intervals. But in the morning he found his horse all right, and after breakfast he again started for the Pawnee Agency.

As he rode south the next day, he crossed the Walnut, and the last traces of civilization disappeared. There were no more farm houses, gardens, orchards, fields of waving grain, and green pastures with sheep or cattle. He had entered the Indian Territory.

In every direction the country swept away from him as far as the eye could see, striking its grassy waves against the horizon. There was not even a tree or shrub, except along the banks of small streams emptying into the Arkansas, and the bright blue sky, clear of even the vestige of clouds, arched down to the prairie floor.

This was the part of the Outlet set aside for the hunting grounds of the Cheyenne, although not occupied by them. They were very jealous of the white man's intrusion, and, unlike other friendlier Plains tribes, never missed an opportunity to avenge themselves. Gordon avoided higher ground, keeping to the natural depressions, and rode in a straight line to cover as much distance as possible.

The second night he camped in a small draw above the Salt Fork of the Arkansas. Riding all day, with little sleep the night before, he was very tired. Staking out his horse, he put his blanket on the ground, rolled in it, and soon was sleeping "as sound as a rock":

In the middle of the night, I awakened violently. As I sat listening with fiercely beating heart, wild shrieks split the stillness of the dark prairie. I was so scared I was shaking all over. My first thought was that I was surrounded by Cheyennes, and they were about to scalp me.

Sticking my pistol into my cowboy holster and carrying my rifle in my hands, I crept through the weeds and grass in the direction of the sounds. The shrieks broke out again in front of me, then behind me and then on all sides of me. If these were Indians, they had me surrounded and there was no escape.

I saw something moving in some bushes near me. This was too close for comfort. I couldn't stand it any longer. I drew my revolver and banged into the brush. With an awful yelp, something bounded out of the brush and disappeared. It was a prairie wolf or a coyote.

I had often heard the Evans boys tell of their hair-raising experiences with prairie wolves, and here I was surrounded by a pack of them. But the wolves didn't bother me or my horse the rest of the night. I was in a cold sweat and couldn't sleep anymore. I built up my fire, then sat by it and waited for daybreak.

He crossed the Salt Fork that morning, and in the afternoon reached the Black Bear River between the Arkansas and Cimarron on the Pawnee reservation. The country now presented a great diversity of scenery.

He crossed several creeks bordered with fine belts of pecan, elm and blackjack, running into the Black Bear from fertile uplands of rich black loam, and rode eastward through valleys with shade in abundance and bluestem grass as high as a man's head. The weather was temperate, enlivening, the sky seemed a deeper blue with a few feathery clouds, and the air bland and pure in golden sunshine.

He passed an occasional grass and mud lodge, a cluster of tepees, and in the evening reached a wooded glen bordered on the right by a lofty limestone ridge, at the base of which a fine spring fed a silver rill. From this valley he rode onto an irregular elevation in the horseshoe bend of Black Bear, where a settlement of cabins was set almost in the heart of the triangular reservation. Across a rocky ford on the opposite bank of the stream, stone and frame government farm and school buildings already were under construction on a plot of 720 acres, where Indian youths were to be taught the habits of industry and civilization.

Blue Hawk had built his lodge on this high peak overlooking the bend of the Black Bear. He came out in front of the lodge with his wife behind him. Though they did not smile, their faces bore expressions of welcome. Blue Hawk said: "My friend, you are good to see."

They went inside the lodge where a fire burned under a big pot in the center of the room. While the squaw brought more jerked beef for the pot, they sat on pallets covered with skins, Blue Hawk with his feet drawn under his legs, and talked about things that had happened since their last visit.

Lillie told him about his trouble in Wichita, and the corners of the Indian's eyes creased in a smile. "It is well," he said, "that you have come to the Pawnee."

The summer of 1875, Gordon lived among the Indians. He got a job in the rock quarry, helping build the first agent's home of native stone, and worked at the government sawmill, cutting trees into short sections, splitting them into shingles, and sawing flooring for the log cabins. He became a personal friend of Major William Burgess, the first agent, who brought the Pawnees to the Territory, and of William D. Bishop, who clerked for Stacey Matlock, the first Indian trader.

Bishop had come from New Jersey to Genoa, Nebraska, in 1873, met his wife Ellen in Omaha and married her in 1874. He had clerked for Matlock at Genoa and come to the Pawnee Agency in 1875. He wore a long white beard, was very efficient in his work and could speak the Pawnee language better than any other white man. The Indians could not say "William," so they called him "Widdiam," and some called him "Ah-ti-out" (grandfather), because he was so patient with them, kind and helpful.

Later, Major Burgess operated a trading post along with Matlock. Government permits for that part of the Territory were secured from Senators John J. Ingalls and Preston B. Plumb, of Kansas, who had been given that political authority by the Department of

Interior. A government inspector came around regularly and made reports.

The traders brought their supplies from Kansas City and St. Louis. They were shipped as far as possible by rail and then freighted overland. The furniture for the agent's home was shipped by rail to Coffeyville and hauled in wagons to the agency. The chief foods for the Indians were beans, flour, cornmeal, coffee and bacon.

The Pawnee lived in four villages in which they built and occupied more than sixty mud lodges and council houses. These villages were all within the vicinity of the agency, and the rest of the reservation was used as hunting grounds.

Gordon hunted and fished up and down the Black Bear with Rush Roberts, a full-blood member of the Too-heets-pee-ott clan of the Skidi (Wolf) band, whose Indian name was Ah-re-Kah-rard (Antlers). He was three months older than Gordon, born in November, 1859, on the plains south of the Platte during a buffalo hunt. His father was La-tah-cots-Kah-La-Haroo (Fancy Eagle), doctor and magician; and his grandfather, Latahcots-te-we-tit (Sitting Eagle), had been one of the most famous doctors and magicians in Pawnee history. Rush Roberts had grown up on the Platte and moved with his people to the Indian Territory in 1874.

He and Gordon made soup of coon and ate roasted opossum they caught by snares and traps. Quail were plentiful, prairie chickens would fly over in clouds, and the timbered ravines abounded with turkey. There was a turkey roost between the agency and Blue Hawk's lodge. Sometimes from the top of the hill Gordon could see deer in the valley.

The Pawnee country from the peak of the hill became his favorite view. Of an evening, he would watch the sinking sun set the valley sky aflame and the smoke from the lodges and tepees rising lazily in the still, heavy air, pungent with burning wood and cooking meat.

Sometimes he would sit in the cool night air until the campfires had died and the red lights glowing from the windows of the traders' cabins had disappeared, staring into the darkness and listening to the quavering complaint of the screech owl, the long-drawn-out howl of a wolf in the distance and the staccato barking

THE FIVE CENT
WIDE AWAKE
LIBRARY

Entered at the Post Office at New York, N. Y., as Second Class Matter.

No. 1052. {COMPLETE.} FRANK TOUSEY, PUBLISHER, 34 & 36 North Moore St., N. Y. {PRICE 5 CENTS.} Vol. II.
NEW YORK, May 30, 1891. ISSUED EVERY SATURDAY.

Entered according to Act of Congress, in the year 1891, by FRANK TOUSEY, in the office of the Librarian of Congress, at Washington, D. C.

Pawnee Bill's Double: or, THE GREAT SCOUT'S Best Trail.
By PAUL BRADDON.

of an Indian dog. And when all was quiet, and the silence seemed
to grow intense, he would doze until Blue Hawk's hand on his
shoulder reminded him it was time to return to the lodge.

Blue Hawk took a fatherly interest in Gordon. In his buckskins,
his face burned dark from the sun and wind, the boy looked like
an Indian. The Pawnees adopted him and called him Ku-luks-Kitty-
butks (Little Bear). Gordon never forgot, as he stood in the lodge
of Eagle Chief, how the old man greeted him with a cordial, deep-
voiced *lau,* invited him to sit down, filled the pipe and talked.

He remembered, too, the stories learned from stalwart Se-tis-tis-
tee (High Eagle). Born in a council house of the chiefs on the Platte
in 1829, he was one of the oldest men of the tribe, and in his keen
brain already was stored nearly half a century of tribal history and
tradition.

He spoke of a time before the white man had visited them, when
the powerful "Pani" and "Pani-mah" tribes, coming far from the
south, had taken by force of arms from the Cheyenne, Arapahoe and
Sioux all the country in the upper Missouri valleys embraced by
Missouri, Kansas, Iowa and Nebraska. Once ten thousand strong,
they had been one of the greatest tribes in western America and
most successful on the warpath. They had protected when necessary
the small tribes like the Ponca, Otoe and Omaha, and because of
their strength and influence, the French had sought their friendship during colonization among them.

His memory ran back to the 1840 visits of George Catlin, the
famous explorer who made notes and maps of the tribe and the
rivers and sketched their pole and mud houses, the first white man's
picture records of Pawnee lodges. He recalled the 1844 expedition
of Major Clifton Wharton, whose military maps located the Grand
and Loup Pawnee villages; the visit of the explorer John Colter,
who mapped the villages as part of his work in locating the old
Santa Fe and Oregon trails; and talked of the 1848 treaty of Fort
Childs, when the Grand Pawnees had ceded a strip of land sixty
miles wide along the Platte, and of the treaty of 1857, when they
had ceded all their lands north of the Platte except a reservation on
the Loup Fork.

Permission had been given to nearly one hundred Pawnees and
their families to leave this reservation for hunting buffalo in 1872.

They had just started the trip when they were attacked by the Sioux and over one thousand Pawnees were massacred. The government then determined to remove the Pawnee to the Indian Territory, and they were brought in groups during the two-year period of 1873-74, the last group reaching the agency in 1875.

The Pawnee had never made tribal war upon the white man, but had been his allies, partly because he had aided them in their eternal enmity with the savage Plains tribes since the days of Coronado and other Spanish and French adventurers and American fur traders and trappers. For ten years Pawnee scouts, under the famous border military man, Major Frank North, and his younger brother, Luther, had been employed by the government against the hostiles. They were usually of good stature, robust muscular development, and possessed incredible endurance. High Eagle had served in every campaign of 1864-65 and 1869-70, and won high praise for his intrepidity and soldierly efficiency.

The old chief grasped one of Gordon's fingers and placed the tip of it in a scar in the side of his leg just above the knee.

"Got him in big fight on Republican Fork in 1869. Big chief Frank North killed Tall Bull as he came out of ravine. We got his squaw. That night Pawnee got many scalps. I bring home scalp of Tall Bull."

High Eagle placed the scalp with its long string of braided hair in Gordon's hands. He spoke of the battle of Summit Springs, and for the first time Gordon realized that Major North was the real slayer of Tall Bull, not his childhood hero, Bill Cody, as alleged by Ned Buntline.

Gordon formed an enduring friendship with another chief, Ruling His Son. Tall, straight, athletic, and the same age as High Eagle, Ruling His Son talked of his early life in Nebraska and the many battles with the Sioux before the Indians had firearms, using only bows and arrows.

Stoic, little given to sentiment, his eyes dimmed as he described the brutal massacre near Norfolk, in which his wife and son had been killed. He then had become a determined slayer of the Sioux and pursued the tribe as an aide to Major North and the United States Army.

As a youth he had been a mighty hunter, and excelled in killing bears. His choice possession was a necklace of huge bear claws, trophies of the chase.

Ruling His Son had never become reconciled to the whites' taking of the Indian lands. The reservation system had seemed the most practical and peaceable solution to the impending difficulties with the Sioux. The government had promised them protection between the Arkansas and Cimarron, far away from their old enemy. It had erected agency buildings; encouraged cultivation of crops; defined annuity articles to be distributed annually; employed a physician, farmer, blacksmith, carpenter, engineer, miller, and teachers for the education of their children; and provided for the necessary appropriation to carry out the terms of the treaties, and the issue of hunting permits on the Western plains. These were tangible evidences of friendship from the White Father in Washington. Ruling His Son had affixed his mark with other chiefs and head men of his tribe, and he never violated his treaty.

Gordon developed a close friendship with Ku-suck-seia (Left Hand), the recognized government Chief of the Pawnee. Left Hand was chief of the Kit-ke-hahk-i band. He was tall, straight as an arrow, with high cheekbones, very dark skin and long hair with scalp lock braided, and fond of Indian dress, such as paint and his headdresses of eagle feathers and scalps taken from the enemy in his younger days. Gordon regarded him as the ideal Indian chief.

His father had been Chief of the Pawnee. The title was hereditary, and Left Hand would have naturally become chief at his death. But a chief without the requisite strength of character might be that in name only. Their government was semi-republican. Each band governed its affairs with a head chief, second chief, third and fourth chiefs. But often some sub-chief or even a warrior of his own or another band might wield more influence than any of these because of his bravery, wisdom and personal popularity. Among the Pawnee, these were important factors in acquiring and retaining authority, and Left Hand's father, being a shrewd man, had told him:

"Before another moon my warriors will be on the trail of the Sioux. I want you to join the war party and gain the favor of your fellow warriors by taking many scalps, and by this way you may be chosen chief."

Left Hand did as his father wished, and upon his return laid before him the scalps of seven enemies, two more than any other warrior. His popularity and renown increased. As a warrior he had no equal, his skill as a hunter, trapper and trailer was unsurpassed, and in the councils of his tribe, he exhibited much native diplomatic and oratorical ability.

Gordon was deeply impressed with these high qualities of Pawnee character. At every opportunity he listened to the many stories of Pawnee heroes and the tales of miraculous doings reflecting that character. He found them an amicable, light-hearted people, keen for the ridiculous and fond of a joke; but in their stories of old manners and rites and ceremonies, there was a poignancy for the old days when the corn and buffalo had furnished them food, clothing, shelter and weapons for war and the chase. Then they had been masters of a prairie empire, roaming over it at will, a cunning, fierce people whose name was terror to their enemies.

Now this was all past. They were few in number, poor, a vanishing race in transition. They faced the task of living by toil, wresting subsistence from the earth, and with new modes of living would come new views, new motives, new sympathies.

Gordon knew what it meant to be transplanted. He was experiencing a transition from Illinois to the wild frontier, and felt like an Indian.

Blue Hawk and his family showed him many kindnesses he had never received from white persons except his blood kin, and he helped them cultivate their ground that had been turned by the government plow, raising corn, beans, squash and pumpkin. The Pawnee had cultivated corn as far back as the elder tribesmen could remember. They called it A-ti'ra (Mother), because it had always nourished and supported them. It had a sacred character, and played an important part in many of their ceremonies.

They still crushed it in wooden mortars with a wooden pestle, which sometimes was four feet in length with a larger upper end to give it added weight. Gordon ate from large gourds and wooden bowls and dishes with spoons and ladles fashioned from horns of buffalo. Blue Hawk taught him to braid ropes from buffalo hair, lariats from rawhide, and that fall his squaw mended a gash in Gordon's buckskins with a bone needle and a thread of twisted sinews.

When in his lodge, Blue Hawk dressed only in a small cloth fastened around his middle. Outside, he wore a breechclout, leggings fringed at the side reaching from thigh to ankle, and moccasins. A buffalo robe, with the hair side turned in, was added in inclement weather.

He wore no head covering. His hair was cut in ancient fashion— the whole head shaved, except for a narrow roach with the hair less than an inch long running from front to back. On special occasions he sometimes stiffened it with grease and used red, white and yellow paint freely upon his face and breast for ornamentation.

The women dressed more heavily than the men. They wore a gownlike upper garment that reached to the hips, a piece of blue or brown calico or buffalo cowskin tied around the waist skirt-fashion, leggings of scarlet cloth or buckskin laced above the knees, and moccasins. In cold weather a robe or blanket was flung on the back, from under which often peered the black sparkling eyes of little papooses.

Children went scantily clad. Except for a string of beads around his neck, a boy went naked until he was several years old when he was dressed in a breechclout. Girls were placed in smocks as soon as they were able to walk. All were loved fervently by their parents and brought up to respect them and the elders of the tribe.

The Pawnee were profoundly religious and had a more highly developed theology than did most of their Plains neighbors. To them there was one supreme deity, Ti-ra-wa, creator of the universe, the Great Spirit. He was intangible, quite as much as the God of the Christians, and governed over all from his abode in the heavens. But, unlike Christianity, there were lesser deities in Pawnee religion—gods of the heavens and gods of the earth, all created by Ti-ra-wa. Some were masculine, some feminine, and each one had a specific function in connection with man. The heavenly spirits, of whom the most important were the Morning and Evening stars, were guardians of the tribe as a whole, and were usually associated with stars. Slightly less powerful were the earthly spirits, normally identified with animals, who were the special helpers of individuals and of the various secret religious societies.

There was an afterworld beyond the grave, and the Milky Way was the long pathway to it. The North Star, associated with death, set the departed on the journey.

The tribe had no written language, so the "sacred history"—a collection of holy objects symbolizing the traditions of the people—was kept hanging in a lodge in a bundle wrapped in animal skin. Among its contents were an ear of corn, a gift from Ti-ra-wa to his children, a scalp representing the wars and achievements of heroes, a bow and arrow symbolical of the hunt, an eagle feather as highly esteemed by them as the national emblem was by the whites, and many other articles representing some myth or tradition about which the keeper was able to relate the details. With the death of each keeper, the tribe lost some of its sacred history, so much of the mythology was known only in part.

There were other Pawnee sacred bundles, associated with the individual branches of the tribe. Each of these had been given to the Pawnee by a heavenly god, and it served as a link between the people and their deities.

There was a genesis. "Ti-ra-wa created heaven and earth," Blue Hawk told Gordon. "He spoke and at the sound of his voice a woman appeared from the earth. Ti-ra-wa then created man and sent him to the woman."

They believed that the bones of the dinosaur which were found on the plains were the bones of giants who had once inhabited the earth and had been destroyed by Ti-ra-wa in a great deluge. Afterward, Ti-ra-wa had promised not to destroy the earth and its inhabitants in this manner again.

"Someday the earth will come to an end," Blue Hawk said. "Ti-ra-wa shall send great storms and fire from the sky. The moon shall turn red and the stars fall from heaven. Many other signs shall mark the end."

The Pawnee did not worship in assemblage, but would go to a hilltop or some other secluded place and pray to Ti-ra-wa in secret. The priest served as the intermediary for Ti-ra-wa and the people, and Ti-ra-wa seemed to watch over him and listen when he interceded for the tribe. His relation to the Pawnees and their deity was like that of Moses to the Israelites and Jehovah.

All undertakings affecting the general welfare of the tribe were preceded by prayer and sacrifice, and in lesser ventures, the parties involved humbled themselves and asked divine assistance. Even their war dance was designed to call Ti-ra-wa to their aid, and in their victory dance success was acknowledged by grateful offerings, in which the victorious warrior sometimes sacrificed the scalp taken from his enemy to be burned by the High Priest in elaborate ceremony.

The corn dance was a prayer for a bountiful crop. At harvest time they danced in thanks to the Great Spirit. There was the wild-horse dance, the deer, bear, dog dance and many others. The musicians always beat the drums with the same rhythm, rattled dried gourds filled with gravel and shook sticks to the end of which the toes of deer and antelope were attached with leather thongs. They sang of former victories of the tribe, incidents on the warpath and in the chase, the tales of prowess of some chief or brave.

Before starting on a buffalo hunt, the hunters and their families prayed that the buffalo would be plentiful, made burnt offerings and offered sacrifices for success and a safe return.

When the Pawnee left the agency on their annual hunt in 1876, Gordon went with them, not as one of the tribe, but in company with an Indian trader called "Trapper Tom" McClain.

4.   The Young Trapper

TRAPPER TOM was a blunt, big-hearted Westerner who had come to Kansas from Illinois in the days of '49, when the country was inhabited mostly by Indians and wild game. He had crossed the plains a dozen times, trapping cougar, bear and beaver and hunting deer and buffalo for their robes, visited virtually every range of the Rockies, and spent considerable time in Denver during its infancy. Here he had become involved in the Occidental uprising, in which fourteen persons were slain, and had returned to Kansas with his traps and guns.

For a while he had traded with the Indians, freighting out of Wichita a hundred and fifty miles south to the reservations of the Kiowa and Comanche, Wichita, Caddo and Cheyenne, and outfitted at the Pawnee Agency to haul flour, sugar, coffee, tobacco, blankets, calico and other goods to the buffalo range for trade with the Pawnee. The Indians had no wagons. They owned large herds of horses and ponies. Practically all of these were ridden or driven and many carried heavy packs lashed to their backs on their journey westward to the Great Plains.

The traders accompanied the bands with their large stocks of goods, which were unloaded wherever the hunting camps were established. Usually the trader was assigned an Indian, called the "trader's brave," who helped him in storing and handling his goods and guarded it during his absence. Trapper Tom took a liking to Gordon Lillie. A young man, roughing it among the Indians, struck him as "a nervy piece of business." He liked grit more than anything, and as young Lillie already could speak the Pawnee language quite fluently, Trapper Tom made him the "brave" for his party.

On their way to the plains, the Pawnee followed well-known trails, camping near wood, water and good pasturage. They built their campfires in holes in the ground to prevent prairie fires. Blankets, robes or strips of canvas flung over brush and tree branches provided temporary shelter. Once they reached the site selected for their permanent hunting camp, lodge poles were cut from nearby streams and tepees of buffalo skin set up and made comfortable.

Buffalo had always been the tribe's staff of life. Failure to obtain meat often had meant six months' poverty and hunger, so their hunts were organized. The chief appointed Indian soldiers to keep order and see that the hunters stayed in camp until the buffalo were sighted. Nobody started on the hunt until he gave the order, then the soldiers took the lead.

They approached the herd from the windward side. The hunters were deployed, half to the left, half to the right, then they closed in, surrounding the buffalo on three sides. As the herd started to move, the chase began.

Gordon was astonished at how fast the great lumbering animals could run. They went over the ground in a shambling lope no faster than a horse could gallop, but they climbed the hills and slopes faster than a horse, and it took a tough little Indian pony to keep up with them. The buffalo ran with their heads down, and the great herd made a mighty noise like the rumbling of distant thunder.

Suddenly they began to scatter. Each Indian selected a buffalo, approaching swiftly from behind. When opposite the beast, he fired, aiming at the spine or side immediately behind the fore-shoulder. One shot in the spine or heart brought the buffalo down, but usually it took additional shots in the vitals to kill one.

The moment the buffalo fell, they were off after another, until the whole herd was killed or the hunters quit the chase. No matter how many animals they killed, no meat was wasted. All were skinned, the meat packed on horses and brought into camp. The men's work was finished.

The squaws unloaded the meat, cut it into narrow slices about an inch thick and three or four inches long, and hung it on poles to be dried in the sun and air for three days. This simple, easy process for curing meat was called "jerking" buffalo. When the meat had dried, it was placed in rawhide sacks or bundles tied with leather thongs. Two of these could be fastened together like saddle bags and flung across the back of a pony for the long trek back to the reservation.

The skins were "fleshed," hung on a frame or spread on the ground and fastened with pegs. Brains were used to dress the hides, then they were moistened and softened by continuous working and rubbing until dried. Skins taken in the summer were used for covering tepees, making moccasins, bridles and other necessary articles. Those taken in the winter bore a heavier crop of hair and were used for rugs and robes.

Trapper Tom taught Gordon how to buy good hides. Valuation was placed on them according to size, condition of the hair, thickness and texture of the skin, and care used in dressing and tanning. They were pressed ten to a bale and loaded on the freight wagons Trapper Tom had brought to the buffalo range loaded with provisions.

The return march to their reservation was a slow process for the Indians. They made frequent and long encampments to feed and rest their horses loaded with cured meat, hides and robes, in addition to their blankets, bedding and cooking utensils. It took nearly two months for all the band to return to the reservation, where they sold many more of their hides at the agency trading post. The traders also bought a large quantity of buffalo tongue, which was salted and packed in barrels for shipment, but they purchased none of the cured meat except for their own use.

Trapper Tom's outfit did not return to the agency, but freighted straight through to Coffeyville, Kansas, where their season's take of hides was shipped to St. Louis and sold for an average price of $6 each.

Gordon was in Coffeyville with Trapper Tom on September 6, when a hundred Pawnee Scouts and warriors marched into town with Major Frank North, their old leader, and boarded the train for Sidney Barracks, Nebraska, to be outfitted to fight in the punitive expeditions being organized against the Sioux and Cheyenne for the fall and winter of 1876.

General George A. Custer and his command had been annihilated on the Little Big Horn. The army had enough men and artillery to wipe the hostiles from the face of America, if it could find them. The Pawnee Scouts knew their habits and tricks of war-fare and where they hid their villages; they could track them after white men had given up; and behind their skill were bitter mem-ories of a century of suffering at the hands of the enemy. Surprise had been an essential element in every victory over the Sioux, and the Pawnee were masters at setting up a surprise attack. So Major North had been dispatched to the Indian Territory by General Sheridan at Chicago to enlist the Pawnee Scouts of his old company.

Frank North had been born in Ohio in 1840. At fifteen he had accompanied his family to Council Bluffs, and a little later, across the Missouri River, settling near Columbus, Nebraska. In the win-ter of 1856, his father, a surveyor, had frozen to death at Emigrant Crossing on Big Pappillian Creek in a snowstorm, and responsibility of caring for the family had fallen upon young Frank. He had tried trapping on the tributaries of the Platte, with small success. In 1860, he found employment with Agent DePuy at the Pawnee Indian Reservation and made the acquaintance of the tribe. He acquired such thorough knowledge of their language that, the next year, he was appointed interpreter by the Indian Commissioner. Frank's younger brother Luther also was employed on the reservation, and gained some knowledge of the tongue. With the outbreak of the Sioux and Cheyenne wars in 1864, they had been authorized to enlist the first company of Pawnee Scouts to be employed against these hostiles.

The Norths had distinguished themselves as fighters with no su-periors for bravery, and the Pawnee Scouts had rendered brilliant service in defense of the Union Pacific Railroad, in the Conner expedition to the Powder River country in 1865, and at the battle of Summit Springs near the Colorado-Nebraska border in 1869. Once Major North and a dozen Pawnees had pursued twenty-seven Cheyennes who had massacred a party of emigrants, and returned to their command with all the plunder and twenty-seven scalps. At the scalp dance following this victory, when the scouts were changing names, as was the custom, the Pawnees gave Major North the name Pa'ni Le-Shar (Chief of the Pawnees), a title conferred upon only one other white man to that time, General John Fré-mont, the "Pathfinder."

Major North had the Indians' welfare at heart. They loved and respected him for his unvarying justice, patience and kindness. His commands were carried out even in the face of great peril or certain death. He was their leader.

"He never said, 'Go,' but always, 'Come on,' " an old chief said. Once in delivering a crushing blow on a Cheyenne village, the Scouts were under hot fire with bullets raining from hillsides all around them, and they wanted to run. "Pa'ni Le-Shar just straightened himself on his old black horse and said quietly, 'The first of my men that runs, I will kill.' We didn't run." Little wonder then that they honored him with the highest rank the Indian could bestow upon a white man.

When he reached the Pawnee Agency, every youth and man had crowded to his office for enrollment. Heading the list were Eagle Chief, Sun Chief, Curly Chief, Ruling His Son, Left Hand, High Eagle, Dog Chief and many others. Gordon Lillie's chum, Rush Roberts, was the youngest of the group.

Major North had objected to taking the boy, but the lad and his father had so insisted that he let him join. Major North had been authorized only one hundred men, but so anxious were the Pawnees to fight their old enemies that many who were left behind, after the quota had been filled, straggled into Coffeyville on foot with a few pack ponies two days after the train had departed, still hoping they might be accepted.

For the Pawnee Scouts, the fall and winter campaigns of 1876 were a series of night rides, skirmishes, escapes and hand-to-hand engagements with the most warlike Indians of the Plains, ending in the capture of Red Cloud's village on Chadron Creek, Nebraska, and the dismounting of his entire band, and General McKenzie's march from Crazy Woman to the Red Fork of Powder River, Wyoming, with the defeat of the Cheyenne and their suit for peace. In all their fighting and trailing, the Scouts lost only one warrior while their enemy lost hundreds.

Rush Roberts participated in the roundup of Red Cloud on Chadron Creek, the Dull Knife fight and the march to Belle Fourche. He proved to be the best of the younger scouts, and when mustered out with the rest in the spring of 1877, made his way back to the Indian Territory with many stories to tell.

High Eagle boasted more scars from wounds received in the battle with the Cheyennes under Dull Knife. He expressed contempt
for Sitting Bull: "Him no chief; Sioux medicine man, him in tepee
with squaw; Chief Gall lead dog soldiers"—and told how the scouts,
with the cavalry, had marched all night in deep snow and cold
to surprise the enemy at daylight.

Left Hand increased his trophies by a half-dozen Cheyenne
scalps, a buffalo calf skin handsomely ornamented with porcupine
quills, a pair of moccasins and a buckskin jacket with a bullet hole
in it taken from a Sioux chief who failed to escape in the hasty
flight of his band from a surprise attack at the headwaters of the
Republican.

Major North returned to his home in Columbus, Nebraska. In
July, he left for the North Platte with William F. Cody, driving
fifteen hundred head of cattle purchased at Ogallala. He settled
down to ranching on Dismal River, and the exploits of Major
North and the Pawnee Scouts passed into history.

Gordon Lillie spent that fall and winter on the Arkansas and its
tributaries with Trapper Tom, hunting small fur-bearing animals
and poisoning wolves for their pelts. Many hunters on the Western
plains were making a living poisoning wolves. There was a ready
market for the skins, which sold for a dollar to a dollar and a half
each, according to size. In the winter, a man could make from
seventy-five to a hundred and fifty dollars a month, and the wolf
family were so plentiful that liberal applications of arsensic and
strychnine had not seriously reduced their number.

The outfit consisted of saddle horses, and a single wagon and
team of mules for transportation of provisions, traps and other
necessities. They began trapping near the present town of Ralston
and proceeded up the Arkansas toward the mouth of the Walnut,
where they found plenty of otter and beaver.

Here, Trapper Tom established headquarters and set up a wolf
camp further west and south toward the Salt Fork. Henry Boch
was camp cook. They called him "Beans," because he was from
Boston and fed them beans three times daily for weeks at a stretch.
But he was a sociable fellow and could skin a coyote while most
hunters were getting ready to do it. He was sent to the wolf camp
with Gordon, and took his regular turn handling "the drag":

The "drag" was a piece of decayed buffalo meat. It was our job to tie this to the end of a lasso, get on a horse and drag it in a circle about five miles around our camp. We would drag it close to the trunk of every big tree on our track. Then we would bore several large holes in each tree we passed and fill these holes with grease and arsenic.

The wolves and coyotes would get on the trail of the decayed meat, and following it, they would pass poisoned trees. At each tree, they would take a lick or two at the grease and arsenic, then follow the trail to the next tree, where they would take another lick. They kept this up until finally they would get enough poison to kill them, and we would find them dead on the trail. It was not unusual to find as high as thirty of them dead in one morning.

The Cheyenne and Comanche Indians were using this part of the Territory for hunting grounds, and were considered "bad" Indians. Gordon let his hair grow long; he talked the Pawnee tongue fluently and knew the Plains sign language well, and had always gotten along well with Indians. He did not think they would harm him.

One morning after I had left camp, seven Cheyennes came up to Beans and asked him for something to eat. Beans refused to give them anything, and they threatened to kill him. He had a big pot of beans setting close to the fire. Beside it was a can of dope I used to poison wolves and coyotes.

Beans decided he had better give the Indians what they wanted, so he put on the kettle, and reaching into my dope can, put into the beans a great fistful of grease and arsenic. It was enough to have killed a dozen Indians.

The Indians ate the poisoned food and went away.

Every time we went out of camp for a week afterward, we expected to find some dead Indians. But we never did, and we never heard of any of those Cheyennes dying from the poison.

Boch never mentioned his home or family, and Gordon always felt that he had left Boston "for a mighty good reason":

One morning I got up with a sore throat and a bad cold. The weather was a little above zero, and there was no promise of sun for that day. Beans got ready to go and stood looking me over. He saw I was ill.

"You look like that last coyote I found yesterday—just about all in," Beans said. "You'd better stay and keep the fire up. I'll go out and re-dope the drags and be back by two or three o'clock."

He pulled out, and I watched till he disappeared. Three o'clock came. Then five o'clock. At dark Beans still had not come in.

I was not alarmed. I supposed he had ridden up to the head-quarters camp. We hadn't seen anyone for more than three weeks, and were nearly out of coffee and matches. So I thought Beans would be home the next sundown. But the next day came and went and so did another.

Finally I saddled up and started for headquarters. I found Trapper Tom in great spirits. He had just come in from the lines with over two hundred skins. He greeted me warmly.

"I was just coming down to haul up your hides," he said.

"Where is Beans?" I asked. "He left camp three days ago, and I haven't seen him since. I thought he might be up here."

"There you are," Tom said. "I knowed that would be the way he'd leave some time."

Then he expressed the same suspicions that had been bothering me.

"Well, I ain't sorry he's gone. I always liked him, but I was afraid he would get us into trouble with the Indians or Uncle Sam."

On their way to the camp with the wagon and mules to haul back the wolf skins, Gordon told Tom about Boch poisoning the beans he had fed the Indians. They stopped at a creek to give the mules a drink. Gordon got down from the wagon to unfasten the reins and remove the bridles. The mules moved to the bank, then snorted and backed from the water:

I looked over the bank, and was astonished to see the naked, mutilated body of a man face down in the stream. Before Tom and I got him fished out on the bank, we recognized what was left of poor Beans. The Indians had killed him.

BEADLE'S HALF DIME Library

Entered at the Post Office at New York, N. Y., at Second Class Mail Rates.   Copyright, 1888 by BEADLE AND ADAMS.   April 17, 1888.

Vol. XXII. | $2.50 a Year. | PUBLISHED WEEKLY BY BEADLE AND ADAMS, No. 98 WILLIAM STREET, NEW YORK. | Price, 5 Cents. | **No. 560.**

PAWNEE BILL

PRAIRIE SHADOWER

THE BLOW WAS A SEVERE ONE, AND HALF STUNNED THE DARING LAD, WHO FELL HEAVILY.

The Gold Queen's Secret.

A ROMANTIC STORY OF REAL BORDER LIFE.

BY COLONEL PRENTISS INGRAHAM,

AUTHOR OF "THE BUCKSKIN ROVERS," "BISON BILL," "BILLY BLUE EYES," "BUCK TAYLOR," ETC.

CHAPTER I.
A DARING ACT.

ALONG a desolate highway, in a far Western State, a horseman was riding one pleasant afternoon.

Pawnee Bill is G. W. Lillie, Government Scout and Interpreter, now living on his ranch in the Indian Territory, near Medicine Lodge. "May Lillie, the Gold Queen," is the wife of G. W. Lillie, and has had a most romantic life on the plains.—THE AUTHOR.

We gave him a decent burial. The next morning, we checked over our stock of salt pork, beans, dried apples, coffee and ammunition. I convinced Tom that the Indians were satisfied, and wouldn't bother us. He agreed to stick it out the rest of the winter.

During the last week in January, one of their mules fell on the ice and broke its hip, and they had to kill him. This left them without a team to pull the wagon. Since they had decided to stay until spring, Gordon volunteered to "hustle another mule," and headed north for one of the settlements above the Kansas border.

The first morning out a cold downpour set in. By noon a cutting north wind began and the temperatures fell below zero. I knew a norther was in the making. It was as much dreaded on the plains as the simoon in the African desert. I tried to make some headquarters as soon as possible, and forged ahead.

Within an hour a howling blizzard was all about me, shutting off landmarks, and I could go no further. I dismounted and tried to build a fire, but all the twigs and branches I could find were wet. With no prospects of the storm abating, and without fire, food or blankets, my position was most perilous. I removed the saddle from my horse and wrapped the blanket around my own body. As a last resort, I had decided to kill the animal and warm my hands and feet in its entrails.

While trying to make a snow bank for shelter, my horse snorted in fright. Looking up, I saw a big man buried to the ears in a buffalo robe coat. He sat his horse, watching me closely.

After a moment, I said: "Stranger, if you will tell me where I can spend the night under shelter, I will be much obliged."

"Young man, if I sheltered you, I might be putting myself and my friends in danger," he replied.

After a pause, in which he seemed to be turning something over in his mind, he went on: "I ain't going to see nobody freeze to death. We have grub, a fire and blankets, but ain't anxious to have our boarding house advertised."

"I don't know where I am, or how I got here, anyway," I said.

The man in the buffalo coat seemed pleased. He waited until I saddled my horse, then I followed him through the blizzard to a shack of a barn. A log fire was burning in a crude fireplace, and it was the most welcome sight I have ever seen.

He introduced me to four men who were sitting around. They brought food to me and after I had eaten, we all turned in and slept until daylight.

In the morning, he gave me some breakfast, reminded me that I was still lost, and started me on the trail with a friendly good-bye....

When I got back to camp with the mule, Trapper Tom was so glad to see me he flung his arms around my neck and hugged me like a grizzly. After a few days, I described the men to him who had saved me from the snowstorm, and he commented that I had spent the night with Jesse James and his notorious gang of train robbers who were known to be hiding out at that time in the Indian Nations.

The rest of the winter being too cold and dangerous to be profitable, we abandoned our enterprise and pulled out for Kansas. The snow had blown away this far north, and we had no difficulty finding a road to Coffeyville.

They sold their furs and wolf skins, and Trapper Tom caught the train to St. Louis. During the winter, he had talked a lot about the big cities on the Mississippi, and Gordon wanted to see them. But being anxious to see his mother and sisters, Gordon returned to Wellington with his season's profits and many stories of his experiences on the frontier.

5.   Hunting Buffalo

HE HAD BEEN HOME in Wellington only a month, when he left with the Evans boys on a buffalo hunt in the Texas Panhandle. Lillie wrote:

We traveled west for three days without seeing any buffalo. On the third day after we had finished supper, we were sitting around the fire smoking and telling buffalo and Indian stories, when we heard a rumbling sound coming from the north. It became more and more distinct.

Finally, I got up on the wagon, and away in the north I could see the dust rising in clouds.

Old Sullivan, one of our skinners, raised up, stretched himself and, putting his hands to his ears the better to hear, said:

"Boys, that's a norther sure as you're born. We better get our wagons corralled and the stock on the inside or we'll lose everything. I was with old Markum's outfit about two year ago, and we was caught in a norther. We lost the old man's favorite buffalo horse and his milk cow. The old man had been raised on a farm and he couldn't live without milk, he said, so he brought a milk cow along with his outfit. It was nearly three months before we got back to the states, but he lived all right without milk and got fat besides—"

"Hand me those glasses, Sullivan," I broke in. "If I don't miss my guess, that's a herd of buffalo coming. If it is, they'll run over our camp—never mind the glasses, I can see them—they ARE buffalo!"

About three miles distant was a solid mass of onrushing buffalo, their front extending from horizon to horizon, running with their heads down and making a grunting noise like distant rumbling thunder.

"Corral the wagons quick! Put the stock inside!"

We had no more than done this when the first buffalo began to pass. We opened fire on the leaders in a line directly north of our wagon. We were armed with Henry rifles and could fire shots quicker than with the old .50 calibre Springfield breech-loading needle-gun so popular on the plains. We dropped them fast and piled them so high on the north side of our camp the herd turned off on either side, leaving our corral free of danger.

We continued to shoot buffalo as fast as we could reload, from a circle on either side and firing into the rear of the herd as it passed. The herd continued to pass all night, and we kept shooting buffalo. By daybreak, we had used up all but 100 rounds of our ammunition.

Then we all lay down to sleep. We had had such a strenuous night that we were very tired and it was nearly noon before any of us awoke. Buffalo were still stringing past, but by the middle of the afternoon, the last of the herd had disappeared. For miles around, the grass was obliterated.

Buffalo were scattered everywhere, some of them a mile from camp where they had fallen and died. We had killed so many it took us two weeks to get them skinned and all the hides dried.

The following summer, young Lillie started another trip, going this time with a government train freighting from Wichita to the Ponca Agency, just established northwest of the Pawnees.

In July, the Ponca Indians had been removed from the Quapaw reservation south of Baxter Springs, where they had been temporarily located in transit from their old reservation in South Dakota. In the large bend of the Salt Fork, two miles west of its confluence with the Arkansas, where there was plenty of cool, sweet water from springs which ran out along the river bluffs, and in an area well-timbered with cottonwood, oak, walnut and pecan, the government had constructed a commissary building with two small office rooms.

Gordon found the Indians living in tents, in one large village, around the agency. Agent William H. Whiteman, who had come down with the tribe from the Quapaw reservation, told him that no attempt had been made to raise a crop of any kind that year, because the tribe had arrived too late in the season, and that the Indians would have to depend entirely upon government supplies for subsistence.

Whiteman already was trying to get the tribe to select the land upon which they wished to make their homes and move upon it, or at least to break up in bands away from the village. The half-breeds had moved to the mouth of the Chikaskia, eight miles west of the agency, and others were considering the matter seriously by the time Gordon made his second trip from Wichita to the agency with the government freight train.

Horse thieves had been quite active in the Territory during the summer of 1878. Thirty-seven ponies had been stolen from the Pawnees in one night, and a few weeks later a dozen more had disappeared. Details of soldiers had been sent in pursuit each time, and in each instance returned with neither the thieves nor the horses. In August, the military turned over to the charge of Agent P. B. Hunt of the Kiowa and Comanche Agency forty-eight Quahada Comanches they had been able to capture.

Pawnee Agent Samuel S. Ely had requested authorization to hire a man who knew the country to lead a detail furnished by the military, but was advised the government was doing all that might be done to put an end to the rustling.

The raids continued. The Pawnees were much discouraged and seemed to think too little effort was being made to recover their property. Lillie recalled:

> We were in camp with our wagons south of the Ponca Agency when a party of about twenty Pawnee bucks in full war paint, each wearing a knife and carrying a gleaming rifle in the crook of his arm, came at us out of the dawn. They had approached so silently that the freighters gasped in amazement.
>
> For a moment, both groups stared at each other like statues. Then the Pawnees placed their rifles on the ground and their chief greeted:
>
> "Nowee! No want fight, we Pawnee brothers. We come to find Little Bear."

Gordon recognized Chief Left Hand, who, after some parley in his own language, told him the Comanches had wounded one of their night guards and stolen nearly fifty head of ponies. They de-

sired Gordon to assist in recovering the animals and punishing the
Comanches for their crime.

I told the freighters I would have to take up the cause of my
adopted tribe, and I went back with Left Hand and his braves and
picked up the trail. The Comanches had divided the stolen horses
into five bunches and gone off in different directions to avoid capture. We divided our Indians into five groups, each going after a
different band of Comanches.

Left Hand and I started out with eight braves. We soon struck
a hot trail and followed it to Skeleton Creek. Here the Comanches
had driven all the horses into the water, and waded upstream for
more than a mile to cover their trail. It took us a long time to find
where they had come out of the creek, and we again hurried on.
The trail was already old. As the main body of our braves was three
or four miles away, we didn't take time to wait for them. We came
upon the enemy about sundown. There were a dozen of them
driving the stolen horses.

We gave chase. When they saw us gaining on them, they did their
best to escape. Their leader wheeled his pony and fired at me. The
bullet went past my leg and into my horse. As my horse went down,
the savage ran at me, shooting as he advanced. His next shot clip-
ped a piece from my hair. I shot him through the arm and he
dropped his gun. He whirled back again, and tried to reach his
friends, but Chief Left Hand shot him through the head. Their
chief dead, the others became panic stricken and fled every
direction, abandoning the stolen horses, which were triumphantly
recaptured by the Pawnees.

We found the dead Indian to be Pretty Bear, who was looked
upon even in his own tribe as a "bad" Indian. Left Hand scalped
him and took off Pretty Bear's belt. On it we found six scalps, one
of these a woman's, with long, silky blonde hair.

Gordon rejoined his outfit at the Ponca Agency, and continued
his trip across the Territory to Fort Sill, which was their destination. His chase after the Comanches had greatly impressed Left
Hand, who told the other Pawnee chiefs of Little Bear's great act of
friendship in their behalf. The freighters reached Fort Sill safely

and started back to Wichita. They were camped on Skeleton Creek
in the Outlet when Chief Spotted Horse of the Pawnees called on
Gordon, accompanied by four United States cavalrymen:

> The old chief dismounted and held out his hand to shake mine.
> This was an unusual thing for a chief to do. White men shook
> hands, but Indians did not. It showed that he had much respect
> for me.
>
> He said to me in Indian language: "I am old man, and have
> come long way for my people." He told me they wanted me to come
> back to the tribe and become their chief.
>
> I went back. Soon afterward, a council was held. Spotted Horse,
> Good Horse, Eagle Chief, Left Hand, Long Feather and the other
> chiefs elected me their white chief. Then they held an elaborate
> ceremony, with feasting and dancing which lasted several days.
> There, with legs crossed, and seated in a circle with the Indians, I
> smoked the pipe of peace. They placed upon me the great coat of
> honor, and I was then a real chief of the Pawnees.

Shortly after Gordon Lillie became their White Chief, Major
Edward Hale Bowman arrived from Fort Bliss, Texas, as agent to
the Pawnees. The Secretary of the Interior thought Major Bowman's military experience particularly fitted him to handle the Indians. Bowman was quick to note the high regard with which the
Indians held young Lillie, and taking advantage of his influence and popularity with them, immediately made him official
interpreter.

Major Bowman told the Indians that the white man eventually
would "crowd them out," and their only salvation lay in moving
onto the land, cultivating it and holding it. He originated the idea
of giving them their land in severalty and obtained permission
through the Department of the Interior to hire a civil engineer to
make these allotments. Fifty-five quarter sections were assigned the
Indians, and the name "Bowman" still appears on stones that mark
surveys of these first choice locations in different parts of the
Pawnee country.

To the first Indians who moved upon their lands, Major Bowman
showed special favor by furnishing them work cattle, implements

and seed, and sending the agency farmer and his helpers to instruct
and assist them. Boys were taught to work and build and farm;
the girls to cook and sew and clean. Within a few months, Gordon
Lillie witnessed a decided improvement in the condition of the
tribe.

By spring, two of the bands had moved from the vicinity of the
agency to their respective breakings, which were cross-plowed for
them, harrowed and put in condition for planting. About six hundred acres were added to the fields already under cultivation, total-
ing more than one thousand acres. Most of the land was planted
with corn; however, many of the Indians cultivated small plots of
onions, beets, tomatoes, cabbage and other garden crops. Some of
the Indians wanted to do more, and Bowman issued them milk
cows, calves and hogs. The Pawnees appreciated this, gave the stock
the best of care, and hoped that by another year they would have
cattle and hogs of their own.

They appeared to understand the necessity of engaging in civilized pursuits other than industry in stock-raising and agriculture.
They went into the woods, cut the trees, split the rails, and hauled
and built them into fences and better dwellings. Nearly eight hundred rods of fence were built, twelve log and two frame houses completed, and more than a score of others were under construction
before summer.

Several Indians found employment as apprentices and teamsters,
helping the government carpenter, blacksmith and farmer, and
there were more applications for these positions, and for general
work, than could be accommodated. Agency improvements and
repairs were made. A gristmill was completed. Early in May, they
finished a manual labor school building capable of accommodating
one hundred pupils.

The Pawnee showed much interest in having their children attend school. Although many lived several miles from the agency,
the attendance during that year reached a good average, and a
request had been made by the chiefs and headmen for another day
school and that the manual labor school be opened as soon as
possible.

Major Bowman instituted other reforms. Some of the Indian
dances were objectionable, and he provided nightly entertainments

for both young and old, with music, singing and speaking, to replace them. Everyone was invited, and Gordon was on hand to explain things to those unable to speak English. These entertainments were called "collections" (of people, not money).

The cares of agent were rather oppressive and exacting at times. Major Bowman was obliged to listen to all complaints and grievances and was the final judge to whom his charges came for justice, protection and redress. He decided to shift some of the responsibility from his shoulders. When the next important case came up, a venire was issued to the captain of the Indian police to summon twelve jurors.

The parties in dispute, jurors and witnesses reported promptly, full of curious interest. The Major called court to session under the spreading branches of a large white oak tree in the yard, and with great gravity, explained to the parties at variance that their differences were to be submitted to a jury of their own people, who would decide under oath from the evidence of the sworn witnesses what was just and right according to their best judgment, and their decision would be final. He explained to all the solemnity of an oath in calling on God (Ti-ra-wa), the Great Spirit, to witness that they told the truth, and told the Indians that Ti-ra-wa would be angry with them if they spoke with forked tongues.

The jurors were sworn and the facts presented: An industrious Indian policeman had raised a nice field of corn, and his fence had been torn down by hungry cattle. There was a village corral for the safekeeping of horses and cattle at night, but a few lazy and dishonest men of the tribe neglected to yard their stock, and the policeman's cornfield had suffered badly. The policeman protested in vain. Finally, in a moment of exasperation, he lifted his carbine and dropped the lead steer of the herd. He notified the owner, who came and dressed the carcass. The meat was eaten and the hide sold, but the owner had lost the money which the growth of the steer would have brought, and his action was to recover this damage.

The jury deliberated long and patiently, then brought in its verdict: Between the policeman and the owner of the steer, things were even. Both had been damaged, and neither should pay the other anything. But the policeman had been damaged by other people's cattle and, therefore, everyone whose cattle had been trespassing should pay him a bushel of corn, and until the corn crop was gathered, should herd the animals by day and corral them at night, so there would be no further damage or shooting.

The verdict was approved, an order of execution placed in the hands of another policeman, and peace again reigned in the village. The right of every man to the product of his own labor had been vindicated in Pawnee. Trial by jury became an established institution, and Gordon witnessed some very interesting trials and heard some astounding verdicts in later cases.

Indian customs prevailed to a greater or lesser extent as they saw the necessity for abandoning them. As soon as a house was finished, a request for table, chairs and bedstead followed. If the owner of the house had several ponies, he invariably wished to exchange one for a cooking stove and culinary implements. A number of Indians exchanged ponies for hogs.

Major Bowman reported to the Commissioner of Indian Affairs:

The Pawnees have awakened to the importance of becoming self-supporting. If encouragement to labor in agricultural pursuits and care of stock is continued for the adults, and a better and more healthful mode of living provided for the children, with improvement of schools, both manual labor and day, so that all those of school age can attend, this question of civilization, which is the work of an age, can approach solution among these people in a generation.

The Pawnees gave up their winter buffalo hunt without trouble. The firm but gentle means of getting them to take allotments and start preparing for their spring crops and fencing their fields had induced them to abandon it, though they occasionally referred to the hunt for the coming summer.

In May, 1879, when Bowman gave them permission to go on their last buffalo hunt, Gordon went with them. The party consisted of fifty hunters with buffalo ponies. The balance were squaws, boys, old men and poorly mounted bucks. There were not a half-dozen guns among them. It was the spectacle of a genuine buffalo hunt with the primitive bow and arrow. Rations of beef, flour, sugar and coffee were issued, and the party headed west, hoping to find buffalo within one hundred and fifty miles.

On June 2, the Pawnees had reached Fort Elliott in the Texas Panhandle, without finding buffalo. Their rations were depleted. The citizens of Wheeler County resented their presence. They accused the Indians of stealing hogs, and sent a highly exaggerated petition to the Governor, charging they were "occupying an extreme outlying frontier position, surrounded and depressed by disorder and lawlessness, with no security for life and property, subject not only to merciless depredations of Indians, but thieves, murderers, escaped convicts, and outlaws from New Mexico, Colorado, Kansas and Indian Territory."

The Texans appeared before Colonel J. S. Davidson, in command at Fort Elliott, and demanded the ponies of the Pawnees in compensation for the alleged depredations. Gordon told the Colonel that "Pawnees hardly ever steal anything," and asked protection from a company of Rangers in the vicinity who were under orders to shoot every Indian found in Texas.

Colonel Davidson kept the Pawnees at the post two days, rationed them, and suggested they start back toward their reservation. A company of infantry under Captain E. H. Liscum accompanied them to Fort Supply in the Indian Territory, where they were placed in charge of the commander, Major Alexander J. Dallas.

The Pawnees were disappointed. They had to be back to their reservation by June 19; they had lost several ponies, and were without rations. Major Dallas took these factors into consideration when Gordon asked that the Indians be permitted to go on a ten-day hunt before starting their homeward trek. Dallas believed they could find buffalo within fifty miles of the post, and sent a captain, lieutenant, sergeant and six enlisted men as escort, to prevent further trouble between the Indians and Texans.

They traveled west up the valley of the Beaver to the crossing of the great Texas cattle trail to Dodge City, then up Kiowa Creek into No Man's Land. They found three buffalo and killed one. The next day they killed two antelope and a fawn. Far out on the plains they made camp, and sent out scouts to search for further game.

Some of the Pawnees were ready to turn back. The big buffalo herds on the northern ranges had been exterminated, and the Indians "looked dejected" upon finding the only range left between Dakota and Mexico invaded and destroyed. Lillie wrote:

The Indians had a legend about the buffalo. There were probably fifty million buffalo on the plains, and they dropped about ten million calves a year. The Indians used to say that it was impossible to kill all the buffalo because they came from a big hole in the ground somewhere, and as they were killed, others came to take their place. White hunters must have believed this too, because they destroyed them by the millions with reckless lack of foresight.

Until 1870, there had been little demand for buffalo hides among the whites. Most of the skins had been obtained by post traders and sub-traders, who mingled and ofter intermarried with the Indians and were familiar with their methods. A fine robe could be had for a few cups of brown sugar, a pipe-clay ornament for the breast, a German-silver ornament for the scalp lock, or a couple of yards of cloth for a breechclout.

This desultory trading had not diminished the vast herds of buffalo. White men had slaughtered them for sheer lust of slaughter. European hunting parties had gone out to see how many buffalo they could kill in one day. Then enterprising businessmen showed Europe and America how the skin could be utilized for leather, coats and rugs, and professional hunters carried out the work of destruction systematically. Others killed them by the score to get their tongues for table delicacies, and left tons of meat to the wolves or to rot on the plains. Hundreds were slaughtered for a single meal from the tongue or hump.

From the first colonies down through the early 1870's the whites had slowly pushed the red man back into the wide, vast region between Canada and the Rio Grande where he had made his last stand. In less than ten years the buffalo hunter had accomplished what the people of all the states had failed to do in two hundred at great cost of blood and property. By simply destroying the food, clothing and shelter of the roaming Indian, they had made it impossible for him any longer to stand in the path of advancing civilization. They had done more to pacify the savage of the plains than had the United States Army.

About noon the scouts reported a herd of thirty-five buffalo grazing on the edge of a deep cut ravine about ten miles away. The
Pawnees killed twenty of these, and spent the next day in camp
curing meat and hides. They reached the head of Kiowa Creek,
found nothing, moved to Duck-Ponds Creek, found only eight
buffalo and killed all of them.

Unbelievingly, the Pawnees turned back to their reservation,
their season a failure. They stopped for a brief visit with their Ponca
neighbors, gave them some of the dried meat, and advised them
there were no longer enough buffalo on the plains to sustain a hunting party. The Indians were convinced that in the future they must
rely upon tilling the ground and stock-raising or starve. Soon they
must adopt the way of the white man in all its varieties, even to
exchanging their small ponies, worthless except for riding, for a
smaller number of large work horses and mules.

Lillie recalled:

This disappointment of the Indians made an impression on me
that grew deeper as the years passed and first put the idea in my
head of trying to preserve to future men and women this noble
animal — the buffalo.

PAWNEE BILL AT THE HEIGHT OF HIS SHOW CAREER, C. 1900. *G. W. Lillie Collection, Division of Mss., University of Oklahoma Library, Norman.*

BUCKSKIN JOE AND PAWNEE BILL, 1888. *G. W. Lillie Collection, Division of Mss., University of Oklahoma Library, Norman.*

MAY LILLIE, AS SHE APPEARED WITH PAWNEE BILL'S HISTORICAL WILD WEST, C. 1890. *G. W. Lillie Collection, Division of Mss., University of Oklahoma Library, Norman.*

PAWNEE BILL'S HISTORIC WILD WEST. Cover for show program of 1894. *Author's Collection.*

Pawnee Bill as Government Interpreter and Teacher at Pawnee Agency, c. 1880. *G. W. Lillie Collection, Division of Mss., University of Oklahoma Library, Norman.*

Pawnee Bill's Wild West in Parade through Streets of Pawnee, Oklahoma, in Celebration of Oklahoma Statehood, Nov. 16, 1907. *Author's Collection.*

PAWNEE BILL AND MAY LILLIE AT CEREMONY CELEBRATING THEIR FIFTIETH WEDDING ANNIVERSARY, TAOS, NEW MEXICO, AUG. 31, 1936. *G. W. Lillie Collection, Division of Mss., University of Oklahoma Library, Norman.*

PAWNEE BILL AND BUFFALO BILL COMBINING SHOWS IN 1908, "the largest merger ever consummated in the amusement field." *G. W. Lillie Collection, Division of Mss., University of Oklahoma Library, Norman.*

6.   Interpreter–Teacher–Cowboy

GORDON continued in the employ of Major Bowman as interpreter and secretary. He was nearly twenty now. As agent, Bowman was in charge of the Indian school, and Gordon, with his previous teaching experience, rendered valuable assistance in its operation.

The large stone building which had been completed in May was used as a dormitory and the small one used for classrooms. There were over a hundred students enrolled, ranging in age from six to nineteen. They were detailed to work, as well as taught English and a book education. A seamstress was hired to oversee the girls in the sewing room. A matron and assistant matron taught and looked after their dining room manners, and supervised the play-room in inclement weather. All slept in the dormitory and made their own beds each morning. An Indian truant officer brought back runaway children.

In the fall of 1879, an Indian youth named Colonel Meacham made life so unbearable at the school that three teachers quickly resigned. Agent Bowman was gravely concerned. In idle jest, Gordon told him he not only could teach the school, but could discipline the boy. To his amazement, Agent Bowman nominated him to the Commissioner of Indian Affairs, who approved his appointment, and Gordon Lillie found himself teaching fifty half-grown girls and boys.

Colonel Meacham was a hulking young brave about Gordon's age, crooked-faced and surly. The first day at school, he "badgered" Gordon with his "aversion to the virtues of obedience." After a particularly hostile display of contempt for classroom discipline, Gordon decided to keep him after school to give him time to reflect on the "error of his ways."

The fire had died down in the pot-bellied stove which heated the room, and Gordon picked up the poker and began to adjust the embers on the grate before adding more wood. For a moment, his back was upon his recalcitrant pupil. He heard a desk scrape, and whirled to see Colonel Meacham rushing up the aisle with a knife.

Gordon couldn't move. The stove blocked his way. There was only one thing to do. As the Indian leaped for his throat, he swung the heavy iron poker. Colonel Meacham dropped to the floor.

Gordon thought he had killed him. Blood spread in a pool under his head. Finally, the Indian moved, and Gordon summoned the doctor.

The youth was in the hospital several days. When he was released, he was transferred to the boarding school to keep down further clashes over the incident. But Colonel Meacham gave no further trouble, and Gordon had no more difficulty in his classroom for several weeks.

One morning Chief Spotted Horse appeared in the classroom with a young brave from his band named Frank West,* and demanded a suit of clothes for him. Gordon explained that he had nothing to do with the government allotment of clothing.

"You will have to see Major Bowman," he said.

"You can get them," Spotted Horse insisted in Pawnee.

"No," Gordon declared. "Frank probably has his clothes, anyway."

The chief's hand dropped to his knife. Gordon shook his head. The knife flashed, and Gordon turned pale. But he kept his nerve, and advanced on the Indian. Either from fear of the consequences of a knifing or respect for Gordon's courage, Spotted Horse backed from the room with no further show of hostility. But his brave never forgot the incident, according to Lillie:

> With the vengeful spirit of all red men, he held the quarrel in his breast. The government had to change their method of handing out beef to the Pawnees. Heretofore, the cattle purchased by the government had been turned loose and the Indians had the fun of running them down like buffalo. It was anything but civilizing to see an Indian chasing a steer half a mile, shooting at it a dozen times, then after death to see squaws and papooses gather around

* As the Pawnees grew accustomed to the white man's ways, they gave white names to their children.

and eat blood red meat still warm. The humanitarians decided this way was too cruel and ordered that the beef be killed and weighed out to the Indians.

The red men were sore. They didn't want their fun spoiled, and it looked like a general uprising. The army sent in troops just in time to prevent what probably would have been a massacre, and the Indians gave in.

One day I was helping butcher some of the beef when Frank West caught me off guard and plunged a tomahawk into my head. I didn't know anything for several days. Everyone thought I was going to die. Meanwhile, the Indian escaped. I never saw him again, but I carried the scar on my head the rest of my life.

Spotted Horse felt sorry and blamed himself for the trouble. He invited Gordon to his lodge, where he treated him as a brother, and accorded him the honor of witnessing a scalp dance in the great council house.

The scalp dance was a very impressive ceremony to the Indian, and jealously guarded from the eyes of white men. In the course of the dance, a warrior appeared with the scalp of a red-haired woman and enacted the scene of how he had gone into the camp and captured her, mimicking her screams as he had taken her scalp. It was the only scalp dance Gordon ever attended during all his years among the Indians.

He had no more trouble as teacher at the school. He was firm, but fair, and the students respected him. He taught many Indian youths who were to make him proud of them in later years.

One of his star pupils was Sun Chief, whose white name was Mark Evarts. He was born in the Nebraska Pawnee village in 1862, the son of Si-ti-he-wa-hoot (They-gave-him-applause-for-doing-good-deeds), chief of the Skidi clan. As a small boy he listened attentively to the other chiefs when they gathered at his father's lodge and learned the ceremonials and rituals of his tribe. He attended the agency school, wearing only breechclout and sheet, finished his education at the Carlisle Indian School in Pennsylvania under its founder and superintendent, Captain R. H. Pratt, who had served in the Indian campaigns of 1874-75, and he returned to become a chief of the Pawnees.

Another of Gordon's students was Tay-loo-wah-ah-who, named William Pollock for an official in the Indian service. After leaving the agency school, he entered the Haskell Institute at Lawrence, Kansas, where he became an outstanding artist. The small Studebaker wagons assembled at the school and sent to the Indians bore his paintings on their sideboards and tail gates. His ability became widely recognized, and his work was exhibited in the Smithsonian Institution at Washington.

When the Spanish-American War broke out, Pollock was among the first to volunteer. As a member of Troop D, First Cavalry, Roosevelt's Rough Riders, he fought with distinction in the battles of Las Guasimas, San Juan Hill and Santiago, and won special commendation from Colonel Theodore Roosevelt. When the war ended, he returned to his people. He died of pneumonia at Pawnee in March, 1899, shortly after signing a contract to appear in Buffalo Bill's Wild West at Madison Square Garden.

In 1880, Gordon's father and mother and two sisters came to the Pawnee Agency, his father to fill the post of government baker and his mother to teach agency women and girls the art of homemaking. Each was paid one hundred dollars a month, and thought they could save enough money to build a real home on their Kansas homestead. Later, Newton Lillie brought overland from Wellington and erected at the agency the first flour mill in the Territory.

On baking days, the Indian boys were detailed to mix the bread in big tubs, and the girls put it in the pans. Newton Lillie would build a fire in the huge rock ovens, then rake out the coals when the rocks were hot enough to bake the bread evenly. Sixty loaves were baked three times a week.

At first, Effie and Lena went to school with the Indian children, then Newton Lillie hired a private teacher for them. They got religious training at the old government-owned Baptist Mission, and the family groceries came from Wellington by wagon and mule team. Finally, Lena got a job as matron at the Indian boarding school, and Albert, who had stayed on the farm in Kansas, began freighting supplies to the Ponca Agency at White Eagle, the Pawnee Agency and the newly established Otoe Agency at Red Rock.

Under the provisions of an act of Congress approved March 3, 1881, the Otoe and Missouri tribes were assigned a reserve of

130,000 acres southwest of the Arkansas and east of the Indian Meridian,* between the Ponca and Pawnee. Albert Lillie followed the old Sac and Fox trail, which ran south from Arkansas City through the Ponca and Otoe reservations, then angled southeast to the Pawnee and south again to the Sac and Fox Agency east of the unassigned Oklahoma Lands in the center of the Territory.

He made the trip from Wellington to Ponca in one day, and on to Pawnee the next. It was a good trail, and all these Indians were friendly. The Pawnee, Otoe and Ponca visited back and forth and held their ceremonial dances and presented gifts of ponies, money and trinkets to the visitors.

The Osage and Pawnee were not so friendly. The Osage had a custom of getting a scalp from a member of some other tribe to bury with their headmen. They believed the owner of the scalp would be a sort of servant to the headman when he reached the hereafter. The Osage took scalps from the Pawnee until the Pawnee put an end to the practice. There were other disagreements over stealing each other's horses and hunting wild game on their reservations.

There were still plenty of deer, antelope and turkey around Pawnee Agency in the early 1880's. There was little meat rationed to the Indians besides the cattle bought and butchered by the government, and the Pawnees lived mostly on the game they shot or trapped. They would jerk the meat and hang it on a line or in a tree to cure, or smoke it. When the tribes held their powwows, the visiting tribes brought the food for the feasts. Albert, through Gordon's acquaintance with the Indians, was able to witness many of their ceremonies and dances he otherwise would never have been allowed to attend.

Gordon Lillie found teaching at the agency the most interesting work of his career, and he became a staunch friend of Major Bowman. Bowman placed him in charge of the day school, with the head

* In 1870 a complete survey of the lands of Oklahoma was begun by the federal government under the public lands survey system. An initial point was established a mile south of old Fort Arbuckle, in Murray County, eight miles west of Davis, and was identified by a stone marker which still exists at this writing. Through this point, the surveyors ran a true north-south line across Oklahoma from Kansas to Texas, a line known as the Indian Meridian.

of the boarding school as superintendent over both. This left Gordon plenty of time to spend outdoors.

He picked up weight and his shoulders broadened. His dark eyes were piercing. A mustache adorned his upper lip, and his thick, wavy brown hair fell to his shoulders. A buckskin hunting shirt, open at the throat, and a huge broadbrimmed hat lent an air of the picturesque. Five feet eight inches in height, but well-muscled, he presented a figure to command respect—a far cry from the fifteen-year-old, undeveloped youth who had come riding down from Wichita to take up life among the Indians.

At the same time he got the nickname by which he is best known to posterity. Few outside his family called him Gordon. The agency employees called him Bill Lillie. But there were already so many Bills in that part of the Territory that they needed something to add to it. The Indians found the name difficult and pronounced it Bill Illy. But, since he lived and worked among the Pawnee Indians, they called him "Pawnee Bill."

The name stuck, and was to become as significant as those of Wild Bill (James Butler Hickok) and Buffalo Bill (William F. Cody) in the history of the West.

Pawnee Bill had been teaching little more than a year when the superintendent accepted another government post, leaving him temporarily in charge until the vacancy could be filled from Washington. Pawnee Bill might have applied for the position, but he lacked political influence and was too young.

When the new superintendent, G. W. Martin, arrived, Lillie formed an immediate dislike for him. From the man's conversation, it was apparent he cared little for the school, and really was after the job of Indian agent.

Lillie told Major Bowman the man was no friend of his. The Major laughed, and reckoned that as long as he ran things right he would keep his office.

A few weeks later, the government inspector visited the agency. He was closeted in the office of the new superintendent for hours. Shortly after, it was rumored that Bowman might be dismissed.

Lillie was indignant, and told Bowman, in the presence of the superintendent, that the latter had lied about him to the inspector. Bowman petitioned Washington for a "square deal." He remained in office, and the superintendent was reprimanded for his conniving.

The superintendent was jealous of Lillie's loyalty to Bowman. One morning Lillie walked into Bowman's office to find the agent greatly agitated.

"Bill," he said, "Martin has brought charges against you."

"What kind of charges?"

Bowman shifted uncomfortably. "What would be the easiest thing to believe on a young man teaching Indian girls? I don't believe them, of course."

Lillie stamped out, face flushed with anger, and barged into the office of the superintendent.

"What's this about you bringing charges against me?" His temper put an edge on his voice.

"I can't have a young man under me whose morals are questionable—"

Lillie struck him. The superintendent tossed up his hands like a man drowning and sprawled backward. His head struck the window ledge, cutting a wide gash in his scalp, and he dropped loosely to the floor.

"I ought to kill you!" muttered Lillie. For a moment, he stood over him, the impulse slow to leave. Then he turned and strode silently out the doorway. Bowman found him later, and appeared deeply concerned.

"Bill, you're lucky you didn't break his neck. He says you tried to. They have taken him to the hospital. He wants to file charges of assault to murder."

Lillie laughed sarcastically. "He's just full of charges, isn't he?"

Lillie's resignation was imperative. He left his papers with Bowman and departed for Wellington. Bowman soon wrote him that the superintendent had recovered and had dropped all charges, apparently satisfied that Lillie had left the agency.

Bowman asked him to come back, and in a letter to the Honorable Hiram Price, Commissioner of Indian Affairs, July 13, 1881, he nominated Lillie for another position:

I forward today for your action the name Gordon Lillie for Shoe and Harness Maker. The reason for it is this: We greatly need a new Commissary Building. Without one properly planned and constructed, it will be almost impossible to induce this people to take the necessary care and forethought in saving seed and roots for future crops. There is a large amount due from the Pawnees in labor for wagons, harness, etc., which by freighting alone will be an almost interminable job to get worked out. I propose, by the authority already granted me, to employ the Indians with their teams to haul stone for the building. But I cannot induce them to provide the stone ready for hauling. I intend to make Mr. Lillie take charge of the business of quarrying and preparing material ready for loading.

He is intelligent, active and zealous in all his undertakings and conscientious in performance of his duties. He has knowledge sufficient and will power to make it efficient. Mr. Lillie was a very excellent, capable and efficient teacher in our school. I nominated him on the recommendation of Hon. David Davis, United States Senator of Illinois. He has proved himself worthy of confidence and does honor to his sponsors. He resigned his position as teacher in the school in consequence of a difficulty with the superintendent, in which Mr. Lillie became exasperated almost to madness by insinuations and indirect charges most seriously affecting his character as a teacher of female pupils. I had the matter under investigation, and would have finished at the next sitting, but under what Mr. Lillie considered intense provocation, he knocked the superintendent down. Of course, this made the necessity for his resigning. I had advanced in the investigation so far that I could see that Lillie was in the toils of a "wire worker." I had told you previously that G. W. Martin had to my intense surprise developed the character and qualities of a "wire worker," but that I had him under control in the agency. I did not anticipate any deviltry in the school. I think this quality of Martin's was the source of the trouble.

I have written at this length that you may have as clear a comprehension as practicable of the circumstances. I believe Mr. Lillie to be a worthy and valuable man. He can talk very well with the Pawnees and is a useful man to keep here. And I think the construction of a good commissary building a matter of prime necessity. . . . I propose, with your approval, to detail Mr. Lillie to take the oversight and management of the quarrying of stone, etc., at the same time keeping the harness in proper repair.

I respectfully ask your approval of the nomination.

Major Bowman's request was denied. In August, 1881, Lillie received his last government check in full payment for his services at the agency, and remained in Sumner County, Kansas.

That winter he worked for Oscar Evans, his cousin, hauling corn to the big cattle ranches in the Cherokee Outlet. Often they found the creeks and rivers swollen so they could not cross. Sometimes they swam their teams and floated their wagons, and when their wagons were empty they had to tie the beds down to the standards with wire or ropes to keep them from floating away. Later, when the rivers and creeks were frozen, they had to unhitch their teams and drive them across to the opposite bank, then tie a long rope or chain from the wagon to the bank and pull their loads across because their teams could not stand up on the ice. They received forty and fifty cents a bushel for corn, and hauled over five hundred bushels to one ranch located near Red Rock.

The whole broad expanse to the west grazed cattle. Everywhere cowboys and their ponies could be seen riding across the prairie. South of the Outlet was the Cheyenne and Arapahoe reservation, bounded on the west by the Texas Panhandle, on the south by Greer County and the Kiowa-Comanche-Wichita reservation, and on the east by the Oklahoma Lands. It was a fertile region, traversed by the Canadian and Washita rivers. The Cimarron formed, for a distance, its northwestern boundary, and its southwestern boundary was the North Fork of Red River.

In the great council at Medicine Lodge in 1867, the Cheyenne and Arapahoe tribes had been assigned this reservation. The Cheyenne did not like these lands, and never accepted them. This tribe numbered nearly four thousand, and were among the wildest and most warlike Indians on the continent. They had written their history in blood throughout the area of the Great Plains from Texas to the Canadian border, and not until the relentless campaigns of 1868-69 were waged against the Indians of this region, including the hostile Kiowa and Comanche, were the tribes located upon their reservation, an agency established, and a force of cavalry placed at Fort Reno for its protection.

Long before 1881, however, ranchmen had seen the value of the rich pasture lands of the whole western half of the Indian Territory. They had fattened their herds on the rich grass since their first great cattle drives from Texas to the Kansas "cowtowns" in 1866. As the railroad extended westward, the Chisholm Trail ran north along the eastern boundary of the Cheyenne-Arapahoe reservation, and as the rails reached Dodge City, the great Western Trail cut through the heart of it from south to north.

From time immemorial, the Cheyenne and Arapahoe had been accustomed to subsist largely upon the buffalo. Once these animals had occupied in great numbers the lands included in the reservation, but when driven further west by the guns of the hunters, the Indian bureau had made contracts with ranchmen to supply the Indians with beef. These beef contractors brought the first cattle to the reservation for actual grazing. They were allowed to pasture their herds near the agency in order to issue a certain number of animals to the Indians each week.

As the buffalo disappeared and the quantity of beef increased, the ranchmen began to seek the privilege of pasturing their herds permanently. While this was contrary to law, the ambitious and resourceful cattlemen found ways to overcome it. They gave the Indians beef and money for pasturing privileges in the northern part of the reservation. By 1882, over 22,000 head of cattle were grazing on a range lying partly on the lands of the Cheyenne-Arapahoe. The cattlemen had leased grazing lands in the Outlet from the Cherokee. White men who had worked for the government and traded among the Indians bought Texas cattle and obtained grazing leases granted by the Osage Council, covering 75,000 acres of their reservation. Others had moved onto the free grass in the Oklahoma Lands on which no Indians had been located, and built corrals and ranchhouses of native logs.

The Secretary of Interior refused to approve these leases, but made no objection to them so long as the rights of the Indians were safeguarded. He reserved the right, however, of cancelling any and all such lease agreements whenever he deemed it for the best interests of the Indians and the government.

Hauling corn to these ranchers was rather too quiet for Lillie's active disposition, and in the spring following his last trip to the Outlet, he went on roundup for the Hutton Ranch, whose range was on Skeleton Creek. In the fall, he got a job on the Zimmerman Ranch on the Skeleton at roundup time:

In our camp was a young preacher from England who had joined the outfit, hoping the life and pure air of the great prairie would repair his health, which had failed through long, hard study. He was a gentlemanly, courteous fellow with a smile and a pleasant remark for everybody, wore a regular toy-shop cowboy outfit and carried a beautiful revolver.

The boys in the outfit had little to amuse themselves, and a preacher in a cow camp was more fun than dancing with each other to the music produced by Shorty on his tin whistle. The preacher became the butt of all jokes, but all the boys were good natured and meant no harm, except one, a surly Mexican, who carried things too far.

The second evening after the preacher arrived, Mex brought out one of the worst broncs on the ranch. He told the Englishman she was gentle enough for even a lady to ride and that he wouldn't even need a saddle. I got to the corral in time to see the preacher climb aboard. Mex gave the animal a lash with his quirt and the mare humped up and went straight in the air. The Englishman had plenty of grit. He hung on about three minutes. Then the mare hit the far end of the corral, dropped her head between her knees, raised up her hind legs and sent him over the fence.

He lay quite still on the ground. His ankle was broken. We had to carry him into our dugout, where he was laid up several weeks. By the time we were ready to trail the herd to winter pasture, he was able to ride, but still pretty sick.

Mex made life miserable for him all the way. One evening after supper, he told the Englishman to dance for him. This was impossible with a broken ankle that hardly had mended. When he refused, Mex began shooting at his feet.

The boys didn't like it, but Mex was such a bad brute none cared to stop him. I couldn't stand it any longer. I told him to quit teasing the poor fellow. Mex squinted his eyes and looked fiercely at me and said if I had any regard for my own health I had better start taking care of it. When he fired another shot at the Englishman's feet, I stepped between them, stuck my face square up to his, and told him not to do it again.

The other boys were so surprised and scared it was a half minute before any drew a breath. They all thought I had gone crazy. Their eyes were riveted on us. They felt sorry for me, I suppose they thought I was too young to know better. Mex was a six-footer, square and muscular, with thin lips and heavy brows hanging over steely eyes. A big scar ran across his face from cheek to cheek, leaving a dent in his nose where somebody had cut through it with a knife. He stood stock still while my threat sank in, then began to reload his gun to shoot at me.

The boys, to prevent what they thought was sure murder, took his revolver away from him, and said I didn't mean anything and would apologize. But I told them I wouldn't apologize to anybody who would take advantage of a sick man. I unbuckled my own belt and let my gun drop on the ground. Then I took off my coat and tossed it to the Englishman, who stood too stunned to say anything.

Mex let out a volley of oaths and rushed me. I sidestepped and hit him hard on the chin. He reeled a little. Then I danced around and gave him another hard punch, getting away quickly before he could hit me. The boys were having a high time, and yelled encouragement to both of us. We clinched and fell, rolled over and over, hitting and punching whenever we got a chance. Then Mex ran his hand back and whipped out a skinning knife the boys had overlooked when they disarmed him.

I grabbed his hand. He struggled and swore, but I twisted his wrist harder and harder until he was forced to drop the knife. Then I got up and left him lying on the ground. A square fight was too clean an argument for a man of his caliber. Mex had talked so long and loud of his strength and daring that all had believed him. The boys looked disappointed.

A few nights later, I was sitting alone near the camp when I suddenly turned to see Mex behind me with his revolver leveled at my head. He had followed after he had seen me come away from the wagon without my gun.

"You know I'm unarmed," I said. "Go ahead and shoot, if you've got the nerve, and be hanged!"

He holstered his gun and walked away. The next morning he had disappeared on one of the horses that belonged to the ranch.

While the cattle were on winter range, Lillie had his first experience with rustlers:

We had trailed the three men for two days, and were getting close to the Gyp Hills, when we came upon them unexpectedly in a gully surrounded by high rocks. The thieves opened fire on us before we saw them, and at their first volley I got a bullet in my neck.

We were going on a dead gallop toward the rustlers, however, and I hardly realized I had been hit. There was a strange sensation in my throat, and later I put up my hand and felt blood running down my shirt front. The wound didn't hurt much, or the excitement made me forget it. In a moment we were in the thick of the fight.

Our dash carried us right over the rocks behind which the rustlers were hiding. We had a hand to hand fight that ended in killing one of the rustlers. Another was so badly wounded he died two hours later, while the third was over-powered and disarmed before he could kill one of us.

There wasn't much ceremony after that. The live rustler met death under the first tree we found. His body was hanging there when we rode away. In the West in those days, cattle stealing was a worse crime than murder. The thief who got caught stood little show of mercy.

The bullet in my neck never troubled me. Soon after the fight, I went to a doctor, and he said it wouldn't do any harm because by that time the wound had healed and there would be no danger from the lead. So the bullet stayed there.

Lillie wrote his mother, telling her how well he liked the exciting life in the Cherokee Outlet. She replied, begging him to give it up, as he would surely be killed—if not from a bullet, then from the strenuous work. Lillie noted:

She was right. Sixteen hours a day in the saddle would, in a short time, shake any man to pieces, and I had never gotten back my full physical strength after my illness as a child — even though life on the prairies and among the Indians had improved my health considerably. I stuck it out until spring, when we drove our cattle to Caldwell.

7.   Caldwell

UNTIL 1870, Caldwell, Kansas, had consisted of a single, dilapidated shack that stood on the Chisholm Trail and served as a saloon.
The last place where liquor could be bought on the way into the
Indian Territory, and the first oasis for thirsty herders and teamsters coming up the trail from the south, it did a good business. In
front hung a weather-beaten sign with the name "Last Chance
Saloon" on one side and "First Chance Saloon" on the other.

In 1871, Captain Charles Stone built a store, and from these
meager beginnings the town grew slowly as the railheads for ship-
ping Texas cattle moved southward from Abilene to Newton, Ellsworth and Wichita. The cattle trail became hemmed in by quaran-
tine laws and barbed-wire fences. A new route was established
further west to Dodge City, and the settlement seemed doomed.

Then, in 1880, the Santa Fe built a branch line south from
Wichita. Caldwell became the roaring terminus of the old Chisholm Trail and "Queen City" of the border.

Gun-toting cowboys from the western Kansas plains, the Cherokee Outlet, No Man's Land and Texas became king in its saloons
and gambling halls. Roughly dressed railroad laborers rubbed
shoulders with freighters and soldiers bound for forts in the Indian
Territory, who stopped to take on food and supplies. Indians came
to haul their own freight to their agencies. A colony of David L.
Payne's Oklahoma "boomers" made their headquarters here, and
there was great excitement over their demand that the government
open the unassigned lands in the Territory to settlement.

In 1876, after Lillie had seen Payne in Wichita, Payne had got
the appointment as assistant doorkeeper in the House of Representatives in Washington. His duties there had given him opportunity
to investigate conditions under which these vacant lands were held
by the government, and since 1879, he had been a thorn in the side

of the government and the cattlemen who had been allowed to use this section for their herds.

On different occasions, from 1880 to 1883, he had led bands of homeseekers into the area, only to be arrested and ejected by the military. Through failure after failure he had become a true action-ist and organizer. To facilitate his movement, he had founded his own newspaper, the Oklahoma *War Chief*, the first issue appearing under a Caldwell dateline in January, 1883. He had stirred up sen-timent in Arkansas and Texas; and all through Kansas, in such then-important cities as Kansas City, Wellington, Wichita, Arkan-sas City and Hunnewell, colonies had been formed in favor of the movement.

To this strange medley of humanity in Caldwell flocked the dis-reputables and criminal parasites that had been run out of Dodge City and Wichita by Wyatt Earp's sawed-off shotgun and Bat Mas-terson's flaming six-shooters. Robberies and killings became so fre-quent that decent citizens were afraid to appear on the streets at night. Law enforcement consisted of preventing only the more heinous offenses, and it became a sacrifice of human life for officials to name a man to preserve order.

In June, 1880, City Marshal George Flat was shot from ambush while walking past an implement yard. Frank Hunt, acting mar-shal of the town, was killed while sitting in the window of the Red Light saloon the night of October 11, 1880, and his murderer was never apprehended. Mike Meagher put on the star, and was killed by the Talbot gang on December 17, 1881. In 1882, George S. Brown was appointed city marshal, and on the morning of June 22, was slain trying to arrest two Texas cowboys who were shooting up a saloon.

In July, the city council pinned the badge on Hendry Brown, formerly marshal of Tascosa, Texas. Brown had ridden with Billy the Kid through the Lincoln County War in New Mexico, and was generally considered a "hard case." For an assistant, Brown chose Ben Wheeler, a tall Texan. Within six months they had quieted down the lower class of humanity which paraded the streets.

When Pawnee Bill arrived in Caldwell with the Zimmerman herd in 1883, the town was living down its reputation as a place where hilarity rode high, wide and handsome with the common fare a dead man for breakfast, and was taking rapid strides toward becoming an enterprising and influential business center.

The cattle were herded into roughly constructed pens and loaded along a railroad spur just south of town. The cowboys were paid, and headed for the saloons and dance halls. Lillie rode in with Zimmerman:

We passed a group of farmers camped with their women and children on some vacant lots along the road. I read the banners on their wagons: "Strike for A Home," "No turn back," "Uncle Sam is Rich Enough; Give Us All A Home in Oklahoma," and other mottoes. The Colonel (Zimmerman) pointed at them and remarked:

"Boomers. It's a shame to see more and more good cattle range plowed up every year. If Dave Payne had his way, the whole Indian Territory would have four families to every square mile and there wouldn't be room for anything but a milk cow." His voice was filled with bitterness and there was a resentful gleam in his eye.

"It will have to come someday," I said. "Maybe not for a while, but Oklahoma will be opened for settlement."

The Colonel looked at me sharply. "Who's been telling you that?" he asked.

"Nobody," I said. "I've seen Payne only once, but he impressed me as a man who usually gets what he goes after. Besides, he has as much legal right in Oklahoma as we have. It's government land."

That shocked the Colonel. "Bill," he said, "I'm real disappointed. Do you mean you're a sympathizer of the boomers?"

I told him if I had my way about it, I'd give the country back to the trapper and the buffalo. But that would be the selfish way to look at it, not because I thought the cattleman or the boomers were right or wrong.

"It's Indian land," the Colonel said. "The Cherokee Strip is owned by the Cherokee Nation, and the cattlemen there lease their range from the Cherokees. The Oklahoma land was purchased by the government from the Creeks and Seminoles for Indian occupancy. Payne's got the fool notion that because they've found no use for it that it's public domain and subject to preemption and homestead settlement. I just borrow my range from the government." The Colonel emphasized the word "borrow", and laughed.

This puzzled Lillie. The government was pledged to the protection of this land and the security of the Indians from intruders. No white person had the right to go there without a permit. The cattlemen had no more right there than the boomers, so he couldn't share Zimmerman's hostility toward Payne and these people.

Zimmerman thought a good drink would make him forget the whole business, but Lillie wanted to look around town a while, and "the Colonel snorted and rode off."

Within a few days, Lillie learned that the problem was not so much the question of whether or not the land was subject to settlement under squatter sovereignty. Rather it was the influence of prominent politicians who owned stock in the wealthy cattle companies using the land for pasture that was causing trouble for the boomers. The Secretary of the Interior had promised to act on the matter, but the homesteaders had seen no effort on the part of the military to remove any of the herds grazing within the limits of the Territory, and charged the secretary with insincerity.

The nature and validity of the treaty made by the government with the Indians in 1866 had been attacked by Judge Baker of St. Louis, who had defended Payne in the United States District Court at Fort Smith in March, 1881. The courts were undecided; the Secretary of Interior and some of the ablest lawyers of the country were at variance, the latter holding that Oklahoma was subject to settlement as public lands.

Payne had been released on a $1000 bond, and following each of his later attempts to settle in the territory, the performance had been repeated. The boomers had been arrested, their property destroyed before their eyes, and they were forced to return to the Kansas border, where they were released. Payne demanded, each time, a trial before the courts.

His latest attempt to colonize Oklahoma had been in February, 1883. He reached the North Canadian Valley, where he again was arrested and thrown out by soldiers. In March, he removed his headquarters from Wichita to Geuda Springs, between Caldwell and Arkansas City, because of growing Wichita opposition to his conduct of the campaign. Some officials of the movement believed their efforts should be directed only to the opening of the

Oklahoma Lands. But Payne now turned his attention to the Cherokee Outlet.

His *War Chief* fearlessly charged that the Cherokee Livestock Association, from its headquarters in Caldwell, had bribed army officers, members of Congress, and other high officials with gifts of shares of its stock into aiding the cattlemen in holding illegally land that was subject to homestead settlement under congressional statute.

He pointed out that under the various treaties with the Indian tribes, particularly the Cherokee, Creek, Seminole, Choctaw and Chickasaw, the boundaries of their immense bodies of land had been accurately defined, except on the west, where outlets had been reserved for the Indians to the buffalo hunting grounds extending to the Rocky Mountains. These loosely defined hunting highways, varying in width from fourteen to over a hundred miles, included most of the western half of the Territory, now occupied by the Plains tribes, from Kansas to the Red River. With the buffalo gone, the purpose of these outlets had ceased, and the whole broad, magnificent domain actually was a part of the public land and subject to entry under homestead laws.

In May, Payne made a lengthy announcement, stating that a new start for the "promised land" would be made on June 25, and the boomers would celebrate the Fourth of July with a barbecue on the banks of the North Canadian. Immediately a proclamation was posted throughout southern Kansas as a warning to all who might be contemplating joining the announced invasion.

Pawnee Bill had decided not to return to the cattle range. He found employment as a waiter in a restaurant in Caldwell, and he paused outside to read the notice that had been tacked up beside the door.

". . . I, Chester A. Arthur, President of the United States, do admonish and warn all such persons . . . against any attempt to so remove or settle upon any of the lands of said Territory. . . ."

There was a lot more to the proclamation, but Lillie skimmed through its stilted phraseology and turned away in disgust.

"It is foolishness or cowardice," he said. "If Congress had any spine it would open Oklahoma and provide homes for thousands of citizens who would turn the land to some use."

His strong conviction and youthful optimism impressed the group of listeners. Before the day ended, his words had been repeated to the famous boomer chief, Payne.

The next morning, a man with a mustache and goatee, the "face of a poet" and the "eyes of a dreamer," sat down in the restaurant, removed the big black hat covering his dark, wavy hair and ordered breakfast.

During the course of the meal, Lillie noticed that the man's eyes followed him, and after he had eaten, he summoned Lillie to his table.

"You are Pawnee Bill, aren't you?"

Lillie nodded. "And you're Captain Payne. I saw you once in Wichita."

Payne surveyed him keenly. "You've grown some."

"I'm going on twenty-four."

"Well, it's a young man's fight. I'd like to see you in it."

"It looks like I am already. At least, my sympathies are with the boomers. I can't see the government letting a few cattlemen get rich at the expense of thousands of people who need homes."

Payne's eyes lighted, but his face was grim. "That is the human side of the case. The troops are so busy running poor people out they can't see the cattlemen. There is a legal side, too. The government knows the land is public domain, but won't do anything about it."

"What could I do?"

"You have been in the Territory a long time, you know the land and the Indians. You could lead a colony."

"I'll think it over," said Lillie.

Payne rose to his feet. "We will be going into the Territory again pretty soon."

"What about the proclamation?"

"Proclamations won't keep us out."

Lillie watched Payne as he strode down the street. There was something so frank and impelling about the man he felt a sudden urge to follow him. Why not throw in with David Payne and see this new country opened to civilization? Certainly it would be more exciting than waiting tables.

Lillie was still pondering the matter when he learned his assistance was needed at the E. H. Beals home on Market Street at once.
Spotted Horse, the Pawnee chief, and one of his squaws had driven
into Caldwell with a team and wagon the night before and camped
in a vacant lot between Main and Market streets. Early that morning, they had gone to the Long Branch cafe and asked the proprietor to give them breakfast. The proprietor had refused, and
they had gone to the Moreland House, where they were given a
sackful of cold meat and bread. The Indians had then gone to
Beals' house, walked in on the family at breakfast, and demanded
to be fed. Beals had cursed them and ordered them outside. Spotted
Horse had drawn a revolver, and there was about to be a killing.

When Lillie reached Beals' residence, the Indians were gone.
Beals stated he had invited Spotted Horse outside to settle their
trouble, and the Indian had put up his gun and walked out, Beals
following him. Outside, the Indian again drew his gun, and Beals
seized a spade leaning against a tree. Grant Harris, a youth who
worked in a local print shop, came running up and told the Indian
he ought not attack an old man. Spotted Horse had cursed him in
the Pawnee language, but finally put up his revolver and left with
his squaw, heading back toward the business district. Beals had
notified the marshal, Hendry Brown.

Lillie hurried back uptown. He met the proprietor of the Long
Branch, who told him the Indians had come back into his restaurant through the kitchen and helped themselves to the food. The
squaw had gone off to the wagon, and Spotted Horse had entered
Morris' Grocery, next door.

As Lillie turned toward the store, he heard a pistol shot. As he
broke into a run, three more were fired in rapid succession. When
he reached the store, he found Spotted Horse dead on the floor,
lying across his blanket with a gun in his hand, and Marshal Brown
holstering his weapon.

At the inquest, Brown testified that he had entered the store and
asked the Indian to go with him to an interpreter; that the Indian
refused, and he took hold of him. The Indian jerked away, reaching
inside his blanket, and the marshal had fired to frighten him.
Spotted Horse kept feeling for his revolver, and three shots were
fired by the marshal, the last one striking the Indian above the right

eye and coming out the back of his head. Witnesses testified that had Brown's last shot missed, the Indian would have killed him, for he had just succeeded in freeing the gun from the blanket.

Lillie always believed that had he reached the store ahead of the marshal, he could have saved the Indian's life.

In the middle of June, Lillie decided to join Payne's colony, and went to Geuda Springs. He found the boomer chief ill, and the planned invasion of the Territory had been called off. The boomers celebrated the Fourth of July at Geuda Springs, and Payne arose from his sickbed to address them. Again he assured them that Oklahoma was public domain, that soon the government would no longer be able to keep them out, and eventually all who joined them would be rewarded with the richest lands on the American continent.

Disappointed, Lillie returned to Caldwell to find a young man named Charlie Burgess looking for him:

> He was the son of Major Burgess, who had spent so many years with the Pawnees in Nebraska and finally brought them down to the Indian Territory. Charlie was working for Buffalo Bill, who had sent him down to the agency to pick up a half-dozen Pawnees to put in a Wild West show.
>
> Agent Bowman had objected to his taking them without first getting permission from the Indian Commissioner in Washington. This had taken the biggest part of a week, as a messenger had to be sent to Arkansas City, seventy miles away, and a telegram sent from there to Washington, and the messenger had to wait a reply before returning.
>
> The Indian Commissioner had given his consent provided the proper bond was made and someone placed in charge of the Indians acceptable to the government. He said, "There is a young man out there who was in the service for a time who talks Indian like a native, wears long hair and is a great friend of the Pawnees." So Burgess had written Buffalo Bill, and Cody had written back to bring me and the Indians.

The show was to be put on in 1883, the first and only outdoor performance of its kind ever given up to that time. Lillie was to be in charge of the Pawnees, whose job was to hold up stagecoaches, slaughter palefaces and otherwise act the part of traditional Plains Indians.

Lillie had seen Buffalo Bill only the one time in Illinois. But the impression Cody had made on him as a child stuck with him, and at various times he had followed the exploits of the Colonel's last years on the plains—how he had scouted the Big Horn country in 1874 with a detachment of cavalry under Colonel Anson Mills, how they had surprised Little Wolf's band of Arapahoes and driven them back into the agency, and again in the Sioux War of 1876, after the Custer Massacre, how, as chief of scouts for the Fifth Cavalry under General Wesley Merritt, he had intercepted the Cheyennes at War Bonnet Creek, and killed the young chief Yellow Hand with a bowie knife.

Lillie wanted to stay with David Payne in Kansas. The conversion of hundreds, even thousands, would hasten the opening of Oklahoma. But he saw a thrilling new life ahead in the show world with the famous Buffalo Bill, enticing the Easterner through the portals of the show arena where they could witness the tribal dances and fancy shooting and scalping acts he would prepare for them. He left at once with Burgess for the Pawnee Agency:

> It took another week to get together a group of Indians, their squaws and children. Meantime, I had a chance to become well acquainted with Mr. Burgess, and found him most entertaining. He had been with Cody three years and had been in every big city in the United States. His stories of Cody's stage career fascinated me.

After the Sioux War, Cody had taken his war trophies back east for a further theatrical tour, starring in a new play colored with his latest exploits and written by the actor J. V. Arlington. It was called "The Red Right Hand, or Buffalo Bill's First Scalp for Custer." It had a highly successful season, but there were changes in his company. Texas Jack Omohundro left him, never to return to the stage. He was replaced by Captain Jack Crawford, the poet-scout, who resembled Cody in appearance, and afterward became his rival in the show business, claiming that Cody never killed an Indian in his life. The company was disbanded; Cody returned to Omaha, went into partnership with his old friend Major North and built their ranch on the south fork of Dismal River, sixty-five miles north of North Platte, Nebraska.

Cody made money in the show business, but he longed for the plains and outdoor life. Yet he could not give up one for the other. The next few years, he spent his summers on the ranch with North, buying, driving and branding cattle, and his winters touring with theatrical companies.

In September, 1877, he appeared at New York's Bowery Theater in a new drama based on the Mountain Meadows Massacre and life among the Mormons. Although the scenes dramatized had occurred twenty years earlier, they were fresh in the public mind due to the long-delayed trial of the villain, John D. Lee, and his recent execution at the scene of his crime.

For the seasons 1878 through 1883, Cody toured again in "The Red Right Hand, or Buffalo Bill's First Scalp for Custer"; and in "The Knight of the Plains, or Buffalo Bill's Last Trail"; "The Prairie Waif, A Story of the Far West"; and "Twenty Days, or Buffalo Bill's Last Pledge."

With his profits he extended the ranch on Dismal River to include seven thousand acres. More than half of this he planted to alfalfa and corn. There was a lake and a wooded area, which he stocked with deer and buffalo, and in the center of the ranch he and North constructed a farmhouse that looked like a castle, which they named Scouts' Rest. Cody also built a house for his family at North Platte called Welcome Wigwam.

Cody had achieved success as a stage personality, but he had no illusions. It was his fame as a scout and plainsman that drew his audiences and increased his capital. How much longer would the dwellers in the metropolis occupy the pit, parquette and gallery while he slaughtered Indians, baffled scoundrels, rescued maidens from terrific prairie fires, and go away firmly convinced that they had beheld a realistic portrayal of life in the Far West?

During his last stage appearance for the season of 1882-83, he sat in a New York restaurant one day and listened to an eloquent young actor and manager named Nate Salsbury describe to him a new kind of show made up of buffalo, wild steers, broncos, and noted marksmen, Indians, Mexicans and cowboys personally identified with the wild enactments and stirring events of the mountains and plains. It would not be presented on a cramped stage, but out-of-doors; yet it would not be a circus, for it would heroically localize the life, hardships and occupations of the plainsmen. By reason of its electrifying realism, it would command respect and admiration of the greatest statesmen, rulers, soldiers, and educators, and sweep the cities of America and Europe.

Burgess told Lillie:

"When Cody got home, he found the people of North Platte making plans for a Fourth of July celebration, an 'Old Glory blowout,' and they appointed him grand marshal. Cody got out some hand-bills to the ranches for a hundred miles around and advertised in the papers the fancy cowboy stunts and the prizes to be given. You never saw such a turn out. Every rancher in the West tried to participate, and the day it came off North Platte had the biggest crowd it ever had before. Cody said later, 'I've tried this on my neighbors, and they lived through it and liked it. I'm going to take this show East.' "

Cody's new partner was W. F. "Doc" Carver, who had been before the public eight years as a great exhibition marksman. A tall, powerful man, he wore long hair like Cody, affected the same elaborate buckskin dress, and advertized himself as "The Evil Spirit." He had achieved his reputation as a remarkable shot in southwest Nebraska at a time when it was estimated there were still twenty million buffalo on the western plains. The winter of 1872-73, he alone killed 5,780 buffalo for their hides, and killed one hundred and sixty in a single day in a record match against Jack McCall (who later murdered Wild Bill at Deadwood), to win the title "Champion Buffalo Hunter." Carver held championships for rifle shooting in the air throughout the world and, when he joined Cody, was fresh from a tour of Europe, where he had set crowned heads buzzing.

Cody wired Nate Salsbury and asked him to join them in the venture, share and share alike. Salsbury replied that it would take a lot of money and another year to get the show in proper shape.

He thought Doc Carver a faker in the show business and refused to have anything to do with the combination.

Cody didn't wait. His business manager, Major John M. "Arizona John" Burke, went to work gathering a staff, preparing programs and posters and planning a route for "The Wild West, Rocky Mountain and Prairie Exhibition." They planned to visit all large cities at the fairgrounds or on race courses, giving exhibitions with a herd of buffalo, a large band of Indians, and various characters drawn from Nebraska ranches who brought with them all the elements of their different lives, including wild steers, bucking horses, and other outlaws of the plains to be conquered and subdued.

Thus, Buck Taylor, who could throw a steer by the horns or tail, ride the worst bronco, and lean from his saddle at full speed to pluck a neckerchief from the ground, became King of the Cowboys; Jim Lawson, the star roper; Seth Hathaway, the Pony Express rider; and little Johnny Baker, another acknowledged crackshot of the world, the Cowboy Kid. Major Frank North came out of retirement to be billed as Pa'ni Le-Shar, Chief of the Pawnees; and a dilapidated Deadwood mailcoach, an original Concord drawn by six horses and capable of seating twenty passengers, bounced around the arena pursued by yelling Indians.

Another star attraction was A. H. Bogardus, widely known exhibition marksman whose shooting was limited exclusively to the shotgun. He had acquired his skill with the smoothbore in duck blinds along the Mississippi. On July 4, 1877, at Lincoln, Illinois, he had whanged away at one thousand glass balls and missed only twenty-seven. In September the same year, he blazed away at the glass targets, missing only nineteen; and later, at Bradford, Pennsylvania, he had missed only ten out of a thousand, setting the highest score he was ever able to establish.

The show was assembled at North Platte, organized at Columbus, Nebraska, and opened at the fairgrounds in Omaha on the west bank of the Missouri. "No Tinsel, No Gilding, No Humbug!" It was "amazing, soul-stirring and authentic."

From Omaha it toured eastward to Council Bluffs, where Pawnee Bill joined it with his Pawnee Indians. Lillie described the shock he experienced at his second glimpse of Cody:

I had been carrying around in my mind for a dozen years or more the picture of Buffalo Bill as I had first seen him, well groomed, with a beautiful buffalo robe coat.

I never was so disappointed in my life. He had been sleeping on the floor of a tent in some hay, his fur coat was missing, his hair was all matted and he was drunk . . .

I found him courteous enough. He was pleased with the Indians and it became my job to assume responsibility for them, to do all the interpreting for them and even to make up as an Indian myself and go on with them.

8.   With Buffalo Bill

LEAVING COUNCIL BLUFFS in its crude form, moving from town to town in sixteen regular railway cars, playing upon the fairgrounds and other enclosures in the open without any seats other than the ordinary grandstands, the show made a triumphant march eastward. A few weeks after leaving the Platte, it "astonished" sedate Boston; the "upper ten" of Newport society turned out with ten thousand other people to fill the Aguidnuck fairgrounds in mid-July; and in Hartford, the conservative *Courant* commented: "It is the best open-air show ever seen . . . Buffalo Bill is the real sight of the whole thing. A perfect model of manly beauty, mounted on his blooded horse, he is an extraordinary figure, and his feats of shooting are perfectly wonderful. He has, in this exhibition, out-Barnumed Barnum." The show eventually located at Coney Island for a five weeks' run, thus establishing a precedent for outdoor exhibitions.

Lillie recalled:

The Pawnee Indian show proved ovation in every town, and its popularity was acclaimed in every city visited.

He described his first meeting with May Manning, the daughter of Dr. William R. Manning, a prominent Philadelphia physician, while the show played in the old Quaker City:

I was standing on the show grounds in front of the main tent when May came by. She was a school-girl then, and carried her books under her arm. I thought I noticed her smile, and I turned and tipped my hat. She thought I was funny with my long hair, sombrero, and buckskin clothes, and just laughed out loud. That's what started it.

That evening, I saw her at the show with another girl, who turned out to be her sister. I sent her a note, telling her I'd like to meet her. We got pretty well acquainted.

He learned that May was attending Smith College, working toward a bachelor of arts. Born on the Delaware River, within a stone's throw of the romantic spot where William Penn had signed his famous treaty with the Indians, she had been surrounded and associated with Quakers from infancy. Lillie was impressed by her quiet and unpretentious demeanor:

It was love at first sight, and I knew that she was the girl for me.

After the performance, Cody looked for Pawnee Bill. A ticket seller told him he had seen Lillie "walking off with a pretty girl." Later that night, Lillie saw Cody and explained: "I met a nice girl —a little beauty. She came to the show with her sister, and we got to talking, and I took her home. I guess I made a fool of myself."

"How's that?" asked Cody.

"Well, her folks had a house full of guests, and her mother resented her bringing in a wild and woolly cowboy. I spent the evening telling her father's friends about the West. They were the biggest bunch of city rubes I've ever seen. They thought the Indians were still massacring whites on the plains, and kept staring at my long hair and clothes like I was a curiosity."

Cody laughed. "That's showmanship, Bill. You haven't a thing to worry about."

"Yes, but I forgot myself and spit on the floor, and that really raised their eyebrows."

Lillie didn't see May Manning again before the show moved on, but he wrote her lengthy letters, giving her detailed, highly exciting accounts of the towns they played as they headed back West. The show continued to give Cody and Carver a good profit, but internally, all was not well.

In the sixteen-car train, one whole car was loaded with liquor. It became an "eternal gamble" whether the show would exist from one day to the next, simply because it was beyond human endurance to stay awake twenty hours out of every twenty-four to cele-

brate the birth of this new amusement enterprise. Every time the
show hit town, the biggest saloon always announced an open house
for the company, and Cody, always the good fellow, would be in
the midst of the celebration, whooping it up, often longer than
anyone else.

There was no management. Cody could draw the crowds, Burke
could get the publicity, but Carver was a liability. Angered by his
bad shooting at more than one performance, he had smashed his
rifle between his horse's ears, and cursed or slugged his assistant
who was throwing up the glass balls he missed. Often, when three
balls were thrown at once and the third fell almost to the ground
while he was breaking the first two, Carver would fire even if the
ball was within inches of his assistant's toes.

Nate Salsbury witnessed one such performance in New York, and
predicted the show would come to a ghastly end if continued under
such handling. Cody continued to drink heavily, and sometimes
grew reckless himself to the point of jeopardizing his life needlessly.
Lillie related one such incident:

> The riding of wild buffalo was one of the acts featured in the
> show. These beasts were ferocious and the show had several damage
> suits to pay because of depredations they committed on the way to
> the grounds from the train and back again. The top riders with the
> show had ridden all the buffalo except one big male, called Mon-
> arch because of his size and majestic appearance. Cody had sug-
> gested several times that they rope and ride him. But they would
> miss their catch or someone would tie onto another buffalo before
> he was caught, and thus up to the day we played Indianapolis,
> Monarch had not been ridden.
>
> About one o'clock in the afternoon Cody drove to the grounds
> with two landaus filled with a party of friends with whom he had
> had lunch at a club. Before the show started he called the men to-
> gether and said, "Now, boys, when we get to the buffalo riding act,
> I want you to rope old Monarch and ride him. I've got a party of
> real friends in the audience today, including the Governor and
> Mayor of this city. Let's give them a real Wild West show."
>
> The boys tried to argue with him, but he just laughed, saying he
> could ride Monarch himself easily. When he stepped away, they all

got together and agreed not to ride him. When the act came, Cody
rode in with us and hollered to Buck Taylor and Jim Lawson, our
two best men, to rope Monarch. Buck caught him a nice throw
around the neck, Jim heeled him, and in a few minutes they had
him stretched out on the ground ready for the rider to mount.

No one came forward, so Cody called to Jim Bullock, our best
steer rider. But Bullock refused, saying it was too dangerous. Cody
then called to one or two of the other boys, and they refused. Dismounting, he said, "I've got more nerve than all of you put together." He walked over and got aboard and hollered to the boys to
turn him loose. Monarch bounded to his feet, ran a short distance
and then started to buck, and finally threw Cody high in the air.
When he struck the ground, he never moved.

We carried him to one of the landaus and he was taken to the
hospital. He remained there two weeks and kept sober until we hit
Chicago.

When he joined us again, he was a different looking man. It was
the first time since I had joined the show that I had seen him free
from liquor. It carried me back to my first sight of him.

In Chicago, the show drew sixty thousand people at its first performance, the largest crowd ever gathered at such an exhibition
with an admission charge. But Cody was too badly worried to celebrate. Salsbury was playing in Chicago at the same time, and Cody
went to see him. He told Salsbury he was "through with Carver";
that he "would not go through another such season with him for a
hundred thousand dollars," and if Salsbury "did not take hold of
the show," he was going to quit.

A new contract set up a partnership between Cody, Salsbury and
Bogardus. Salsbury went on with his Troubadours, meanwhile lay-
ing plans for the reorganization of the Wild West show; and in
October, 1883, Cody and Carver met at Omaha, where the show had
begun, and by the toss of a coin, divided their assets horse for horse,
steer for steer and wagon for wagon.

The fact that Cody won the Deadwood Coach did not keep Carver from having a Deadwood Coach in his own show, which he now
promptly organized. With Cody's old enemy, Captain Jack Crawford, as an added feature, he took to the road duplicating many of

Cody's acts. Carver was to outlive his former partner by eleven years, and, when he died in 1927, was still in the show business; too old to shoot, he was making the rounds at state fairs, exhibiting a diving horse.

Pawnee Bill returned to Kansas. A new agent had taken over at the Pawnee Agency, and his parents had returned to their farm near Wellington. He lived at home the next few months, taking a position as teacher in a school in the Whaley community. His sister Paulina had remained in the Indian Service at Pawnee, but Effie went to school to her brother, and recalled braiding his hair while he taught that winter.

When the term ended, his father offered to let him take over operation of the mill, but Pawnee Bill had other ideas.

"I'm buying some cattle and selling them," he said. "I've got the money I saved from my Wild West tour. They've had a drought in Texas, and cattle can be bought cheap. I'll ride down there and drive them back to Kansas. I'll pasture them this spring and sell them at a nice profit. I don't know how many head I'll buy, but I've got over six hundred dollars, and I'm going to invest all of it. I'm aiming to accumulate a fortune, and this is the first step."

Instead of buying Texas cattle, Lillie met a rancher in the Choctaw Nation named Billy Dunlap. Dunlap had been in Texas on the same mission, and said the talk of a drought there was a lie and that better cattle could be purchased in the Nation at a cost of six dollars per head.

Lillie bought a hundred head from Tandy Walker, nephew of ex-governor Walker of the Nation. Dunlap bought some cattle at the same time, and together they drove across the Indian Territory by way of Red Fork to Buffalo Springs, where the Cheyennes had waylaid and massacred Pat Hennessey and his wagon train in 1874. On the Salt Fork, they separated. Dunlap went to the Quinlan Ranch in the Cherokee Outlet, and Lillie drove his cattle to Cedar Creek in the Gypsum Bluffs on the plains of Barber County, Kansas, west of Medicine Lodge.

To make some money while his cattle fattened, Lillie decided to go on spring tour with Buffalo Bill's Wild West show. Cody asked him to bring his Pawnee Indians. Philadelphia was on their route again, and Lillie wanted to see May Manning. He wrote his brother Albert to meet him in Medicine Lodge and take over his ranch and cattle.

Pawnee Bill left Cedar Creek the morning of April 30, 1884. A heavy rain was falling, making the roads slippery and filling the ravines with water, so he rode slowly, reaching Medicine Lodge shortly after 10 o'clock.

A few minutes before, four riders had entered the town from the west ahead of him. Because of the rain, few persons were on the streets, and the quartet rode unnoticed up to the coal shed behind the Medicine Valley Bank. One man remained with the horses. A big, bearded man entered the front door of the bank, and the short, thin-faced leader, with the fourth member of the quartet, entered through the side door.

Inside the bank, they produced pistols, walked directly to Cashier George Geppert, and demanded that he open the safe and hand out all the money. Geppert started to comply, but the president, E. W. Payne, who was sitting at his desk, reached for a gun. The leader promptly shot him. Geppert turned the knob which locked the vault, and the big, bearded man shot the cashier. Geppert died almost instantly, but Payne lived long enough to make a statement as to what had happened.

Reverend George Friedly was just across the street. He heard the shots and gave the alarm. City Marshal Denn ran up the street and exchanged shots with the robbers as they mounted their horses. A group of men, mostly cattlemen and cowboys, who were playing cards together in a saloon nearby, left in a body to join the battle.

By this time, the robbers were riding out of town. Pawnee Bill saw them as they thundered past, took cover and emptied his revolver futilely at the flying figures. As the news spread, large posses were organized, and Pawnee Bill rode out on the trail of the gang with one group of infuriated citizens determined to avenge the deaths of Geppert and Payne.

The bandits fled safely south to Medicine River, but at the crossing, the big man's horse bogged in the quicksand and he was forced to abandon it. They started on with him and one of the others riding double. This delay brought the first pursuing party in sight of the robbers, and the fugitives turned and opened fire.

While this fight was going on, Pawnee Bill, Charley Taliaferro and others circled to the south and cut the escape route of the robbers, forcing them to turn west toward the Gypsum Bluffs. Pawnee Bill was familiar with the rough, broken country, a part of his cattle range, and headed the fugitives into a blind canyon.

The single outlet was occupied immediately by eight men under Tom Doran, a Medicine Valley rancher. The others surrounded the canyon, and Doran and his men crowded the robbers deeper into its recesses. The fugitives abandoned their horses and fought back on foot until they stood waist deep in water that filled the pit at the base of the bluff. Hopelessly trapped, benumbed by cold and outnumbered, the four men surrendered.

Lillie was startled as he recognized their leader—Hendry Brown, the city marshal of Caldwell, who had killed Spotted Horse, the

Pawnee chief. The big man with him was his deputy, Ben Wheeler, and the others were identified as William Smith and John Wesley, two Texas cowboys who had worked for a while on the T5 range near Caldwell.

A few days before, Brown confessed, he and Wheeler had left Caldwell for the Cherokee Outlet, allegedly to search for horse thieves for whom a large reward had been offered. They had been joined by Smith and Wesley and ridden north to rob the bank.

The prisoners were taken to Medicine Lodge, given dry clothing, shackled and fed. About 3 o'clock, they were photographed and lodged in a small frame house which served as a jail.

All afternoon parties of silent men gathered on the street corners and in the stores. Albert Lillie arrived from Wellington, and Pawnee Bill rode with him back to the ranch. The next morning, a messenger rode out from Medicine Lodge to tell them the bank robbers were all dead.

About 9 o'clock that night, a mob of three hundred men had overpowered the sheriff and broken into the jail. The prisoners had tried to escape. Brown got only a few yards before he fell, riddled with buckshot. Wheeler, Smith and Wesley were wounded. They were then taken a half mile east of town and hanged to a tree by Elm Creek.

In June, Pawnee Bill was on the road again with Buffalo Bill. Cody had greatly increased his company and extended the scope of the exhibition by adding bears, a herd of elk, more buffalo, and over one hundred Indians from various tribes, including Sitting Bull and others who had participated in the Custer tragedy on the Little Big Horn. Nate Salsbury, in addition to his duties as manager, was press agent, and Major Burke the announcer.

During that summer, performances were given in all the large cities to good audiences. In Philadelphia, Lillie saw May Manning again:

> I adored her above any young lady I had ever met, and I was bold in declaring my sentiments. The result was that she consented to marry me in the near future.
>
> I got a cool reception from her mother. She had burned my last two letters to May without letting her read them. But her father

and I got along fine together. I told him about my cattle venture
and my ranch out West. I told him I was in love with May, and that
she had consented to marry me. I was more determined than ever
to convince them that I would make a suitable son-in-law.

Although the season was generally successful, it had its disasters.
At Hartford, in July, while the show was playing at Charter Oak
Park, Cody lost his great friend and ranch partner, Frank North.
During the opening dash down the track at the afternoon show on
the second day, North's saddle girth broke, and he was trampled
beneath galloping hooves. His ribs and spine were injured, and he
was left behind in a hospital while the show continued on tour.
During the winter, his condition grew worse. He was sent home in
March. A week later he died.

In August, Pawnee Bill picked up an Eastern daily and read that
his old boomer friend David Payne had been arrested by Federal
troops again and lodged in jail at Fort Smith. Payne had led 1500
boomers to the north bank of the Chikaskia, about five miles south
of Hunnewell, in the Cherokee Outlet. They had set up tents,
covered wagons and dugouts, and erected a frame building for the
War Chief.

Payne's appeals through the columns of his newspaper had attracted men in responsible positions. He had sold colony shares to
doctors, judges, railroad officials, and big dailies like the Kansas
City *Times*, the Chicago *Times*, and the Topeka *Commonwealth*.
Buffalo Bill had purchased forty shares, and offered Payne a handsome salary to join his Wild West show. But the boomer chief was
too busy with his own show.

In January, 1884, he had gone on a speaking tour as far east as
St. Louis and Springfield, drawing enthusiastic crowds and en-
rolling homeseekers. More than two thousand colonists launched a
movement at St. Joseph, and letters of inquiry poured into his
Arkansas City headquarters from Iowa, Illinois, Ohio, Kentucky,
Indiana and New York.

In February and March, he was in Washington, "pulling all the
wires" and causing the "Cattle Lords to look down their noses."
Everywhere—on the streets, in crowded hotels, and executive offices
of the Capitol—this handsome, well-groomed frontiersman, who

had been variously listed in newspaper headlines as the "notorious Captain," the "Oklahoma outlaw," and the "border dead beat," told how he had been hunted down by vindictive civil and military forces of the Federal government, though his only crime was his determination to seek a home for himself and his people upon public domain. A congressional committee was appointed to investigate the expulsions. But nothing happened.

Payne stayed in Washington until his funds ran out, then returned to Kansas. In April, he began preparations for a new invasion of the Indian Territory, and early in June, moved his colony on the site at a ford of the Chikaskia. On August 7, soldiers surrounded the camp, seized his newspaper, set fire to the office, and arrested its editor J. B. Cooper, Payne, his lieutenant William L. Couch, and Couch's two sons, and the colony surveyor. The rest of the boomers were marched back across the Kansas-Indian Territory border. The prisoners were placed in irons, taken three hundred miles to Fort Smith, and discharged without the formality of a warrant of arrest or a trial.

On Thursday evening, November 26, Payne addressed a large crowd of citizens and Oklahoma boomers at Wellington. He "never spoke more fluently," and it was his "finest effort" in the "justice of his cause." He retired to his room in the DeBarnard Hotel. As he was waiting for breakfast to be served the next morning, he fell dead.

The body of Captain Payne lay in state and thousands passed to pay their last respects. The funeral was the largest ever held in that city. More than five thousand persons followed the body to its last resting place in Woodlawn cemetery, and among them were William F. Cody and Pawnee Bill.

Nate Salsbury had left Cody that fall to go on a western tour with his Troubadours. He had made arrangements for the Wild West show to tour south to cover expenses and reach New Orleans in December at the opening of the Centennial Exhibition, commemorating the anniversary of the exporting of cotton from that port. They would settle down there for the winter, and play the South in the spring. Cody and Pawnee Bill left by train to meet the show, which had been put on a Mississippi river boat for New Orleans.

Off Rodney Landing, Mississippi, the boat rammed another steamer and sank in mid-stream. The mules, steers, elk and buffalo proved no match for the tawny current. All the animals except a few horses were drowned. All the equipment was lost except the Deadwood Coach and the band wagon.

The twenty thousand dollar disaster might well have ended the show. Cody wired Salsbury, who was playing in Denver: "Outfit at bottom of river, what do you advise?" And Salsbury replied: "Open on date planned, have wired funds."

Cody scoured the country for animals and equipment. Within two weeks, he had replaced his losses, and opened on the advertized date.

Then for forty-five days it rained and drizzled, and turned the show ground into a bog.

Cody lost heart. Salsbury insisted that he keep the show going. That winter they lost sixty thousand dollars.

Bogardus cut his losses by retiring. Already past fifty, he thought it was time for him to settle down and quit trying to defend his title as champion shot of the world. A smiling nineteen-year-old girl from Ohio named Annie Oakley, and her husband, Frank Butler—a celebrated shooting team of the variety theaters and circus—took his place. Salsbury set out to raise money to keep the show going.

Pawnee Bill decided to return to his ranch at Medicine Lodge. "I've got my cattle in mind again," he told Cody. "It's an investment that needs looking after."

Cody understood. Before Lillie left, he presented him with a handsome, solid gold medal in appreciation of his services:

PRESENTED TO
GORDON WM. LILLIE
"PAWNEE BILL"
INTERPRETER
OF THE
PAWNEES
BY
WM. F. CODY
"BUFFALO BILL"

Back in Kansas, Lillie found the boomer movement had gained new impetus. There were ugly rumors that Payne had been poisoned by those opposed to the opening of the Oklahoma Lands, and the boomers were filled with resentment. The *War Chief* re-minded its readers that Moses had led the Israelites to the edge of Canaan and died just before they went in to possess the Promised Land.

Payne was dead, but not his spirit. At a mass meeting of the Oklahoma Colony, Captain William L. Couch, Payne's faithful aide and most trusted friend and adviser, had been elected presi-dent. An intelligent, persistent man, who knew all the treaties, laws and court decisions affecting the Oklahoma land problem, he lost no time in asserting their claims.

On December 8, 1884, he left the Kansas line at the head of more than three hundred armed men bound for the unassigned lands. Four days later they set up winter headquarters on Boomer Creek near the present site of Stillwater, and vowed not to surrender to the military. Between January 7 and 24, they were surrounded by six hundred troops under Colonel Edward Hatch, who cut off their supply wagons and reinforcements. With only enough stores to last five days, they were forced to abandon camp and return to Kansas, flanked on either side by cavalry. After three days of strenuous travel over ground covered with snow and sleet, they were a cold, hungry lot of men. Couch and twelve others were taken before the United States District Court at Wichita and charged with treason, but when Colonel Hatch and officers of his command failed to appear as witnesses, their cases were dismissed.

The other boomers found food and warmth in homes in Arkansas City, Caldwell and Wellington, where Pawnee Bill talked with many of them. He was struck by the courage with which they had lifted the banner from their dead chief's shoulders and borne it so proudly. Even in the face of one defeat after another, they promised that they had just begun to fight, and again asked him to join them.

Lillie attended their meetings at Caldwell. The failure of the government to prosecute Couch and the others at Wichita was new fuel for propaganda. There were new tales of hardship and suf-fering and cruel treatment at the hands of soldiers who had driven them from the territory at the points of their sabers, and despite the stories' lack of authenticity, they grew into a "mighty accusation of persecution and martyrdom."

David L. Payne had been "crucified," and photographs of this "sad-eyed man with mustache and goatee" decorated all maps and were tacked on the walls of thousands of homes and public places. At a mass meeting of the colonies at Topeka on February 4, the leaders denounced President Arthur for his use of the military, reasserted their homesteader rights, and arranged to send a delegation headed by Couch to Washington. Grover Cleveland was soon to be inaugurated as the first Democratic President since the Civil War, and they believed he would be sympathetic to their cause.

In Washington, Couch was told that the Indian Territory still was regarded as country acquired and reserved for Indian occupancy only; that no white persons had the right to go there and reside without a permit, and that the government was "pledged to the protection of it and security of the Indians against intruders." However, Secretary of the Interior L. Q. C. Lamar did promise him that cattle would no longer be permitted to graze on the unassigned lands.

Couch returned to the boomer camp south of Caldwell and made his report. He had remained in Washington long enough to learn that many members of Congress favored the boomers' demands. Congressmen Sidney Clark of Kansas, and James B. Weaver of Iowa, were especially acting in their behalf. On March 3, Congress had passed an act directing the President to begin negotiations with the Creeks and Seminoles for a clear title to the unassigned lands, and with the Cherokees for the Outlet. But the boomer leaders failed to catch the full significance of the move. They were discouraged by Couch's report, and when the military made no effort to remove the cattlemen from Oklahoma, charged Secretary Lamar with insincerity.

Editor Samuel Crocker, in the columns of the *War Chief*, described the range as over three million acres, enough land to provide homes for 100,000 people, controlled by seven cattle kings at a rental of two cents an acre. He demanded to know whether the money was being paid into the United States Treasury "or to United States troops for arresting and chaining United States citizens to the back end of a wagon and dragging them from the land that is rightfully theirs, like a hog," and took such other verbal thrusts that he was arrested July 10, at Caldwell, for "seditious conspiracy and inciting insurrection and rebellion against the United States government," and lodged in the Cowley County, Kansas, jail for several weeks through the hottest part of the summer before his case was dismissed and he was released.

His incarceration added flame to the movement. The boomers renewed their attacks on the cattlemen, and spread their grievances throughout Kansas and into neighboring states until legislators in Washington could no longer ignore them. In the summer of 1885, a Senate subcommittee consisting of Senators Dawes, Jones and Morgan, was sent to the Territory to investigate the whole affair. Couch was given a hearing at Caldwell, in which he offered to prove that many of the leases to cattlemen had been secured by bribing the Indians; that government officers had both given and received bribes; and that cattlemen were permitted to occupy large parts of this land while the homesteaders were denied the same right by "inhuman outrages" inflicted by the army.

Senator Dawes was impressed. After the committee left Caldwell, the boomers returned to their homes to await action by Congress. By fall, nothing had happened, and they grew restless. They had all but exhausted their resources on the invasion cause, and could win now only by persistent effort. Couch realized that if something were not done to satisfy them and their disaffection should spread to others, it could result in complete disintegration of the movement. So he planned a new invasion.

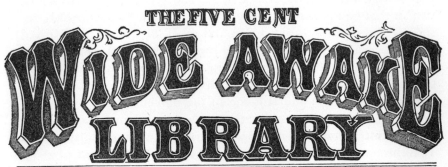

THE FIVE CENT
WIDE AWAKE
LIBRARY

Entered at the Post Office at New York, N. Y., as Second Class Matter.

No. 1031. {COMPLETE.} FRANK TOUSEY, PUBLISHER, 34 & 36 North Moore St., N. Y. {PRICE 5 CENTS.} **Vol. II.**
NEW YORK, February 14, 1891. Issued Every Wednesday.

Entered according to Act of Congress, in the year 1891, by FRANK TOUSEY, in the office of the Librarian of Congress, at Washington, D. C.

Pawnee Bill's Shadow; or, MAY LILLIE, THE GIRL Dead Shot.

By PAUL BRADDON.

9.   The Land Boomer

BY FALL, Lillie was back in Medicine Lodge with a growing ambition. His executive ability and untiring patience in managing Indians had made him a success with Buffalo Bill and Doc Carver. If other people could make money off Pawnee Bill, why couldn't he make it for himself?

"This Wild West show business is bound to pay if it's run right," he told Albert. "If I can raise the money, I may go on the road with a show of my own."

When the Healy and Bigelow Company of New York and New Haven decided to test the box office value of the Indian by adding to their already elaborate medicine show a Wild West act for the season 1885-86, Pawnee Bill gathered a large company of Indians and headed east. The show played across the country to San Francisco, staying two weeks on the Pacific Coast.

Love seemed to have struck the Lillie family that season. Albert got married in Chicago, and his sister Effie married William Judy of Quincy, Illinois, at Wellington. Letters bearing a Philadelphia postmark kept coming to Pawnee Bill until "there was no doubt as to the seriousness of his affair." May Manning had graduated from Smith College, the product of all the refining influences on the Atlantic Coast and hardly material for a wife on the Western plains. But Pawnee Bill was determined that she was the girl for him. When the show closed in Denver that summer, he wrote May that he was coming East to marry her.

> August 31, 1886, was the turning point of my life. On that date, May and I were married. Thereafter, I decided to make it my business to pile up money and make a good name for myself at the same time.

Philadelphia newspapers noted that "a Quaker girl in pigtails was given in marriage, at the Siloan Church, to Gordon W. Lillie, of the plains country." The ceremony, arranged by her parents, was performed in the presence of a large number of invited friends, "whose hearty congratulations were received." An hour later, Pawnee Bill and his bride were on board a train for Kansas:

> May had her misgivings about the West. She was going into a new country where there were none of the society and conveniences of Philadelphia, and I didn't want her to be disappointed. When the train reached Wichita, I telegraphed some friends that we would reach Wellington that evening and I wanted them to make our arrival as exciting as possible.
>
> Fifty or sixty gentlemen and ladies turned out with a band to receive us and gave us a serenade. When we got off the train, May looked around and said, "Where's the carriage?" A spring wagon rattled around the corner of the depot, and I said, "That's it." We all got into spring wagons and drove to South Wellington to the home of my sister Effie, who gave us a fine reception.
>
> This made May happy, and she decided the West wasn't such a rough place after all.

May Lillie was small and vivacious, and very much in love with her husband, but ranch life "utterly bewildered" her. She grew homesick and lonesome while her husband was "gallivanting around the country with a bunch of wild Indians." She "never thought of asking Gordon to give up his prairie life," for she "knew how much he loved the freedom of the plains." She described the tragedy that changed her life:

"In the natural course of events a baby boy came to us in June, 1887. Gordon was away. Babies were important only to the immediate parties most concerned in those days, so a country midwife was the only hope and consolation at the blessed event.

"I was proud of my ten and a half pound son, and when Gordon rushed home to see us three days after his birth, I foolishly arose from my bed to greet the proud father. The consequences of that rash act were terrible. To add to my suffering, our son lived only six weeks.

"A serious operation was necessary to correct complications which caused recurring illness. When I learned that I could never bear another child, I took an interest with my husband in western affairs."

Pawnee Bill and the cowboys at the ranch taught her to ride side-saddle and shoot. She "cultivated a taste for the rifle," and at her first shooting match, "carried off the laurels by missing the object not a single time."

From that day, the prairie, the cattle and the horses were her inheritance. The Boston *Journal* said: "She took to them as most girls gravitate to ballrooms and pink teas. When her classmates were debutantes, entering upon the social whirl of conventional life, she was learning the tricks of the lariat. While they were making conquests of city hearts, she was roping steers and studying the art of remaining comfortable on the hurricane deck of a bucking mustang. Her recitals and soirees became target matches with the rifle and six-shooter. She brought the entire culture of the East into the cow camps of the West, and she exchanged her beneficent influence for the skill of her new companions."

That summer, Lillie took her on a hunt with the Pawnees in Indian Territory, where she again proved her skill with a rifle, killing eight prairie chickens and sixteen wild turkeys in one afternoon. The Pawnees were so pleased they presented her with a colt, which she named "Hunter," and he became her favorite horse. She trained him herself, and was the first person to mount him. That autumn, during the Kansas fairs, she rode him in competing for prizes and was never defeated. She was acclaimed "the most graceful lady rider in the state," and created a sensation with her expert marksmanship from the back of her fast-moving pony.

Her parents almost disowned Lillie:

I tried my level best to get May's picture in the best show paper of the day. Finally I succeeded. Under the picture it said May was an Indian girl. We visited her folks in Philadelphia that fall, and May's aunt was all het up.

"Gordon," she said, "how did that awful paper get May's picture? May hasn't a drop of Indian blood in her."

On November 12, May gave an exhibition at the Pennsylvania State Rifle Range. Shooting at two hundred yards, she scored twenty-four points out of a possible twenty-five, the best score ever made by a woman at that distance. Her Philadelphia friends presented her with a handsome solid gold medal inscribed:

PRESENTED TO
MAY LILLIE
CHAMPION GIRL SHOT OF THE WEST
BY APPRECIATING FRIENDS
AT PHILADELPHIA
DEC 5, 87

While Lillie was in Philadelphia, Charles M. Sothwell, who was John McCaull's business manager at the Broad Street Opera House, talked him into taking out a show similar to Buffalo Bill's:

Charlie had a lot of experience. We were to form a partnership and split the profits, if any. Believing I could make money with a Wild West show, I sold my cattle at Medicine Lodge for a good profit, borrowed $400 from my father, and spent the winter lining up my Indians and negotiating for animals and performers.

By the spring of 1888, Pawnee Bill's Wild West was ready to be launched. The Philadelphia *Dispatch* said: "It far surpasses any previous attempt in that direction in magnitude and variety of performance. In this exhibition 165 horses, mules and broncos, 84 Indians, 50 cowboys and Mexicans and 30 trappers, hunters and scouts are used. Among the various tribes represented are the Pawnees, Comanches, Kiowas, Kaws and Wichitas.

"This great assemblage was brought together on Pawnee Bill's ranch. Brussels, in Belgium, was their destination, they having a guarantee from King Leopold for $3,000 per week and expenses for a period of six months at the Grand Exposition to be held there. The train was waiting at Wellington to convey them to New York, when a cablegram was received announcing the death of Emperor William, and a consequent suspension of all amusements. The contract, of course, was cancelled, and the dates were immediately made for this country."

The show started northeast. At St. Joseph, Missouri, the afternoon of May 24, it "drew a huge crowd at the fairgrounds and rendered great satisfaction." Forty additional Indians from the Pawnee Agency joined the show at St. Joseph.

On June 1, the Kansas City *News* reported: "Pawnee Bill and his Wild West is making a fortune at Exposition Park. There is a big crowd at every performance." The Kansas City *Times* gave Trapper Tom top billing: "He has been a miner, prospector, hunter and trapper in Missouri, Indian Territory, Colorado, California and Wyoming. In Missouri, he lived as neighbor to the James boys, and spent weeks in company with them and the Younger brothers. In Colorado, he was a partner of Billy the Kid, and played a title role in the famous Munn-McManus fight on the border of New Mexico."

It criticized the cowboys for their "bashfulness before an audience. Some of them are fancy shots with a revolver, but they are afraid to give exhibitions. Al Lillie can hit off-hand small objects thrown in the air with certainty for his own and his friends' amusement, but before the grand stand he gets stage fright and would miss a bale of cotton." But it said: "John Eaton, the crack-rider of the company, is the gentleman, who, a short time ago, converted a Santa Fe plug local train into a through express by drawing his Colts and inducing the conductor not to stop at any way stations, and stands ready to ride anything that can be caught and saddled," and "the shooting of May Lillie is something wonderful . . . .

"The Cheyennes were immensely pleased yesterday at seeing Colonel D. B. Dyer, now of Kansas City, but formerly their agent at Fort Reno. Colonel Dyer stated that very few men had the knack of managing Indians. Pawnee Bill is one of them. He is quiet, and that suits them; he is patient, and that suits them better; he is personally brave, and that suits best of all, as the Indian has a contempt for any emotional weakness. The Pawnees are devoted to him.

"He is the first man in any sort of show business ever seen in Kansas City, but is too modest. Nobody would imagine that he has already performed a dozen feats which would have made some men celebrated."

The *Times* closed its report: "Together, the Indians and cowboys afford no end of study for the dweller of cities. A stroll among them after the performance is worth as much as the riding and lasso throwing. By observing them closely, one can imagine what life is in Oklahoma."

At Indianapolis, two weeks later, Pawnee Bill's cowboys and Indians "gave a very entertaining representation of wild Western life. The riding itself is daring, the feats on horseback thrilling." The *Journal* commented: "In exhibitions of this kind the features are somewhat limited, but this company introduced novelty to keep the interest of the spectator alive to the general excellence of the show."

Again May Lillie was the star performer. "Her work with the rifle is remarkable. She is the only woman in the world able to break targets thrown in the air while riding at full speed on her mustang." She picked up a vast knowledge of the parade and the arena, was "unusually attractive," and the equestrian acts which she developed for the program were "the most extraordinary performances with horses ever introduced to the public." On the road and on billboards, she was "May Lillie, Princess of the Prairie," and the "World's Champion Woman Rifle Shot," who "challenges any woman her age from $500 to $5,000 a side" to duplicate her feat at rifle shooting.

The press made "liberal mention" of Lillie himself as White Chief of the Pawnees, a "young dare-devil who performs miracles with a rope and six-shooter and rides like a fiend on a big black stallion."

The show proceeded east to New Jersey. Although crowds in attendance were large, money was not coming in as fast as Lillie had anticipated.

"I can't understand it," he told Sothwell. "We've got a good show, and the weather as a whole has been favorable. It must be a bad year."

At Gloucester, they determined to increase the box-office receipts, and formed a combination with Buckskin Joe's show, the star performer of which was Annie Oakley, the famous woman shot of Buffalo Bill's show.

Cody had recuperated his 1884 losses in the summer of 1885 at Erastina, Staten Island, where the show had played to crowds that packed the twenty thousand seats. During the winter of 1886-87, through arrangements made by the circus great, Adam Forepaugh, Cody had given his exhibition in the heart of New York at Madison Square Garden, where, for the first time in covered space, the great Wild West show was transformed into "a spectacular, scenic production of the age," called the "Great Drama of Civilization."

MAY LILLIE.

NEW RIFLE QUEEN.

The following March, the show had departed for London, played six months as an adjunct of the American Exhibition, moved to Manchester for the winter and returned to New York in May, 1888. But Annie Oakley's popularity in England had led to jealousy. Cody was bringing his autobiography up to date and did not mention her name in the account of his European tour. When the London season ended and the show moved to Manchester, the well-loved "Little Missy" left Buffalo Bill on a tour of her own, and had just returned to America when she joined Buckskin Joe and Pawnee Bill.

They opened at Gloucester in July, with two performances daily, "the stars of the company being Gordon W. Lillie (Pawnee Bill), May Lillie and Miss Annie Oakley, all of whom do some exceedingly skillful work with the rifle." Eleven thousand people witnessed the exhibition in the afternoon and evening.

Lillie spiced his regular programs with special features designed to increase attendance. Once Annie Oakley was matched for a purse of $200, to kill forty out of fifty live pigeons with a 20 gauge gun, three-quarter ounce shot, a feat that "has never before been attempted in this country." Again Lillie startled a crowd of 5000, at the close of an afternoon performance, by letting them witness the marriage of Wah-Ki-Kaw, the Kaw Chief with the Wild West show, to Miss Annie Harris, a white woman. The ceremony was performed by a Justice of the Peace, and afterwards performed according to the Indian custom by Pawnee Bill, White Chief of the Pawnees, "present-making being the chief feature of the latter ceremony, and which included almost everything from an Irish jackass to pie, lemonade and blankets." Then followed the wedding dance, and in the evening, a pet dog was sacrificed in honor of the event.

On July 29, "the management of the fireworks drama at Gloucester cancelled all contracts for the city, claiming that to continue the naval battle would be a losing investment, the public having gone 'wild' over Pawnee Bill's Wild West." The *Advertiser* of August 12 said: "Pawnee Bill's Wild West enters upon its fifth week today at Gloucester Beach; the show has up to date been visited by 150,000 people, and as yet there are no signs of abatement in the popular interest." And on August 19: "The thousands who daily visit this great show are proof sufficient of its merit, and it is admitted on all sides to be the most realistic illustration of Wild West life ever attempted."

The attack upon the stagecoach and the massacre of the occupants were scenes "not easily forgotten." Pawnee Bill performed the feat of breaking a glass ball while it revolved in the air, with a rifle shot from the hip. May Lillie made many difficult shots with a rifle from the back of her racing pony. The Pony Express act, lasso throwing, the chase after wild steers, the buffalo hunt "added much to the show." Picking several handkerchiefs from the ground from horseback was the "most dangerous feat of the cowboys." The capture and punishment of a horse thief by Judge Lynch "excites interest and even sympathy as he is trailed about at almost lightning speed across the field to a convenient tree." The rescue of a little child, the only survivor of a mountain train massacre, "is pathetic and real."

A special engagement was made with the Bennett family of sharpshooters, comprising F. F. and W. E. and Miss Annie Bennett, whose claim to the world's championship at revolver and pistol shooting, backed by a standing challenge of $1000, remained undisputed. "Some of the shots accomplished by the Bennetts have never been attempted by any other marksman. They break, with single bullets, balls from Miss Bennett's head, wheel and fire while holding the revolver sideways."

The show went into its sixth week with an attendance "as large as ever," and in September, toured south. The return of Buffalo Bill's show from England was hazardous competition for Lillie. While Pawnee Bill played at Gloucester, Buffalo Bill's show again took a stand at Erastina, Staten Island. It now toured southward to Richmond. Since joining Buffalo Bill in 1884, Annie Oakley had been as great an attraction in the show as Cody. The temporary rift between them had left a hole that Cody easily felt, and he and Nate Salsbury used against Pawnee Bill every weapon known in the fierce warfare of showmen. They plastered his billboards in advance with announcements: "Wait for the big show; Buffalo Bill is coming."

Annie Oakley fought back. She gave interviews, performed press agent stunts on foot and horseback, and displayed the numerous cups and medals won in shooting exhibitions in America and Europe. Pawnee Bill gave her top billing, and the crowds flocked to see her.

But the show played at fairs through the states, and Pawnee Bill and Buckskin Joe lost money due to unfavorable contracts with fairgrounds people. Then the weather turned bad. Day after day rain cut attendance and drained the money from their small treasury. Buckskin Joe withdrew from the combination, and Pawnee Bill and Sothwell went on alone.

The bad weather continued. Late in October, they were in Maryland, playing small towns, trying desperately to recoup their losses. At Easton, they ran into more rain and into a sheriff with an attachment for the livestock and equipment.

Lillie remembered:

> We went on the rocks at Easton. The show lacked fare to move to another town and had no money to pay its eighty odd employees. It happened there was a very prominent citizen in town named Senator Gibson. When he learned of our plight, he wrote a petition to the people to help "the Westerners" get on their way. Senator Gibson signed first, subscribing $25 to the fund, and it was not long until we had enough money to send the Indians back to Oklahoma.

After taking care of the other employees, Lillie was unable to pay his hotel bill, and the landlord kept his trunks with all his clothing. May Lillie wired her folks for enough money to reach Philadelphia. The trunks remained in Easton.

In the mail, when Pawnee Bill reached Philadelphia, was a letter from the Wichita, Kansas, Board of Trade, asking him to come to Wichita immediately, as they desired a man of his type for a leader in the movement to open Oklahoma to settlement.

Something more tangible than sentiment had developed in support of the boomer cause. The Santa Fe had built railroads north and south across the Indian Territory. An act of Congress approved March 2, 1887, had granted the Rock Island charter right to cross the Indian Territory and Texas to Galveston. Steel rails were rapidly being constructed through Wichita and Caldwell to make this line the main connection between Fort Worth and Kansas City. The railroads foresaw the business potential of these vast, undevel-

oped lands. The cities of Kansas envisioned a great market to the
south of them. If the gates could be opened, settlers would swarm
into the territory, creating an immediate demand for Kansas products, and Kansas would grow richer. These uninhabited Indian
lands were retarding Kansas' growth.

The Boards of Trade in Kansas cities got busy. Numerous peti-
tions were sent up to Congress, with no immediate results, and as a
climax to their efforts, delegates from all states bordering the Indian Territory met in a rousing convention at Kansas City and
drew up a memorial stating that since the Territory in its present
condition was an obstacle to the social, agricultural and commercial
interests of the whole Southwest, and to the moral, educational,
financial and political interests of the Indians themselves, at least
its western half should be opened to settlement, with compensation
to the Indians for all lands taken. Couch and eighteen other prominent boomer leaders were selected to present the memorial and
other resolutions in Washington.

They scored a signal victory in February, 1887, when President
Cleveland signed into law the Dawes Act, providing for the allotment of lands in severalty to the Indians and permitting the President to negotiate with a tribe for any surplus lands after allotments
and to dispose of these to settlers in tracts of 160 acres, with the
exception of the lands of the Osage, Peoria, Miami, Sac and Fox,
and the Five Civilized Tribes.

For months, Wichita had been interested in the opening of the
whole western half of the Indian Territory. David D. Leahy, city
editor of the *Eagle* and a remarkable writer, by extolling the glories
of the new land and the opportunities that awaited the settlers there
had been a tremendous factor in stirring up interest. But it was
largely Marsh Murdock, publisher of the paper, who saw with pro-
phetic eye a trade area that would make Wichita the biggest city
between Kansas City and Denver, and set the Wichita Board of
Trade and City Council to work formulating plans to open the
country at the earliest possible moment.

Through their efforts, an Interstate-Oklahoma Convention was
held on November 20, 1888, in the Opera House on Douglas Avenue. General James B. Weaver, champion of the boomer cause,
Congressman William M. Springer, Congressman Charles Mansur

of Missouri, and other members of Congress were in attendance. The Opera House was "filled to suffocation," and many speeches were made. Captain Couch, Sidney Clark and Samuel Crocker were selected to go to Washington to push the Oklahoma bill through Congress. They labored in vain. After a few weeks, they found it so completely pigeon-holed that they began getting up a substitute bill in the closing days of the session.

Meanwhile, in Wichita, Murdock and the Board of Trade had begun organization of a vast movement. And it was the idea of some of the members of that body like W. S. Corbett, its president; H. L. Pearce, its secretary; J. P. Allen, Mayor of Wichita; A. W. Oliver, C. A. Walker, William Mathewson, M. W. Levy and others, to send a letter to Pawnee Bill, asking him to come to Wichita and assume leadership of the boomers, in a position similar to that of the dead Captain Payne. If Congress did not pass a bill to open the Territory, the people of Kansas were prepared to enter the country en masse and settle.

Lillie gave this account of taking over the boomer movement:

I didn't have much enthusiasm about becoming a Captain Payne for them, but I did want to get back West. I didn't have the money to go on. I had not given the letter any particular consideration, in fact I had not read it all. The next day I encountered an old friend of mine, James R. Hope, who asked my intentions as to the future. I said if I could get back to Wichita I could do what this letter wanted me to do. He read the letter.

"Do you want to go?" he asked.

I had trouble enough of my own without taking on any more. It meant bucking Uncle Sam, and I recalled what it had done to Captain Payne. Of course, I answered, "Yes; but why did they pick me?"

"Who else?" asked Hope. "My friend, Pawnee Bill, Indian interpreter, pioneer, showman, a national figure who will command the confidence of the people and has the nerve to force a showdown."

"That doesn't mean I can lead a bunch of settlers into the promised land and keep them there where Payne, Couch and others have failed."

"I expect it's up to you to find a way or they wouldn't have sent for you. Have you no better clothes than those you have on?"

I told him my trunks were in Easton, held for our hotel bill. He advanced me money to get my trunks and pay my fare to Wichita. I did not have the nerve to ask for enough so I could take my wife. May remained in Philadelphia.

Pawnee Bill wired Wichita that he was coming:

As the train pulled in, I saw the platform, the street, in fact all the open space in sight literally packed with people all "Hurrah-ing" and waving handkerchiefs and flags in the throes of the greatest excitement. As the train quieted down, I could hear the strains of a brass band playing "The Conquering Hero Comes."

"What's going on?" I asked a gentleman standing next to me. By this time everyone was on their feet peering from the windows of the coaches.

"Why, Pawnee Bill is on this train. He is coming here to organize and lead the boomers into Oklahoma," he replied.

I almost sank in my tracks. Never before had I been received in such glorious manner, and here I was, dressed in a threadbare suit, worn by a season's work, and actually holes in the crown of my big sombrero. And I to be the center of this enthusiastic reception.

As I reached the platform of the coach, I was grabbed by leaders Marsh Murdock of the *Eagle,* George Dixon, Harry Hill, Joe Rich and a number of others.

I was rushed to an open carriage with the brass band in the lead, and with this great crowd following, they escorted me to the Delmonico hotel, which was to be headquarters of the colonization company of which I was to be president and leader. That evening I sat at a formal banquet in the Delmonico and responded to speeches of welcome. The Pawnee Bill Oklahoma Colonization Company was formed. I would promote the project, they guaranteeing all expenses and immunity from harm.

Every man in the drama had a different perspective, but Lillie saw the whole thing as a dramatic test of the psychology of the show business:

The only thing Captain Payne lacked was a good press agent, and I tackled it from that point of view. It would make hot copy, and would help my show no end.

Nevertheless, there was nothing phoney or tawdry about his position. He was a boomer, and proud of it. He earnestly wished to settle the new empire and build it into a great commonwealth. He had been a friend and admirer of Captain Payne, and believed that the homeseeker should have the right of way over free-range cattle interests.

He said that they would organize branches in every city and state possible—dues, two dollars to join, and two dollars a year—but predicted that within a year the Territory would be opened.

The others felt his enthusiasm. "But what are we going to do— wait for it to open?"

"We'll force the government's hand this time!" Lillie replied. "We'll organize this winter. Before spring, we go in—and stay."

"Rebellion? Bloodshed?"

"I hope it won't be necessary. Rebellion is one thing, resisting the government with a show of force is another. If the government knows we're ready to rebel—if they realize how serious the situation is—they'll do something. By that time I'll have a plan."

That night the *Eagle* telegraphed out 800 words about the boomer plan, proclaiming Pawnee Bill the new leader. Following that, for three weeks, there were from 200 to 300 words placed on the wire by the *Eagle* every day. And these stories were carried in every large paper in the United States. "Send all the news you can get about the opening of Oklahoma," they telegraphed. At one time Marsh Murdock showed me thirty telegrams asking for stories on the project. The whole country got interested. I was deluged with mail. There were letters of inquiry. Some condemned the project. Most wanted to know how to join it. I don't say this to brag. The American people knew about my show career and started talking Oklahoma. You see, it took showmanship.

The *Eagle* described a visit to the Delmonico headquarters in late December: "Pawnee Bill was found busily engaged answering

letters, giving evidence of unusual fast work and everything presenting a lively appearance. Before him on the table was a pile of
letters unanswered and on the floor a basket filled with those whose
contents had been noted.

"In the course of a few minutes conversation he stated that the
movement had assumed gigantic proportions more rapidly than he
had anticipated. He showed a number of papers that had given
space to the movement and honored the same with editorial
comment."

As part of its efforts to keep the public interested, the *Eagle*
printed, with a proud boast, "the best map of Oklahoma territory
ever produced." It showed the 2,000,000 acres which lay in the
center, fully surrounded by Indian reservations, with all roads
leading into Wichita as the trade center of this large territory, if
it could be extended. On the map were the familiar faces of the men
who loomed large in boomer affairs. In the upper left corner were
David L. Payne and William Matthewson, known in Kansas as the
"original" Buffalo Bill. Under them was the picture of Colonel E.
C. Cole, president of Cole's Oklahoma Colony, one of the founders
of Kingman and a leading businessman. Below Cole were Pawnee
Bill and George Harris, president of the first Oklahoma town company and one time mayor of Wichita. In the upper right corner
was Harry Hill, another man who knew his Oklahoma and whose
memory was to be perpetuated.

Branch colonies had organized as far away as Omaha. Within a
few weeks, both sides of the Arkansas River at Wichita were lined
with boomer camps of people from every state and territory. A New
York *World* correspondent described Pawnee Bill's colony as having 3600 registered members, living in and around 1200 covered
wagons and buggies. The *Eagle* said: "The farmers for miles around
drive in to verify the stories in the newspaper, and few leave home
without throwing in sacks of feed, potatoes, chickens, turkeys, geese
and other provisions for the larders of the boomers. One farmer
even brought in a three-year-old steer, which was used to give a big
barbecue celebration when it was learned they were starting for
Oklahoma."

Entertaining little hope for the passage of the Oklahoma bill in
Congress, sub-colonies in Colorado, Nebraska, Arkansas and Texas

sent councils to Wichita to confer with Pawnee Bill. It was decided
by unanimous vote to make the entry into Oklahoma on February
1, 1889, from four directions, and in this way thwart the troops
who had instructions to expel all boomers and arrest Pawnee Bill
on sight.

On January 28, Pawnee Bill moved his colony to Arkansas City,
preparatory to the invasion.

> We were met by Captain Woodson and the Seventh Cavalry, re-
> inforcements having been sent from Ft. Leavenworth. Chiefs Mayes
> and Bushyhead of the Cherokee Nation had ordered their mounted
> Indian police to assist the cavalry, and they had orders to shoot me
> if I set foot in Oklahoma.
>
> In the night, on January 29, we moved on to Hunnewell. The
> next day, Lieutenant Elliott and a detachment of cavalry followed.
> We camped on one side of the line and the soldiers on the other.
> My men wanted to attack the troopers at once, but I intended to go
> twelve miles further west beyond Bitter Creek and the Chikaskia,
> which were swollen by recent rains, and thus place two impassable
> streams between us and the soldiers, then enter the Outlet.

At 3 o'clock that afternoon, a courier arrived from Wichita,
carrying two messages for Pawnee Bill. One was from the Board of
Trade, telling Lillie that the House had passed the Indian appro-
priations bill for the forthcoming fiscal year with a rider opening
Oklahoma to settlement. The other was from Captain Couch to
the Board of Trade, telling them to "prevent Pawnee Bill from
going into Oklahoma at all hazards, as it will jeopardize the bill in
the Senate."

> I was glad this had happened, for we did not want a fight with
> the troops if we could get our rights without it. We had succeeded
> in our mission, as we had woke up those fellows in Washington.

Instead of returning to Wichita, Pawnee Bill held his colony as
a threat on the border. The Caldwell Board of Trade notified him
that every vacant lot and building and the fairgrounds were available for his 3600 followers. Lillie accepted the invitation and

moved to Caldwell on February 2, and there he and his motley
army of homeseekers were quartered on March 3, when word was
received that the opening bill had passed the Senate and President
Cleveland had signed it into law.

On March 23, Cleveland's successor, President Harrison, issued a
proclamation setting the opening of the unassigned lands to
white settlement for twelve o'clock noon, April 22, 1889. Cannons
boomed and bonfires burned all across southern Kansas as the
boomers celebrated their victory. Two weeks before the opening so
many people started for the new country that it looked as if the
towns were being evacuated.

Two days before the opening, Pawnee Bill's colony crossed the
Cherokee Outlet to the southern boundary of what is now Garfield
County. Here Lillie learned that the Seventh Cavalry was collect-
ing all settlers on the line at Buffalo Springs and holding them
under guard until noon, April 22. Realizing the disadvantage of
having his colony thrown in with this "miscellaneous mass of 7000
people," he at once changed course, heading due west to the bank
of Big Turkey Creek, where he went into camp until the morning
of the 21st, "when the march due south was begun across open
country." A scout reported the appearance of Pawnee Bill and his
colony on the Oklahoma line just a few minutes before Lieutenant
Elliott fired the signal that opened Oklahoma to the boomers.

The spectacular events of the "Run"—the great masses who gathered on the borders, the shots which signaled the start, and the mad
stampede across the prairie for the choicest lands—have been por-
trayed by novelist, playwright and artist. A correspondent of the
New York *World*, who made the run with Lillie's colony in the
camp cook's wagon, wrote a simple story for the May 5 issue, under
the title "How Pawnee Bill Rode In":

"The colony, with one grand rush, bore south over the old Chisholm and Fort Dodge trail with all the speed their teams possessed.

"Pawnee Bill, in the lead, rode his 12-mile racing mare, Bonny
Bird, and made the 20 miles in 65 minutes, being the first man to
reach the mouth of Turkey Creek and locate the townsite (now
marked by Dover). There was no quarreling among the colonists,
but some trouble was had with the brushmen who had slipped in
and located claims the night before. A man named Charles Afbach

shot and instantly killed a man named Evans over a disputed claim. Afbach is held under guard. A brother of Pawnee Bill was accidentally shot through the fleshy part of the arm, but was not seriously hurt."

Lillie recalled:

> An uncle of mine, member of our colony, took a claim, and so did my brother, Al. When Al reached his claim, although he had made a fast run, there was another man ahead of him with a cellar half dug. That ended Al's homesteading efforts.

The number of persons making the run of 1889 have been estimated at sixty thousand. Certainly there were more people than there were homesteads for them, and many of these were taken by men who had slipped past the border patrols before the date of the opening. The entire country was taken that first day, and Guthrie, Oklahoma City and Kingfisher arose as cities of tents and shacks before dark. Within a few weeks provisional governments were organized and functioning.

Captain Couch made the run to Oklahoma City and staked a claim adjoining the town on the west. He was elected its first mayor and served with honor one short year. On April 14, 1890, he was wounded in a gun fight with J. C. Adams, a trespasser. He died April 20, and on April 22, one year from the date of the opening, was buried in Fairlawn cemetery.

Like Captain Payne, he had given the best years of his life for something he did not live to enjoy.

Lillie did not take a claim. He didn't want one. The show business was in his blood. At the time, he expected little personal return from the enterprise. It was as he stated later, an "unpaid" job.

But the morning following the run, when the Associated Press dispatches sent the story to the waiting world, he discovered that he had made himself famous. For days afterward, every paper in the country carried accounts of the settlement of Oklahoma, and many featured the name "Pawnee Bill."

Gordon Lillie was a national figure. He at once reorganized his Wild West show, and this time, Buffalo Bill, who had had the field virtually to himself, recognized that he had a real competitor.

10. Pawnee Bill's Historical Wild West

THE NEW SHOW was called Pawnee Bill's Historical Wild West, Indian Museum and Encampment. It was described as "America's National Western Entertainment, depicting true scenes of Rocky Mountain and Frontier life, headed by the famed guide, government interpreter and Oklahoma Hero, Major Gordon William Lillie (Pawnee Bill), and May Lillie, champion girl shot of the West and the most daring and graceful bronco rider in the world."

From Texas and Indian Territory, he picked a band of the "most scientific horsemen and lasso-throwers of the plains," who, at each performance, "will rope and brand cattle, ride wild mustangs, pick up coins from the ground, mount and dismount with their horses running at full speed." Albert Lillie's experience with a rope and his agility in the saddle while foreman of Pawnee Bill's ranch on Medicine River from 1884 to 1886 had made him quite famous among his cowboy companions; he was starred as "Oklahoma Al," king of the cowboys. Prince of the cowboys was Mustang Walter. As a trick rider and roper he stood unexcelled. Another champion was "Horse-Hair" George Esler, who had spent a lifetime riding and branding wild horses for some of the most prominent ranchmen in the West. John Eaton, champion bronco rider who had traveled with Pawnee Bill in 1888, was starred as "Cyclone John." The champion steer rider was Wichita Jim, named by White Bull, chief of the Wichitas. At a bull fight in Dodge City in 1885, he had ridden four mavericks in succession. Pawnee Bill offered $1000 "to any man who can surpass him."

George Hooker did the Pony Express act. He had gained his fame carrying dispatches through Nebraska and Kansas during the Cheyenne raids in 1878, and was depicted in many of his narrow escapes and hand-to-hand encounters with Indians and renegade whites.

Wilbur Collins had begun his career as a cowboy on a Montana ranch at the age of twelve. He had fought horse and cattle thieves, and rendered valuable service as a detective in the Wyoming rustler wars. A remarkable shot with a Winchester, he displayed his skill as "Deadshot Dick."

From Chihuahua, Mexico, Lillie brought the "finest and largest band of Mexican vaqueros ever to visit the United States." Billed as the "most daring and graceful riders of all mankind . . . their tricks with the lasso seem the work of a conjurer, yet they do actually catch a horse by any foot called for by the audience; lasso and throw wild buffalo and then mount and ride him, an act never before attempted." In charge of this famous band were Don De Anza and Señor Francisco, who "hold the distinction of being the only vaqueros who can rope a steer or buffalo, running at full speed, from horseback, and throw and tie him in twelve seconds from the start-off, this test to be given at each performance of Pawnee Bill's Wild West."

Rejoining Lillie were Trapper Tom and Professor E. J. Hoyt, the celebrated musician-scout of the Ute Indian country, first to organize a Wild West band and known for thirty-five years as "Buckskin Joe."

Lewis Vosburg, a French half-breed, last survivor of Kit Carson's band of guides and scouts, played the role of "Iodine, the Trapper." A veteran of the Indian wars on the Yellowstone, he possessed a magnificent collection of Indian trophies and firearms.

In Washington, Lillie presented his credentials to the Commissioner of Indian Affairs, told him how many Indians he wished and from what reservations, and posted bonds for their safe return. Chief Left Hand brought his band of Pawnees, with Jo-pe-dict (Bright Star), "The Handsomest Indian Princess in the World." She was "possessed of extraordinary charms and valued by her father, Big Bear, at fifty ponies—he has repeatedly refused thirty-five ponies for her, thirty being the largest number ever given by a Pawnee for a squaw."

Stumbling Bear, war chief of the Cheyennes, with fifteen warriors, and White Wolf, chief of the Comanches and oldest war chief of the tribe, with twenty braves in charge of Emmet Cox, their interpreter, joined the Encampment. It was White Wolf's band who had led the combination of southern tribes against the man-eating Tonkawas on the Washita in 1860. They were the first band of Comanches ever placed on exhibition.

Lillie was assisted by G. De Fuerst, "Eagle Eye," government scout and interpreter and White Chief of the Winnebagoes, who had spent thirty-two years among the Indians of the Western plains. His wife, the Princess Neola, was a full-blood, educated by the government and the champion Indian pianist of the world. She was the granddaughter of the late John Mount Pleasant, head chief of the Iroquois Confederation, and niece of Eli S. Parker, who, during the Civil War, had been secretary to U. S. Grant, and the only Indian ever to gain the rank of general.

The Indian village added to Pawnee Bill's Wild West was not a peaked tent or two, artistically daubed by some contemporary artist, as seen in many so-called Indian villages and encampments, but a "bona fide Pe-haw-e-rat village of wigwams with lodge-poles and trappings . . . illustrating the modes of living and the habits of the red man in his forest home, showing the squaws at their bead-work, sewing moccasins, tanning hides, and the braves in council smoking the peace pipe, or playing with their chieftain's young."

In his travels from the Atlantic to the Pacific and from Mexico to Canada, Pawnee Bill had gratified his desire for curios, especially from the hand of the American Indian. His museum was one of the largest private collections in the country, and the most valuable, consisting of the rarest handiwork from nearly every tribe in America, many single articles being "possessed of a charm"—medicine garments, bags, gourds and broken torus, and an endless array of instruments of war, farming tools, leggings, drums, beads, seventy kinds of wampum, Indian history written on buffalo and deer skins, bows and arrows, shields, old metals and silver ornaments for the scalp lock, sheaths, headdresses of eagle feathers, genuine scalps, buffalo-hair saviets, porcupine-quill-trimmed body robes and travois.

There was a corral of spotted ponies from the prairies of the Indian Territory, a bivouac of Mexicans from Quendero, a pack train of Mexican burros, and herds of mountain elk, antelope and buffalo.

Buffalo Bill had his Deadwood Coach, but Pawnee Bill obtained

the historic stagecoach of the Cheyenne and Fort Sill line to play
the leading role in the "Deadwood Robbery and Massacre." A
Concord, with perches, packs and braces of unusual construction,
intended for a train of from six to eight horses, it could carry up
to three thousand pounds of freight, with a heavy leathern boot
behind capable of holding eight to nine hundred pounds of baggage. It would seat seven persons inside and four on top besides
the mail agent and guard. Chosen by the Paymaster-General of the
army and the paymaster of the Indian Department to deliver them
and their treasure, it had carried much gold, and although "details
of mounted soldiers had often escorted her to her destination, she
nevertheless had met with several defeats . . . not less than nine
persons had met death within her walls."

"A Fatal Drag," the manner of dealing with horse-thieves by
Judge Lynch in the Western country, was "faithfully enacted," as
was the "most thrilling and daring expose of border life," the
Mountain Meadows Massacre. As a "life-like portrait of savage
modes" it had no equal. "The approach of the war party, the uncon-
cern of the campers, the Indian concealment, the sudden surprise,
their unearthly yells and attack, the resistance fight and dare-devil
massacre of the men, women and children, and flight of savages on
wing-footed steeds arouses enthusiasm and inculcates a lesson of
the most useful and strange character."

Organized at the Pawnee Agency and in Philadelphia the winter
of 1889, with business offices in Philadelphia, the show toured the
Southern states and the North from Michigan to New York and
Montreal, Canada, in 1890, 1891 and 1892. The Montreal *Herald*
of August 21, 1890, called it "the best Wild West ever visiting
Canada." The Atlanta *Constitution* of October 19 called it "the
best Wild West ever visiting the South. . . . Crowds cheered vo-
ciferously at the success of each feature. . . . the grandstands
echoed with applause almost continuously while the show lasted."
The New York *Times* said: "May Lillie is rapidly improving in
the art of breaking the glass target and attracts large crowds which
are amazed at her skilful performances." Philadelphia newspapers
proclaimed her the "New Rifle Queen," and predicted that within
a year she would "make Doc Carver look to his laurels."

Writer Paul Braddon recognized Pawnee Bill's "dime novel"

appeal, and Frank Tousey's Five Cent Wide Awake Library of New York published "Pawnee Bill Doomed, or the Great Scout in No Man's Land"; "Pawnee Bill's Shadow, or May Lillie, the Girl Dead Shot"; "Pawnee Bill's Double, or the Great Scout's Best Trail," and "Pawnee Bill's Gold Hunt, or the Lost Treasure Train." Beadle and Adam's Half-Dime Library published "Daring Dick, Pawnee Bill's Pard, or the Red Cavalry Raid"; "Pawnee Bill, the Prairie Shadower, or the Gold Queen's Secret," and "The Buckskin Avenger, or Pawnee Bill's Pledge," written by the Buffalo Bill novelist, Colonel Prentiss Ingraham. These brave titles were the forerunners of a long line of dime novels about Pawnee Bill.

Gordon Lillie had achieved fame greater than he had even dreamed while reading Buntline's novels back in Bloomington, Illinois. While obliged, through the management of his show business, to be absent from Oklahoma most of each year, he kept in close touch with the development of the embryo state and maintained a warm interest in every plan for its benefit. From 1889 to 1893, Oklahoma Territory had grown rapidly.

In the spring of 1890, negotiations were completed with the Cherokee for relinquishment of the unoccupied lands of the Outlet west of the 96th Meridian, and with the Iowa, Sac and Fox and the Pottawatomie-Shawnee, whose reservations lay east of Old Oklahoma. In June, negotiations were made with the Cheyenne and Arapahoe for their lands south of the Canadian and west of the region opened in 1889. These tribes took allotments in severalty and agreed to the opening of their surplus lands to white settlement. The Iowa, Sac and Fox lands and the Pottawatomie and Shawnee were opened September 22, 1891, adding two new counties and enlarging four of the original seven. On April 19, 1892, the Cheyenne and Arapahoe country was opened by a third run, and six more counties formed.

No land districts had been established for either of these openings. The lands were apportioned to Guthrie and Oklahoma City offices, at a great disadvantage to settlers living long distances away, and "sooners" took much of the land as in 1889. Many failed to obtain homes, and large groups of dissatisfied settlers gathered on the northern border of the Cheyenne and Arapahoe country and the southern border of Kansas, pressing for entry into the Outlet.

In December, 1891, the Cherokee agreed to cede their unoccupied lands to the United States. In November, 1892, the Pawnee agreed to take allotments in severalty and cede their surplus lands in the Outlet to the government. Believing the government would open the land at an early date, many settlers along its borders brought their families and were "living up their means." Congress ratified the agreement of 1891, but made no appropriation to cover the purchase. This bred discontent. Some of the settlers invaded the Outlet, and the soldiers burned their buildings and drove them out.

Pawnee Bill's parents had sold their home in Kansas following the opening of 1889 and returned to their old jobs as baker and cook at the Pawnee Agency under Indian Agent D. J. M. Woods. Paulina Lillie was appointed assistant matron at the Pawnee School under Superintendent T. W. Conway in 1891 and 1892. From 1889 through 1892, Pawnee Bill made his home at the agency between show seasons.

The build-up on the borders of Kansas and the Cheyenne-Arapahoe country caused him again to enter a movement to force government action in Oklahoma. In the fall of 1892, shortly after his show closed, he was called to Arkansas City by the Board of Trade to organize a group of "Cherokee Strip Boomers" to enter the Outlet.

Title to the land still lay with the Cherokees. On December 9, 1892, Lillie aproached Judge G. W. Saunders of the Cherokee Nation at Fort Gibson to draw up such leases as the Cherokees would agree on to rent to white settlers to farm in the Outlet.

"Our people are becoming very impatient," Lillie told Saunders. "There will be no difficulty in securing five hundred to go in at once, and thousands will follow."

On January 6, 1893, press dispatches reported that Pawnee Bill had gone to Tahlequah, Indian Territory, for the purpose of negotiating a lease on the Cherokee Outlet for five years, and that he would then sub-lease this land in 160-acre tracts to settlers who would move in immediately, regardless of the order or laws of the United States.

This action caused a flurry in the office of the Secretary of State of the Cherokee Nation at Tahlequah, and officials in Washington demanded to know "if any lease is under consideration by your people or if any arrangements have been made authorizing this party to lead the unsuspecting homeseekers to lease this land and take possession of same."

On March 3, Congress made an appropriation to purchase the Outlet, and authorized the President to open it to settlement. Helen P. Clark, an allotting agent, was sent among the Pawnees, and by August 5, their allotments had been taken and approved by the government and their surplus lands purchased at $2.50 per acre. Grover Cleveland had returned to the White House for a second term as President after four years' absence. On August 18, he issued a proclamation opening the Outlet, and on September 16, 1893, this entire northern portion of Oklahoma was changed from an open prairie to a land of farms and cities.

Townsite No. 13 had been established in the horseshoe bend of the Black Bear River, across from the Pawnee Agency. Around this nucleus of the fertile country that had been the Pawnee reservation, a tent town with a population of one thousand sprang up within twenty-four hours after the run. The people voted to call it Pawnee, and the county, known as "Q" County, was named Pawnee in the general election of 1894.

Freighting was a major industry, and the mail came by stagecoach daily from Red Rock and Perry. There was no railroad to Pawnee, but there were two surveys crossing the county seat that within a few years would give the town a direct route to St. Louis, Chicago, and the East, and a short route to the markets of the Gulf. It was destined to become one of the commercial centers of the Southwest.

The black sandy loam along the Black Bear, far more productive than the red soil of the country to the west, yielded grain and fruit in abundance. The Pawnee, Osage and Cherokee Indians each year spent thousands of dollars of their semi-annual payments from the government with the merchants, and while much money was wasted for trifles and luxuries, a certain portion was invested by the Indians in tools, farming implements and furniture. They were looking to the future. Pawnee County, the farthest east of any in Oklahoma Territory, was a center of the border liquor industry. Nine saloons in the little town drew thousands of visitors from the nearby Indian Territory, where the sale of whiskey was prohibited.

The town was the site of one of the largest federal courts in the

United States. The vast Osage country was attached to Pawnee County for federal court purposes for several years, and many lawless persons were brought from the Osage hills for trial. One of the Dunn brothers, notorious in early outlaw history, was killed on the streets of Pawnee by Frank Canton, fearless United States marshal who had his headquarters there. Bill Doolin's gang robbed the Farmers' and Citizens' Bank in 1894, and the town witnessed other killings and pitched battles between officers and territorial bandits. Heck Thomas, who finally tracked down and killed Bill Doolin, was another federal marshal who operated out of Pawnee. Thomas, Canton and Pawnee Bill were close friends.

The Lillie family purchased lots in Pawnee after the opening. From that day, Pawnee Bill made it his permanent home when not on the road with his show. He had made his influence felt in both the opening of 1889 and the Cherokee Outlet. Newspapers called him the "Little Giant of Oklahoma," and he grew famous around the world. He was solicited to run for high public office, but his sense of duty compelled him to decline the honor. The demands of the show business made it impossible for him to give state affairs the time they would justly exact, but Oklahoma always got his support in things pertaining to its material and moral growth.

He returned East with a greatly enlarged show and Mexican Hippodrome, consisting of two-horse standing races, and races between Mexicans, cowgirls, cowboys, Indians, and two two-horse and four-horse chariots. May Lillie was billed as the "$5000 Challenge Horseback Shot." Added features of his Historical Wild West were a Mexican contra dance on horseback, a Mexican band of twelve pieces, an Indian band of ten pieces, a cremation by the Mojave Indians, and Little Virginia Ellis, the "only survivor of the Mountain Meadows Massacre."

There were museum side-shows starring the Five Ali Brothers, Arabian Acrobats; Professor William Malcomb, the Human Pin Cushion and Fire King; Wilfred Grigway, contortionist and India rubber man; Mlle. Winona, Snake and Alligator charmer; Senor LaGuara and Senorita Mijares in a Knife and Battle-Axe Impalement act; Eugene Berry, the Big-Footed Boy; and Marie, Rose and Fannie Anderson, the Spotted Sisters, performing Sioux, African and American song, dance and acrobatic feats.

Included in the Encampment were the Sioux chiefs, Young-Man-Afraid-of-his-Horses and Spotted Tail, with their wives, children and bands of warriors; and Princess Standing Holy, daughter, Ko-Ko, second wife, and Queen White Buffalo Robe, third wife, of Sitting Bull, with their guide and interpreter, Captain A. G. Shaw.

The show moved northeast through Pennsylvania, Maryland, New Jersey and New York, crossed into Canada from Buffalo, and toured Ontario, Quebec, New Brunswick and Nova Scotia. Returning to the United States, it toured Maine, Massachusetts, Connecticut, the District of Columbia, the Carolinas and Virginia, closing a very successful season at Alexandria, November 4, 1893.

Pawnee Bill now was invited by King Leopold of Belgium to bring his show to the World's Fair at Antwerp. He spent the winter making preparations, and in April, 1894, the show sailed aboard the Waesland of the Red Star Line for Europe. Lillie wrote:

> I went there to give the people a vivid idea of our far western life, and took with me the largest exhibition of the kind that had yet visited the Continent—160 people and 100 horses, buffalo and cattle.
>
> Our show caught on at Antwerp. The exhibition was received at every performance with ovations. It was gratifying to me that many of the dignitaries honored us with their attendance. Minister Ewing visited the show several times with members of his family, as did the boroughmaster and governor of Antwerp. His Royal Highness Leopold and the royal family occupied the royal box in July, and requests came to me from several of the chief cities of France, Germany, Austria and Great Britain to visit them before I returned to America.

Press releases bore such headlines as "Vivid Idea of the Far West Being Given the Continental Folk," "Pawnee Bill Causing Excitement Among Nobility," and "Pawnee Bill Makes Stupendous Hit in Europe."

May Lillie "performed difficult shooting feats from a galloping horse, which she rode side saddle," and was "the toast of the Continent." She gave private exhibitions to many of the nobility,

including King Leopold, Baron Muratus, the Viscount DeNewland
and others.

We made good money and had good crowds, but we made a mis-
take. When the Exposition was over, we took our show around
other parts of Belgium. That is a very small country, not as large
as one of our states. Most of the people had already seen our performance, and only handfuls paid admission.

Pawnee Bill knew the value of publicity stunts, and he missed
few tricks. Sometimes, however, they did not work. While playing
to acres of empty seats in one Belgian city, he noticed that a balloon
ascension was getting a big play in the papers. He got in on it. The
balloon broke away and for two days he and the balloonist sat in
the basket and gestured to each other. Neither spoke the other's
language. And the stunt was a dud.

He tried in every way to save the show before reaching the limit
of his resources. After securing passage for his people back to the
United States, he had nothing left to pay expenses. The gendarmes
seized his animals and equipment.

I couldn't sleep that night. Downstairs next morning I was eat-
ing breakfast when in walked a Belgium nobleman who had seen
our show many times.

"You make very bad business?" he asked.

I nodded.

"You want to make some business with me?" he asked again.

I said, "Sure."

He persuaded me to go over to Holland, where not so many
people had seen the show. He counted out 3,500 francs on the table,
and I went out and started paying up the bills to get my show back.
One of the creditors I paid gave me a receipt, but refused to release
my wagons. I threatened to turn my Indians loose on him, and I got
the wagons.

After a few weeks in Holland, Pawnee Bill was able to settle with
his benefactor. But his experiences were of more value to him than
the money:

One evening a man came up on horseback and dismounted in front of my tent. He looked like George Washington. He wore a pair of short silk pantaloons, bagged at the knees, and had a silk coat and vest with a ruffle of lace around the neck and down the front of his shirt. He wore yellow silk stockings and big patent leather slippers. He had a wig with a pigtail on it and all powdered white. On his head was a large three-cornered hat.

He held a large envelope which bore the Coat of Arms of Holland. He demanded to see me. I didn't know the laws of the country, and I thought I might have done something he was going to arrest me for.

When I came out, our handsome gentleman was bowing and scraping to me. He then laid his large envelope on a big silver platter and held it out for me to take.

I ripped open the envelope, but the letter was written in French. I couldn't read French. I passed it to one of my men who could. To my delight I found that it was from Queen Wilhelmina of Holland. She commanded me to hold a special performance on Sunday afternoon for her and all her ladies and noblemen, in honor of Princess Victoria of England.

When Sunday came, everyone in the show was anxious to do his or her part well. Even the Indians were ready to outdo themselves for the "Heap Big White Squaw."

After the show, Princess Victoria sent for me to come to her box. Chevalier DeHunt went with me because I did not know just how to act. The Princess was introduced to me by one of the attendants and I held out my hand to shake with her. She laughed greatly at this, but she took my hand and we shook like two Americans. Chevalier DeHunt told me afterwards I had made a bad break. He said I should not have offered her my hand, but should have waited until she offered me her hand.

We talked for more than half an hour and had a great visit. I was also introduced to Queen Wilhelmina, and we got along royally. When I was finally about to depart, Queen Wilhelmina asked me what I desired in payment for the performances.

I told her I wanted no money at all for it—that it had been a pleasure and a high honor to be permitted to entertain her and her suite.

She then asked if there might be some favor that she could grant
me. I had wanted for a long time to have regular performances every
Sunday, because we could make money on that day. But the laws
of Holland did not permit it. So I told the Queen I would be pleased
to receive permission to show on Sundays. This she readily gave
me, and from then on our stay in Holland was a great success.

After a tour through France, Pawnee Bill was able to return
home with his show, but his funds were depleted. He went
into winter quarters at Chester, Pennsylvania, and through the
friendship of a lumberman, was able to rebuild his wagons.

I also went in debt $10,000 for hardware in refurbishing my
equipment, and when the next season opened, the hardware man
refused to let me leave town until I had paid him.
Again the lumberman came to my rescue. He told the hardware
man he would quit business dealings with him if he seized my show.

In three weeks, Pawnee Bill had the hardware bill paid. He took
all the money he could spare from each day's receipts, wrapped it
in newspapers and expressed it back to Pennsylvania. He ended a
successful season with all debts paid and $30,000 in cash to carry
him through the next year's first appearance.
That year May Lillie won another medal as "Champion Lady
Horseback Shot of the World," presented by F. B. Leys of the
Western Fair Association at London, Ontario; and in October,
1897, Frank Tousey's Five Cent Wide Awake Library published
one of the best in its series of dime novels: "Pawnee Bill, or the
White Chief's First War Trail."
The show went into winter quarters at Frederick, Maryland,
and as always, Pawnee Bill added new features and new personali-
ties. One of these was a great horseman and roper, José Barrera, of
San Antonio, Texas. As "Mexican Joe," leader of the vaqueros, he
became one of the show's top attractions when it toured New York,
New Jersey, Pennsylvania, Ohio, Michigan, Illinois, Indiana, Kentucky, Tennessee, Georgia, and the Carolinas the season of 1898
with the finest Wild West ever presented.
While Joe's skill with a rope was surpassed by many hemp artists,

it was his willingness to dab a loop on anything with four legs that
made him a hero of the show world. While playing in Albany, New
York, the show parade was routed down an exceedingly steep
street, and the brakes on the band wagon failed. As the wagon
gained momentum, the lead team of the six-horse hitch became
frightened and started running down the hill. Mexican Joe, who
always carried his loop ready, dashed up and roped both horses.

With his rope anchored to the saddle horn, he used his cowpony
to try to bring the team to a halt. But the weight of two heavy draft
horses was too much for a 900-pound cow horse. He fell to the
pavement, breaking Joe's leg. However, the rope held and the
weight of the fallen pony was enough to slow the runaways until
the cowboys from the rear of the parade reached them and got
them under control.

Meanwhile, the wagon had swerved into the curb. Without Joe's
quick thinking and skill with the rope, many of the spectators who
lined the parade route would have been injured or killed.

Mexican Joe was taken to the hospital and his leg put in a cast.
In two days he was back with the show, and within a week, he was
riding in the parade again, needing assistance only in mounting
and dismounting from his horse.

On August 30, at Battle Creek, Michigan, he was again injured
when he made a jump for a bucker that refused to let him mount.
At Ypsilanti, Michigan, September 1, he rode Dynamite, a bay
bucker. In order to mount he hitched the halter rope about the
horse's forelegs, but as he started off, the rope caught, throwing both
horse and rider. Joe landed in the reserved seats, severely lacerated
about the head and legs.

He never seemed to get enough. At Coldwater, Michigan, two
weeks later, the bucking horse he was riding went into the horse
tent and took canvas and all with him. The only casualty was a spectator, under the influence of liquor, who injured himself when he
fell through the seats.

When it came to handling show stock, Joe was "tops." His proficiency at roping and doctoring wild buffalo was surpassed only
by his ability to butcher the King's English. In bringing the buffalo
from the train to the show grounds, Joe's cowboy helpers often became too enthusiastic in driving the cows and calves. Joe's voice

would boom out above the cowboys' yells: "Damee, no runnee the lilly buffalo!" He became Pawnee Bill's right hand man, and remained in Lillie's employ until his death.

Pawnee Bill ended the 1898 season with all expenses paid—he owed no man a cent and had $65,000 cash. Back in Oklahoma, the Arkansas Valley Bank, a new institution for Pawnee, had been organized and chartered and a building was being erected for its operation. Its principal promoters were Dr. G. W. Sutton of Cleveland, a gentleman of considerable wealth and a member of the Territorial Council; Captain Frank M. Thompson, a financier of much experience, and C. W. Rambo, of the firm of Fletcher & Rambo, groceries and general merchandise.

Pawnee Bill associated himself with the enterprise. During the years he had toured the United States and Europe, most of the remaining Indian reservations in Oklahoma had been settled. The Kickapoo reserve east of Old Oklahoma and comprising most of western Lincoln County was opened by the last great run, May 25, 1895. In the southwest corner of Oklahoma, a section known as Greer County, consisting of the counties of Harmon, Jackson, Greer and part of Beckham, was claimed by Texas. The Organic Act of 1890 had defined the Oklahoma boundary as the south fork of Red River. On March 16, 1896, the Supreme Court upheld the 1890 act, and Texas lost this area.

The Wichita and the contiguous country of the Kiowa, Comanche and Plains Apache—over two million acres—was settled by a land lottery August 6, 1901. On April 21, 1904, Congress abolished the reservations of the Ponca and Otoe-Missouri lying on the eastern border of the Cherokee Outlet, divided the lands and attached the areas to the counties in which they were located.

The railroad reached Pawnee in 1900, and it boomed as a modern city. It had plenty of honest energy and capital. Almost every line of business was represented, and the businessmen were liberal and enterprising. Fine stone and brick structures soon adorned the business section. A water works and electric system were installed, both owned and operated by the city. Bonds were voted for a sewerage system, concrete sidewalks and street crossings were being built, and other public improvements progressed rapidly as Pawnee took its place among the first-class cities of the Territory.

The Arkansas Valley Bank, organized as a state institution, was nationalized in 1900, with deposits over $300,000—the largest line of deposits of any bank in that part of the Territory—and resources of more than one half million. Pawnee Bill became vice-president, a position he was to hold for several years, and in newspapers and the show journals he was characterized as the "Jekyll and Hyde of the West":

"On Wall Street, in the national financial district, and in the gathering places of men of affairs, they know Pawnee Bill, showman, only as Gordon W. Lillie, president of the Arkansas Valley National Bank, chairman of the Board of Trade, the local school board, and distinguished private citizen of Pawnee, Oklahoma. Clad in the quiet habiliments of commercial life, with his flowing hair concealed under the crown of his ample hat, there are only his virile and jaunty figure and alert, vigorous movements to distinguish him from the men with whom he associates and consults. He is immersed, like them, in the responsibilities of everyday routine avocations.

"Through the winter he toils, concerned with bond issues and bank notes, presiding at meetings of dignified bank directors and of city officials, rejoicing over municipal improvement and spending pleasant evenings in the seclusion of his home. His is a complacent, sedate existence of familiar type. There is no Pawnee Bill.

"Spring comes. It is nature's annual imperious summons for the passing of Gordon W. Lillie. In his stead appears the figure of a mounted man, straight poised in the stirrups of his heavy saddle. A coil of rope hangs on his saddle bow. A loose belt swings a revolver low down upon his hip. A wide hat tops the brown locks that dangle to his shoulders, and a deep handkerchief flutters at his neck. The small and sinewy steed beneath him is as quick and jaunty as he. Red coated bands are blowing, horses stand saddled, plumed, and caparisoned, the steam calliope is shrieking, gorgeously gilded chariots await the signal to start the parade. Crowds are gaping. Indians, cowboys and Mexicans slap and salute him fondly and familiarly, and small boys gaze at him with fascinated awe. He shakes himself and emits a whoop. Pawnee Bill, scout, plainsman, cowboy, hunter, guide, Indian leader, has returned to life."

11.   Friend of the Buffalo

FOR SEVERAL YEARS Pawnee Bill lived these two curiously opposed lives with distinguished success, and amassed a comfortable
fortune. He realized that in only one short quarter century the Old
West had so changed that the present generation had to depend
almost entirely upon history and the Wild West exhibition for a
fair conception of its grandeur and dangers. No longer did the wild
horse and buffalo roam the vast prairies. The passing of the buffalo
had been unnecessarily harsh, if not brutal.

It hardly seemed possible that these animals, numbering in the
millions less than a generation before, had become a rare curiosity.
The original range of the animal had included the Pennsylvania
mountains, the Mississippi delta, northern Mexico, to the upper
shores of Great Slave Lake—nearly two-fifths of the North America
continent. By 1790, the last buffalo east of the Alleghenies had been
killed; by 1810, few were to be found east of the Mississippi. In
1879, those that were left were confined to two great herds on the
Western plains; by 1900, not one was left in the United States except those in captivity, and they had been so intermixed with wild
cattle of various breeds that less than three hundred genuine bison
were in existence.

The Alvord herd in Montana consisted of about sixty; the Goodnight herd in the Texas panhandle, about forty; the Conrad herd
at Kalispell, Montana, about thirty; the government herd in Yellowstone Park, about sixty; the Zoological Gardens of Chicago, Cincinnati, New York and Philadelphia, about eighty in total; and
there were a few small private collections of forty to sixty head, like
the Casey herd of Missouri, the Austin Corbin herd of Blue Mountain Forest, New Hampshire, the James Philip herd at Fort Pierre,
South Dakota, and the Whitney herd of thirty-two at Lenox, Massachusetts. Only twenty per cent of the genuine buffalo existing were

cows. The buffalo cow increased the herd by but one calf every other year, and about seventy-five per cent of the buffalo calves were male. Only the greatest care would succeed in keeping full-blood specimens from being a thing of the past.

Buffalo thrived best and multiplied better on wide free range, summer and winter. A buffalo calf could survive a blizzard that would mean death to the toughest of ranch cattle, and buffalo could find food in the deepest snow, through which ranch cattle would not be able even to move. Nature had taught them to defy the winter, and provided them with a coat of sufficient warmth to keep them from suffering from the cold. Those herds that were permitted to wander in the mountains and valleys in which forage was abundant gradually increased. The herds that were captives were decreasing.

With this object in view, Pawnee Bill purchased the Casey herd, for years the pride of Missouri, and searched for a ranch large enough for them. Naturally, he looked toward his home, Pawnee, in whose broad and wild expanses he had years before given vent to his boyhood energies. When the Pawnees came, the country between the Arkansas and Cimarron was still a buffalo paradise. Here the finest and largest specimens had been found by the buffalo hunters, and the country now, as then, abounded with a rich growth of buffalo grass and cool streams of spring water. To these natural conditions he attributed the enormous size and splendid quality of the early buffalo. Here a sincere effort could be made to give the buffalo all the conditions under which it had flourished in the past, and it was Pawnee Bill's purpose to develop the finest specimens of the animal in remembrance of his early days on the plains.

The only area available that had not been cut up in farms was several tracts of inherited and non-competent Indian lands. By an Act of Congress approved May 27, 1902, certain tracts in the Pawnee reservation were made eligible for purchase and offered for sale. Pawnee Bill bought nearly two thousand acres of hills and valleys southwest of Pawnee, and established his buffalo ranch.

His homesite he purchased from Blue Hawk, the Pawnee chief and medicine man. When the Pawnees took their allotments prior to the opening of the Cherokee Outlet, Blue Hawk had selected the tract of land on high ground overlooking the bend of the Black

Bear, where he had built his lodge and lived when Lillie came to the
reservation as a boy from Wichita. On this point, only a few miles
from the Pawnee Agency where as a young man he had taught
school, and fifty miles from the mouth of Big Turkey Creek where
on April 22, 1889, he had led his famous boomer colony into the
land of Canaan, Lillie built a rambling cabin of native logs, and
named it Blue Hawk Peak, after the Indian chief.

Between show seasons, Pawnee Bill lived there and devoted his
time to building up his ranch and his buffalo herd. He collected
all the pure-blooded buffalo he could buy, and spent most of his
time studying their traits:

> I had seen the buffalo many times in their palmy days on the
> plains and hunted them with both white men and the Indians. At
> my ranch, I had the experience and knowledge of the older Pawnee
> Indians to rely upon when I needed the right kind of advice. The
> Pawnees knew more about the buffalo, no doubt, than any other
> tribe, and perhaps killed more of them.
>
> I discovered that I had far better luck with the buffalo calves if
> I took them away from the cows in September. Both the cows and
> the calves do better. This fact was among those I gleaned from the
> Pawnees about the animals, and it was a very important and profit-
> able one. The calves, by September, were old enough to look out
> for themselves and to feed on pasture and roughness, while their
> mothers were permitted to strengthen and grow fat during the fall
> and winter months.

He kept all the female calves and purchased cows whenever possible to increase his herd. He also was careful to preserve the true
color and hair of the original buffalo, and when an imperfect calf
was found in the herd, it was taken away while young and sold.
Generally, such calves were shipped to New York and sold for beef
at fancy prices.

The cost of buffalo at that time was enormous. In 1904 Lillie
wrote:

> I have one bull that is considered the finest specimen of his kind
> in the country. He is conservatively estimated at five thousand dol-

lars; and, to be candid about the matter, I would not take double
the amount for him.

Experience had shown that seventy-five per cent of buffalo calves
born in captivity or subject to restrictive range were males. Lillie
believed that this might be overcome by raising cattalo, the off-
spring of buffalo and ordinary cattle. Colonel Charles Goodnight
was reported to have had considerable success in this line on his
Texas ranch, and it was being attempted in other parts of the country. Within a few years, Lillie changed his mind entirely:

> The experiments I have made in crossing the buffalo with the
> common domestic cow are expensive, to say the least, and in many
> cases have failed utterly. I have discovered, however, that the black
> Galloway turns out what may be considered the best results. The
> Jersey returns the largest percentage of calves, but this crossing
> lightens the coats to such a degree that the results are not what are
> to be desired. The big-boned Texas longhorn, with which Good-
> night has had success, is fairly well adapted to the purpose; but I
> have found the Galloway the best. The genuine Texas cow leaves
> a white mark along the back and flank, while the Galloway produces
> a long, silky, glossy robe which is a bit darker than the genuine
> buffalo robe.

The hybrid was of finer hair and produced better-flavored meat,
which was in great demand. But the equality in sex could not be
preserved by crossing. Lillie's greatest trouble in raising cattalo lay
in the actual breeding of them:

> I have had but little bad luck in raising the calves *after* they were
> born. There is a fact, not generally known, that cuts a big figure in
> this interbreeding of the two animals. It takes eleven months for a
> buffalo calf to mature and only nine for the calf of ordinary cattle.
> Naturally this interferes greatly in the breeding and quite fre-
> quently results in the death of the cow before the calf is born.
>   Another thing—if there is a white spot anywhere about the cow
> that is bred to a buffalo, that white spot invariably appears on the
> calf. To my knowledge, it has never failed. I doubt very much if a

sturdy race of cattalo will ever be developed. And again, if I can have success in raising the original buffalo, what is the use or what have I gained by experimenting with the hybrids?

Lillie's studies and experiments pointed up the importance of preserving the original buffalo. By 1906, he had increased his herd to sixty, the third largest privately owned collection of pure-bloods in the world. He had proved that the buffalo could be preserved and in part restored to their place in the country, but only by the most conservative and careful methods. It was an impossible task for an individual:

> We must come to a more rational mode of procedure, and what more natural or just than that the national government should come to the rescue of this one-time monarch of the plains? The whole matter, now lying in private hands, must be taken over and conducted upon an intelligent and scientific plan, otherwise the bison is doomed to extinction.

Many reasons have been given for the almost complete extermination of the buffalo. Pawnee Bill summed up his:

> Man's reckless greed; his wanton extravagance; his destructiveness and improvidence in not husbanding the resources that come to him by the hand of nature ready made; the fatal preference on the part of the hunter generally, both white and red, for the robe and flesh of the cow over the bull; the phenomenal stupidity of the animals themselves, and their indifference to man; the perfection of the modern breech-loading rifles and other sporting firearms in general; and the total and inexcusable absence of protective measures and agencies on the part of the national government and the Western states and territories.
> While all these causes acted against the buffalo, there cannot be found one restraining or preserving influence.

As early as March 13, 1871, Congressman R. C. McCormick, of Arizona Territory, had introduced a bill to prevent the ruthless slaughter of the buffalo. It was ordered printed, and that was the end of it. On February 14, 1872, Senator Cornelius Cole, of California, offered a resolution requesting the Committee on Territories to inquire into the expediency of a law protecting the buffalo running wild in the territories. This was agreed to, and on February 16, Henry Wilson, of Massachusetts, introduced a bill in the Senate restricting the killing of buffalo on public lands. It was read twice by title and died in the Committee on Territories.

The same thing happened to a bill introduced by Representative Fort of Illinois, in March, 1874. Even when both houses had succeeded in passing a suitable bill in June, 1874, it went to President Ulysses S. Grant for his signature, only to be pigeonholed and die a natural death. On January 31, 1876, Fort introduced a second bill, which never came back from the Committee on Territories. A bill he introduced on March 20, 1876, to tax buffalo hides, was referred to the Committee on Ways and Means and never heard from again.

Since 1880, the private buffalo ranches for breeding of the animals in captivity had been established through the country, and agitation for the establishment of a national buffalo preserve in the West was kept alive by such men as James Philip, Colonel Goodnight, Charles J. "Buffalo" Jones of Kansas, and others.

In the summer of 1904, Ernest Harold Baynes' series of appeals began to appear in the Boston *Transcript*. His influence spread to the presidential chair; and when, on December 8, 1905, fourteen men organized the American Bison Society, with Dr. W. T. Hornaday, chief taxidermist of the National Museum as president, and Baynes as secretary, Theodore Roosevelt was made honorary president.

For the next two years, the members of the society delivered lectures, wrote articles, encouraged others to do so, and otherwise did everything to revive interest in the buffalo, even to the old dream of making fabrics from its wool.

In Oklahoma, Pawnee Bill's enthusiasm flamed:

All these failures in the past did not deter me. I was quite positive that I would be able to convince congress that what had been shamefully neglected in the past might even in this eleventh hour be remedied.

Through the agency of Congressman Bird S. McGuire, of Oklahoma, he prepared and introduced a bill "providing for the appropriation at once of a sum to purchase outright a sufficient number of such pure-bloods as were existent with which to form a herd to be maintained for breeding purposes alone, the purchase of a tract of land far removed from civilization, the fencing of the same, and an appropriation for its maintenance."

The natural haunt of the buffalo was the Great Staked Plains. Here grew that peculiar quality of grass on which the animals had thrived and lived their best. In the Great Staked Plains, a reservation could be purchased for a nominal figure, and it was there that the hope of the buffalo lay, if anywhere.

But Lillie thought of the 61,500 acres in the Wichita Mountains of southwestern Oklahoma near Fort Sill that Congress had set aside as a national forest reserve when the Kiowa and Comanche Indian reservations had been opened to settlement in 1901. In the neighborhood of this preserve, in 1883, the last great Indian buffalo hunt had occurred, in which representatives of ten different tribes —the Arapaho, Cheyenne, Kiowa, Comanche, Wichita, Caddo, Tonkawa, Sioux, Delaware, and Apache—had contested to determine who could kill the largest number of buffalo with a single arrow without dismounting from his horse. The contest had lasted several days. The victor was William Elk, a Cheyenne, credited with ten buffalo; his closest competitor, a Kiowa, killed five.

Numerous buffalo wallows still marked the prairies, and the bones and horns of the animals were scattered where countless numbers had roamed the foothills of the Wichitas. Here they had been as ruthlessly slaughtered as in other portions of the West in the 1880's, and stories of big killings were still related by old hunters and plainsmen. What better place than this, where the buffalo made his last stand, for breeding and preserving them to posterity!

When Lillie appeared in Washington in February, 1906, he asked Congress to set aside 26,000 acres of the government reservation, and allow a modest sum for fencing part of it:

The buffalo must have room if he shall multiply. The preserve in the Wichita mountains offers such a home, and I predict that the herd there will increase rapidly. In my opinion, all other herds in

the United States should be brought to the Oklahoma preserve as
soon as possible. I mean by that, the pure-bloods, for in preserving
the buffalo he should be kept with a pedigree unchallenged.

Lillie's bill failed to pass Congress, but he succeeded in interesting President Roosevelt in his suggestion, the American Bison Society took a profound interest in the proposition, and interest in the
entire nation was so manifest that the transition of the Wichita
reservation into a national game preserve for buffalo, elk, antelope,
bear and wild game birds met with little opposition. Congress ap-
propriated $15,000 to enclose 8000 acres with a steel-wire fence
seven and a half feet high. When the fence was completed, Dr.
Hornaday carefully selected six male and nine female buffaloes
from the society's Bronx Park herd, and these were shipped to the
preserve on October 11, 1907.

It was the first herd established by private enterprise placed
under government protection, and proved to be a highly successful
experiment. It became one of the finest herds in the country. In
1908, the government set aside another 12,500 acres in the Flathead
reservation, Montana, and the society stocked this range. By 1925,
these herds, and the herd in Yellowstone Park, had become so large
the government authorized the killing of a certain number each
year. By 1926, there were 4,376 buffaloes in the United States.

When it came to buffalo, Pawnee Bill was a sentimentalist. When
Señor José Banjio, a sporting enthusiast from Mexico, dropped into
Lillie's office at the Arkansas Valley National Bank just before
Christmas, 1906, wanting to buy some bulls to cross with native
Mexican cattle, the showman lent an attentive ear. He showed
Banjio about his ranch and spent hours telling him just how such
inbreeding would produce a robe almost as serviceable as the old-
time buffalo robe, and the meat would prove excellent. The Mexi-
can purchased seven bulls for $3375, with an agreement to pay the
balance of $1000 when the animals were loaded on the train in
Oklahoma for shipment to Juarez, then departed.

Apparently he made for the local newspaper office as soon as he
reached Mexico, for the next issue of the *Hairless News* told of
Señor Banjio's return from Pawnee, Oklahoma, where he had made
arrangements for a series of fights at Juarez.

Like most showmen, Lillie subscribed to a clipping bureau. A
few days later, a marked copy of the newspaper found its way into
his mail, and he read how the theater-loving populace of Juarez
and other towns across the river from El Paso were going to have
a treat. In the words of the local paper, "seven of the largest and
most ferocious buffalo bulls in the United States will be pitted
against our most savage Spanish bulls and skillful matadors."

Lillie described his reaction to the clipping:

> I immediately returned the purchase money with the notification
> that I would positively not deliver my buffaloes for the murderous
> purpose planned, and telling Senor Banjio what I thought of his
> deceitful tactics.

A few days later, Pawnee Bill received a letter from Banjio's attorney in New York stating that his attempt to cancel the contract
for sentimental reasons did not affect the legal status of the case, and
unless Pawnee Bill advised by return mail that the buffalo bulls
would be shipped at once, he would institute suit in the United
States Court for the specific performance of the agreement and for
such damages suffered by his client.

Lillie continued:

> When the lawyer set into the game, I decided the only way to
> save my seven bulls from slaughter was to get the buffalo people
> interested. The first two I thought of were Dr. Hornaday and Fred
> Thompson, who had at Luna Park, New York, the summer before,
> a herd of buffaloes which loved him like a father. Thinking that
> Thompson had more spare time than Dr. Hornaday, I appealed to
> him first:
>
> "Judge Eagleton of this city looks after my legal affairs and I have
> placed the money in his hands. Please engage competent counsel
> in New York and have communication entered into at once with
> Judge Eagleton, sparing no expense or effort, for my mind is fully
> made up not to sacrifice these survivors of the now almost extinct
> animal."

Thompson hurried to the Bronx Zoo to see if Dr. Hornaday could find something in the revised buffalo laws to prevent Banjio from carrying off Pawnee Bill's buffalo to furnish a holiday for the sport-loving Mexicans. "There is nothing in the statutes to prevent him from buying up all the 1,200 surviving buffaloes in the country for bull-fighting purposes if he can," Hornaday replied.

However, an interesting point was raised. The contract had been made in a territory of the United States where bull-baiting was prohibited by law. Contracts against public policy, or contracts the fulfilling of which was in violation of the law, were null and void. Did a buffalo bull come within the meaning of the law?

Lillie's attorneys believed so, and the showman advised Banjio, through his attorney:

> Whites and Indians out here are wrought up over the episode. My buffaloes, as you know, are popular pets. The Indians are especially attracted to them. My corral is daily the assembling place of warriors and squaws, to whom the herd has a unique fascination, bringing to them memories of the wild, free days of the early West. There will be stern opposition, if not violence, if any attempt is made to convey the seven to Mexico to fight bulls.

The case never came to trial.

Lillie continued to increase his herd until at one time it was estimated he owned the second largest private collection of pure-blooded buffalo in the country. He kept them all on his ranch, with the exception of a few that accompanied his show.

Pawnee Bill was one of the most picturesque products of the early West. Twenty years' career as a showman had made him financially independent, and his pride and ambition centered in the organization which bore his name. As in the propagation of the buffalo, he strove to gather not merely a good, but the best, show of its character ever put on the road, and was continually adding new attractions, notably a herd of trained camels and elephants.

One of his most successful seasons was 1905, when he opened at Carnegie, Pennsylvania, and played back through Ohio, Michigan, Illinois, Iowa, Missouri, Kansas, Oklahoma and Indian Territories, and Arkansas. "The juvenile contingents of the cities always turned out in all their glory to do homage to his Wild West show. . . . The small boys were up at dawn to watch the circus come in, and there was no thought of breakfast or anything until the last elephant and the last glittering wagon had lumbered from the scene."

Crowds often lined the streets before 9 o'clock for the parade, and "although the pageant did not usually arrive until almost 1:30, the thousands along the way never tired of waiting, and did not withdraw until the brilliant spectacle had unfolded to their hungry view." Almost before the calliope bringing up the rear had tooted its way past, there was a wild rush for street cars and other conveyances, and from that time until 2:30, there was "a ceaseless stream of humanity in the direction of the show grounds." Almost every available seat in the enclosures was occupied when the grand entree was made, afternoon and night, and "from start to finish, there was always something doing."

Many believed Pawnee Bill had Buffalo Bill's show "skinned a block." Buffalo Bill had a larger number of performers in his Congress of Rough Riders of the World, but he had no such "stage settings" as Pawnee Bill. Buffalo Bill made little or no attempt at "stage setting," while Pawnee Bill had one of the most elaborate ever carried by any outdoor show, including the famous Barnum & Bailey and Ringling Brothers. "The trappings of the animals in Buffalo Bill's show always seemed dingy and old, while Pawnee Bill's were bright and new."

Lillie said:

> It came to a place where our show could go into a town with, before, or after Cody, and make as much money as he did.

In 1906, Pawnee Bill decided to branch out. "The Great Train Robbery," a spectacular Western melodrama in two scenes, in which a locomotive engine and train of cars were utilized showing the famous Dalton Brothers in one of the tragic episodes of their checkered careers, became one of the central and conspicuous features of the program. Arthur Voegtlin, famous for his New York Hippodrome triumphs, was its originator. It had been featured at Luna Park the summer of 1906, and instantly became the legitimate

sensation of outdoor theatrics at the Coney Island resort, running
747 performances. Pawnee Bill secured the exclusive traveling
rights to the show the winter of 1906. It was to be produced in his
tent under Voegtlin's personal supervision, the most ambitious
undertaking of tented amusement history.

Lillie allied himself with Edward Arlington, who was for years
identified with the Barnum & Bailey organization as James A.
Bailey's confidential adviser, and announced his intention of going
into the big cities. Heretofore, he had limited his routes to small
towns, and had usually been ignored by Ringling Brothers and
Barnum & Bailey, the "Circus Trust."

Now his show was the biggest Wild West on the continent. Buf-
falo Bill was playing in Europe in 1906. He was ordered back to the
United States at once, and a circus war was launched against Pawnee
Bill.

12.   Pawnee Bill's Great Far East

CODY AND NATE SALSBURY had fought Pawnee Bill at every turn in 1888. After Lillie closed his show at Easton, Maryland, Annie Oakley had gone back to Buffalo Bill's show. They became friends once more, and Cody was happy. While Lillie was engaged in the boomer movement in Kansas, Cody and Salsbury had planned a Continental tour. There was to be a great Exposition Universale in Paris, and an arena and grandstand had been built for the Wild West the previous winter in the military zone outside the old walls of Paris, at Neuilly. In the spring of 1889, while Lillie led his boomer colony through southern Kansas into Oklahoma, Cody's Wild West took ship again. When Lillie went on the road with his show following the Oklahoma opening, Cody's Wild West was playing in Paris, its domestic competition forgotten.

In the fall of 1889, Cody's show went to Barcelona, Spain, then crossed the Mediterranean to Naples, Italy, where it opened January 26, 1890, then moved to Rome. In 1890, it toured Austria, Hungary and Germany, visiting all the leading cities, including Vienna and Berlin.

The exhibition was at Strassburg, Alsace, when Cody received word of the Sioux Indian outbreak at the Pine Ridge Agency, known as the "Ghost Dance War," in a telegram requesting him to come to Chicago at once to act again in his capacity as scout against the tribes. He left the exhibition with Salsbury in winter quarters at an old castle near Banfeldt. Major Burke and the contingent of Indian chiefs and warriors sailed from Antwerp to Washington, where, at the request of President Harrison, all promised to act as peacemakers.

At Chicago, General Nelson A. Miles prepared to take command of a campaign against the Indians. Sitting Bull had chosen the Badlands of North Dakota as the battlefield. Sitting Bull trusted

Cody; he had worked in his Wild West show. Cody suggested that he be allowed to contact him and attempt a conciliation, and Miles agreed. But President Harrison was advised that such a move would precipitate the conflict, and Cody was recalled. Had he been allowed to complete his mission, he might have prevented the bloodshed that followed. Hostilities were short-lived. Sitting Bull was killed, and without their great leader, the Indians surrendered. When Cody sailed from Philadelphia to rejoin his exhibition, April 1, 1891, he took with him Kicking Bear, Short Bull, and twenty-five other rebellious Sioux leaders, held as hostages, at the request of Generals Miles and Schofield, who, like Cody, believed that travel abroad might convince them the white man was not trying to oppress them and that their only hope was the maintenance of peace and good will.

Re-opening at Strassburg, April 19, 1891, Buffalo Bill's show played the cities along the Upper Rhine and Brussels, sailed across to England, visiting the provinces of the British Isles, and exhibited that winter, housed in the Exposition Building at Glasgow, Scotland. He opened at Earl's Court, May 7, 1892, and was commanded to appear before Queen Victoria on the Lawn Tennis Grounds of Windsor Castle, where no entertainment had been given for twenty-five years following the death of the prince consort.

Closing the season in October, he returned to America, opening at the World's Columbian Exposition at Chicago in April, 1893, and, in 1894, played in Ambros Park, Brooklyn, while Pawnee Bill's Historic Wild West was touring France, Belgium and Holland. On the road in 1895, in 1896 following the Barnum & Bailey show in Madison Square Garden, he toured the United States and Canada for five consecutive home seasons through 1899 under the direction of James A. Bailey, who had now acquired an interest in the show.

In 1902, Bailey sent Cody and his Rough Riders of the World back across the waters. He appeared that winter at Olympia, London, making farewell tours of England, Scotland and Wales in 1903-04; duplicated his previous Parisian triumph on the famous Champ de Mars in 1905; opened at Marseilles in 1906, and made a final Continental tour, including Italy, Hungary, Galicia, Slavonia, Bohemia, Croatia, Belgium, Austria, and Germany, before returning to America in November, 1906.

By this time, interesting and significant developments had arisen in the increasingly competitive field of outdoor show business. Two important consolidations had taken place. Edward Arlington had purchased half-interest in Pawnee Bill's show, and would take an active part in its management. At the same time, the Hagenbeck and Wallace circuses had effected a combination and announced that they would tour the country under one name and one canvas.

But, most important of all, a great new force had risen in the show world. It was the Circus Trust—a combination of the Barnum & Bailey, Buffalo Bill, Ringling Brothers, and Forepaugh-Sells organizations. This Circus Trust was dominated by John Ringling. Since the death of James A. Bailey in 1906, he was regarded as the foremost circus man in America. He and his brothers had grown from a small wagon circus to an institution comparable with Barnum & Bailey, and they had risen from a place where they were ignored to a position where they could now dictate terms to all other amusement enterprises.

The Ringlings owned the Forepaugh-Sells Brothers circus, and Barnum & Bailey controlled the Buffalo Bill show. Before the Ringlings bought the Forepaugh-Sells Brothers circus, that organization had been owned jointly by them and James A. Bailey. The change in ownership by which Ringling Brothers became interested dated back to the death of Peter Sells, three years before. At that time the combined shows had been owned by Peter Sells, William Sells, W. W. Cole and Bailey. The Ringlings obtained complete control after the death of Bailey, the sale being made in the settlement of the Bailey estate.

Before Bailey's death, Ringling had made a long term contract with the management of Madison Square Garden by which Barnum & Bailey and Forepaugh-Sells were the only circuses to be admitted to the Garden, the only possible place a circus could exhibit in Manhattan Borough. While this contract barred any show bearing the Ringling Brothers name, it permitted other circuses owned by them to encroach on territory long exclusively the preserve of Barnum & Bailey. Thus, the Ringlings stayed away from New York, Brooklyn, Jersey City and contiguous territory, and alternated in Boston, Buffalo, Philadelphia, Washington and other eastern cities.

A few years before, the Ringlings had become strong enough to bar Barnum & Bailey from Chicago, St. Louis and other Western cities. When James A. Bailey died, the Barnum & Bailey circus was owned by an English syndicate of which Bailey held a third interest and was managing director. For a short time after his death, his confidential adviser, George A. Starr, became acting manager. He was succeeded by W. W. Cole, who was elected through the support of J. T. McCaddon, a brother-in-law of Bailey, and executor of the Bailey estate.

John Ringling was ambitious and had fretted for years at being barred from New York. As long as Bailey was alive he did not feel like making an open breach by insisting on the right to take his show to the metropolis and comforted himself by getting as good territory as possible. When the time came for renewing the territorial agreement after Bailey's death, Ringling refused to accept the usual territory.

He became the dictator, instead of the man who took what was doled out to him, and for the season 1907 scheduled his show for appearances in Brooklyn, all New Jersey cities, and Philadelphia, and had "first calls" on Buffalo, St. Louis and other large cities in the West. Barnum & Bailey could not appear in these cities until Ringling Brothers had visited them, and no Barnum & Bailey paper could be displayed until the Ringling engagement had closed.

Under this agreement, Ringling Brothers with their two shows, and Barnum & Bailey with Buffalo Bill's Wild West, made warfare on other circuses and Wild West aggregations. There was no clashing of dates, and money was not wasted in fighting each other, while they were always ready to join forces to fight any rival circus that became troublesome. And Pawnee Bill's Wild West had become troublesome.

The Pawnee Bill show was undergoing a metamorphosis in winter quarters at Cumberland Park, Nashville, Tennessee. With Edward Arlington, Lillie had conceived the idea of blending the romance and adventure of the Western border with the marvels of the dreamy and imaginative Orient, mysterious Hinduland and savage Africa and Australia, called "The Great Far East," and they had created an entertainment different from all others.

Their agents ransacked many remote countries for amusement novelties and sensations, and returned with a heterogeneous horde.

The result was an exhibition "never before granted startled American eyes."

"Every trick which for centuries have puzzled Western scientists and laymen" was included in each performance of the Great Far East—"apparent miracles, passing all understanding and conception." A blooming, fruit-bearing bush grew in ten minutes before the eyes from a freshly interred mango stone; a Hindu was buried under six feet of earth and emerged directly from the midst of the audience; a girl was confined to a small wicker basket and apparently butchered, and lo! the receptacle was empty; pigeons flew from eggs; balls were thrown into the air to fade slowly from sight; and deadly snakes bit grinning performers to no purpose, but inserted their fangs in dumb animals which died on the spot.

A nautch girls ballet "brought the art of rhythmic motion to the highest degree of perfection attained by human feet and bodies," with Damayanti, their premier danseuse, concluding each performance with the egg dance of Sahmakin, "one of the most difficult feats ever essayed by modern terpsichoreans." Singhalese executed the dexterous evolutions of the "stick and silver" dance. Cannibals from the Dark Continent showed their flesh-eating proclivities. There were Boers, Kaffirs, Abyssinians, Zulus, and Hottentots.

From Madagascar came a band of oxen cavalry. The governor-general of this country, "where no horse could be obtained for love nor money," had "instituted this innovation in warfare." These savage soldiers rode barefoot, without stirrups. The oxen possessed great fortitude and endurance, and were neither slow nor easily frightened in battle. Advancing with horns pointed forward, they created havoc among horse cavalry. The members of the corps joined Pawnee Bill with government permission.

Australian Bushmen gave demonstrations of their prowess with the boomerang. From the pampas of South America came Gauchos, whose skill with the bolo was "the marvel and despair of every nation." Arabs with their superb native horses demonstrated the customs and habits of the desert, and whirling dervishes carried on ecstatic observances with their violent pirouetting and vociferous shouting and chanting.

The equestrianism of a band of wild-riding Cossacks, headed by Prince Luca, a Russian nobleman, was "unmatched in rash courage and skill." With them were three brothers, who the winter before had figured in an uprising in Russia and were arrested. They had fled to Siberia, one under sentence of death, and escaped to America. "Their appearance alone is well worth the price of admission."

Edward Arlington sailed for Tangier to penetrate the interior and communicate with Raisuli, the brigand chief, and lure him to America to exhibit himself. He was at war with the Sultan's troops and in hiding. Arlington was prepared to let him set his own terms in gold, but the trip was unsuccessful.

Pawnee Bill also failed to secure the release of Geronimo, the great Apache leader who had been in captivity for years at Fort Sill. Government officers objected on the grounds that other Apaches would become restless should they not be allowed their freedom also, and President Roosevelt decided it unwise to grant the aged warrior the privilege.

Charlie Owns-the-Dog, cousin of Geronimo, was permitted to join the Wild West aggregation, with the famous Sioux warriors, Standing Cloud, Flatiron, Charlie Black-Eye and Chief Big Turkey, who had played major roles in the Custer massacre. Standing Cloud, despite his seventy years, was one of the fleetest sprinters with the show. Flatiron, ninety-three, was reputed to be the greatest orator of the Sioux nation, and had harangued the Indians before they went into the Custer battle. Chief Big Turkey had commanded the Brulé Sioux in the Custer fight. Too old to do active work with the show, he was taken along for his good influence among the Indians, and ability to quiet them when they became restless or dissatisfied.

Pawnee Bill's show typified the two extremes of the earth—the Wild West and the Far East—and Chief Big Turkey of the Sioux nation, and Chief Rangihaeta, from the innermost depths of Africa, pictured the world's two opposites.

Rangihaeta, a rampant cannibal, had been lured to America with no appreciation of his dietetic deprivation. His house, the council place of his tribe, was named Kai Tangata (Eat Man), in pleasing memorial of the feasts held within. His luxuries barred by custom and law in the United States, he grew thin and lost interest in existence. Pawnee Bill's ample table held no attractions.

It looked as if he would have to be left behind when the season's tour began. A systematic campaign was started to save his health. Rangihaeta would positively not eat flesh other than human. The ham of the herdsman of his native land had been his sustenance since childhood, although plenty of cattle and sheep were at his disposal, and tireless persuasion was futile. Then the American vegetable, unknown in Africa, was suggested. Rangihaeta tasted gingerly, smacked his lips, rubbed his stomach and grinned delightedly. His life and job were saved.

Pawnee Bill's Wild West and Great Far East opened in Nashville with a spectacular night parade April 16. Sky rockets, Roman candles and colored lights were used to enhance the beauty and impressiveness of the "first circus of its kind ever witnessed in the South." Its first performance was on the site of the old Coliseum near the intersection of 22nd Avenue and Cedar Street. "The spacious tent was filled to capacity, the performance was all its title implied . . . an instructive, true insight into the manners, customs and habiliment of the peoples of the pioneer West and the nations of the Orient. . . . The grand entree and general introduction, presenting wonderful riders and important personages from all parts of the world, was a splendid array of gorgeous costumes and a show of mounted military maneuvers. Pawnee Bill, about whom the gay cavalcade was formed, was greeted with roaring applause." The show played two days in Nashville, the last day being Confederate Day, and a portion of the receipts went to a fund for erecting a monument to the Confederate private soldier at Centennial Park. It took forty railroad cars to carry the tents, paraphernalia, animals and other accessories and its 587 people as the show left Nashville to tour the South until the weather was warm enough to venture into other parts of the country.

At Dickson, Tennessee, the *New Idea* called it "the largest and best show of the Wild West variety now touring the United States." It paraded the asphalted street of Memphis "with trappings of gold and crimson, the splendor of native costumes and the atmosphere of the distant West. The line of march was careful and the contrast of nations and people appealed with forcefulness to the general sympathies. . . . Those who saw it were convinced, and both afternoon and night, its big tents were filled to capacity."

The performance began with the usual assembly of nations, and the introduction of May Lillie, champion lady horseback shot of the world, and Major Gordon W. Lillie (the title of "Major" had now been tacked to his name by his show personnel), White Chief of the Pawnees, hero of the plains, and noted historical figure. His long hair flowing, he faced the center grandstand and eloquently introduced his kaleidoscopic extravaganza, and the show was on. Different acts followed in quick sequence, until the final spectacle, the Great Train Robbery.

At Paducah, Kentucky, the *News Democrat* of April 26 called it "a modern revelation" that "brought forth many expressions of wonder from the throngs which packed the streets until there was barely room for the animals and vehicles to pass." It visited Evansville, Indiana, April 29, reached Vincennes, to play that city, April 30, and spread its tents in Terre Haute on May 2. Leaving Indiana, the show headed west, making its introduction to St. Louis, where the engagement was "most auspiciously conducted."

From St. Louis, it played ten daily "stands," then moved to Chicago, moving here three times, giving the north, south and west portions of the city opportunity to see its "veritable colony of nations" and glittering mass of color and animation. "Major Gordon W. Lillie has returned to the arena with rifle and shotgun, after an absence of several years. His accuracy of eye and aim have not been impaired. He breaks glass balls with the regularity and frequency which makes Captain F. F. Bennett, champion rifle and revolver shot of the world, exert himself to the utmost to surpass." And May Lillie told Chicago women: "Let any normally healthy woman who is ordinarily strong screw up her courage and tackle a bucking bronco, and she will find the most fascinating pastime in the field of feminine athletic endeavor. There is nothing to compare to increase the joy of living, and, once accomplished, she'll have more real fun than any pink tea or theater party or ballroom ever yielded."

On June 10, Joliet turned out to see this "congress of nations," and at the head of the parade, with big sombrero and flowing hair, rode the "picturesque figure of a man known far and wide on two continents." The week following, at LaSalle, at Davenport, Dubuque and Oelwein, Iowa, and at Rochester, Minnesota, its tents were unable to accommodate the crowds that sought admittance.

"Of all the great wonders of the show, none is more brilliant and beautiful than May Lillie's demonstrations of the wonder-products of skill and patience and gentleness in animal training. She has courage, determination and love of her art, and endows her public performances with charming grace and finish of manner, movement and method. Her equestrian accomplishments range from simple to complex and from artistic and polite to intrepidly rough. No equine spirit is too wild or purpose too savage for her to quench and rule. She is an equestrian empress whose throne is her saddle and whose four-footed subjects are her devoted pride. Guided solely by her voice and gesture, they execute a multiplicity of exacting feats that illustrate the extreme possibilities of equine expositions. Beyond this extraordinary performance it is impossible to go. . . ."

The show arrived at Minneapolis over the Great Western Road in its two trains of forty cars and pitched its big tents at Fourth Avenue South and Thirty-fourth Street. On June 17, the Minneapolis *News* said, "The Great Train Robbery made a tremendous hit." The parade, stretching more than a mile long, was "a gay and gorgeous pageant." The exhibitions of rifle shooting and equestrianism are "exciting numbers, vivid realism prevails throughout," and the "collected representatives of twenty different races comprise a remarkable ethnological gallery."

Frank L. Sylvis' way of earning a living was to be dragged prostrate around the arena and hanged twice a day by Pawnee Bill's cowboys. How he survived the ordeal was a source of ceaseless wonder to the crowds.

"Sylvis is the luckless victim who impersonates a horse thief. Jose Barrera, Mexican man of the plains, is at the head of the band of vigilantes who swoop down upon the maurauder. A lasso descends upon him, and he is dragged from his stolen mount. Away gallop the captors, Sylvis flat on the ground at one end of the rope. Around the big arena Barrera and his men dash, their prisoner struggling vainly with his bond, and his person the target of a continuous round of ammunition. A telegraph pole at one end of the arena is the destination. The rope is looped over the cross-piece and Sylvis, half strangled and choking with smoke and dust, is hauled high in the air. His life seems to go out with a last few spasmodic kicks, and he hangs limp until cut down by the sheriff and posse.

" 'I fear every time I feel that lasso around me and am jerked off my feet that it may be my last hanging,' Sylvis relates. 'It's the best paying job with the show, and I'll stick to it till they put me out of business.' "

The show folded its tents ending the season at Denison, Texas, November 9. It had traversed eighteen states and taken a hurried look at Mexico. After leaving Minneapolis, some of the larger cities visited were St. Paul, Omaha, Kansas City, Denver, San Antonio and Dallas. The patronage was immense. More than two million persons sat under its canvas. Pawnee Bill brought his show back to his buffalo ranch for winter quarters, and arrived for the gala occasion of the celebration of Oklahoma's new statehood.

On June 6, 1906, the part of the Kiowa-Comanche-Caddo holdings reserved from settlement as common grazing grounds in the opening of 1901, had been dissolved, and these pastures, aggregating nearly 80,000 acres, were attached to Oklahoma Territory. The Osage Indians and the Kaw Indians northwest of the Osage Nation, had resisted all attempts at allotment of their lands, covering some 1,600,000 acres. There was such bitter opposition that the Dawes Act of 1887 had not applied to their reservations. Political strife developed within the tribes. The half-breeds wanted allotments, the full-bloods fought against it, until their consent was finally given, and on June 28, 1906, Congress provided for the division of lands and funds of these Indians.

Oklahoma was two separate regions: the eastern half Indian Territory, occupied by the Five Civilized Tribes, and the western half Oklahoma Territory, the lands opened to settlement. By 1906, Oklahoma contained over 600,000 souls clamoring for either single or double blessedness. Congress passed an enabling act June 16, 1906. A constitution was drafted and ratified by a large majority vote of the people; Charles N. Haskell was elected as first governor; and at 10:16 o'clock the morning of November 16, 1907, President Roosevelt signed a proclamation declaring the two territories a state of the Union.

Lillie arrived at Pawnee with his Wild West on November 11. The city had made big noises before and had some "swell doings," but this time it decided to "cut the guy ropes and go straight up" in a three day "free-for-all," where the pent-up feelings of seventeen

years were to be turned loose in rejoicing. The entire United States
had drawn from Pawnee County for entertainments of this kind,
for this was the home of Gordon W. Lillie, the most widely known
Wild West showman on earth, and now the town was going to "do
herself proud" by utilizing its own resources.

His heavy train of forty cars arrived at noon over the Santa Fe,
and by nightfall over 400 head of horses and ponies, Filipino cattle,
camels, elephants, buffalo, and circus wagons galore, were domi-
ciled at his ranch southwest of Pawnee. Edward Arlington, Secretary Oscar J. Krause, and other executive heads and a hundred
minor employees, who were required to look after the property,
found rooms about town, and Pawnee became the active winter
headquarters for the show.

Pawnee Bill immediately set to work assisting with arrangements
for the statehood celebration. He asked that the place of exhibition
be changed to his own grounds south of the city. Then he agreed
to furnish tents and seats to accommodate the public and to put
on many of his attractions.

Word went out to all parts of the Pawnee country and the Osage
reservation. On November 16, Pawnee witnessed one of the largest
crowds that ever congregated in its streets. And Pawnee Bill, with
his Wild West aggregation, re-enacted the thrilling experiences of
by-gone years to tell the young what frontier life meant to those
who participated in the making of the West. Major Lillie did more
than any other individual that day to help Oklahoma Territory go
out in a blaze of glory.

It was a fitting climax to the most successful season in the show's
history. Pawnee Bill's Wild West and Great Far East now ranked
among the great tented organizations of the country. But it had
achieved its greatness under the most adverse circumstances. Rain
had been almost unceasing from the first parade on April 16 at
Nashville, until the conclusion of the Chicago engagement on
June 2. Cold weather had added to its woes. At Chicago, Lulu Parr,
one of his champion bronc busters, was badly injured when thrown
by an outlaw, knocked senseless and dragged almost a hundred
yards before being rescued by the lasso of Mexican Joe.

Another serious incident occurred in Chicago when the Sioux
warrior, Charlie Black-Eye, got drunk in violation of a stern rule

of the show and went on the warpath. The camp was in a frenzy until Pawnee Bill knocked the Indian down, disarmed him and handed him over to police. He served ten days in jail and reappeared in Minneapolis, full of broken-English promises of permanent reform.

The other Indians warned Pawnee Bill against Black-Eye. Chief Big Turkey told of his bad reputation on the reservation and of his boasts that he always "got square" for real or fancied injuries. An Indian with whom he once quarreled had mysteriously disappeared. A few days later his body was found with a knife wound through the heart.

Pawnee Bill failed to heed the warning. Black-Eye was put back to work. So apparent was his reformation that a few days later, when Pawnee Bill's personal stableman left the show, Black-Eye's pleadings were answered with the job.

It was the aboriginal's patiently awaited opportunity for revenge. It was fulfilled when the show reached La Junta, Colorado. The moment Pawnee Bill mounted his superb stallion, Dandy, for the parade, the animal became unmanageable. The muscular plainsman's strength and skill were no match for the equine's fury. With clenched teeth, flaring nostrils and flaming eyes, he dashed madly among the assembled riders and vehicles. Two cowboys tried to grasp the bridle and were trampled. Mexican Joe hurled his lariat, but missed the careening target. At breakneck speed, straight into a towering chariot, he plunged. The impact was terrific. Pawnee Bill was thrown to the ground and lay senseless between the hooves of the unconscious beast.

Black-Eye was the only spectator who did not hurry to the rescue. Instead, he turned back to his tepee, muttering. Pawnee Bill was quickly revived with injuries no more serious than a wrenched arm. The trembling horse was led back to the stables.

Black-Eye's behavior aroused suspicion. Brought before Pawnee Bill, he denied any knowledge of the cause for the horse's sudden derangement. Lillie was not convinced. He ordered Black-Eye's belongings searched. In a pack which the Indian had guarded carefully was found a supply of loco weed.

Faced with the evidence of his guilt, he confessed. He had vowed to kill Pawnee Bill when he found himself in jail in Chicago, and had returned to the show for that purpose. The poisonous plant had seemed the most effectual method without casting suspicion on himself. He had administered the weed four days before it took effect. Black-Eye was placed in irons and made a prisoner in one of the show cars.

The veterinarians with the show fought to save Dandy's life, using potassium permanganate in an effort to oxidize and destroy the poisonous alkaloid. The horse lived, but continuously champed his jaws and was deaf and blind to the end of his life. He was brought to Denver in a specially built box-stall. Pawnee Bill carried an arm in a sling, and that afternoon, Black-Eye was taken back to the Rosebud Agency in South Dakota and turned over to government authorities.

There were many other difficulties with the weather, the show and employees, but Pawnee Bill suffered most from the war waged against him by the Circus Trust. The Buffalo Bill advertising had already appeared in the newspapers and on the billboards of Chicago when Pawnee Bill arrived there, although its appearance was months away. All the way to Chicago from Nashville, Pawnee Bill's advance cars found both the Barnum & Bailey and Ringling shows competing for billboard space. When they arrived at Davenport on June 12, the found the Barnum & Bailey show billed for August 19, and across the Mississippi River at Rock Island, the posters of the Ringling show announced its coming there on July 16.

At Evansville, Pawnee Bill's agents found him on the unfair list of the local typographical uion. Members swarmed through the streets pleading with shopkeepers to remove the gaudy lithographs displayed in their windows, and much of the picture paper was ignominiously destroyed. In the afternoon, men and boys flocked through the city with arms full of black-typed dodgers condemning Pawnee Bill as discriminating against organized labor.

Pawnee Bill's agents tried to convince labor that he had done them no wrong. This was accomplished after several busy hours of telephonic corroboration from Edward Arlington, general agent of the show then in St. Louis, and from Pawnee Bill himself, who was with the show in Covington, Kentucky. By midnight they had learned all the facts.

A slow-thinking manager of Pawnee Bill's advance car had rolled into town on Monday without a supply of "dates"—the slender strip of paper pasted beneath each lithograph to tell the time and place of performance. The Barnum & Bailey manager chuckled to himself and advised a local non-union shop, and Pawnee Bill's man had the work done at this boycotted establishment. The typographical union got the news soon after the lithographs were in place, and began their retaliatory tactics.

When these facts were disclosed, the labor leaders promptly gave Pawnee Bill's show a hearty endorsement, commending it as a union amusement enterprise and rescinding all charges they had brought. The Barnum & Bailey car had left the city with its manager "rejoicing over the commotion he had caused, but blissfully ignorant of the final satisfactory settlement."

It was different at Vincennes. Pawnee Bill's men slipped in and plastered the city and surrounding country with bills advertising the date of the show's appearance before the Barnum & Bailey opposition car could arrive to begin the fight.

Probably never before in the annals of the circus had a tented organization been subjected to such combative tactics. The Circus Trust preceded the show, city to city, using every artifice known to these cunning circus men to detract patronage. So bitter and determined became the warfare against this independent amusement institution that the newspapers, billboards and store windows of the cities were employed to advertise the coming of one of the trust circuses three months in advance.

Still Pawnee Bill refused to divide territory, abandon his parades, or enter any secret agreements, and the big people openly declared they were "after his scalp." But the veteran plainsman and showman had not preserved his headgear through all these years to allow any tenderfeet to remove it. He was sufficiently big and favorably known to make his declaration of independence. Everywhere the trail of his combination conflicted with the routes of his two competitors, and in the face of their persecution, he did a tremendous business all season.

To Minneapolis the Circus Trust sent a score of expert bill-posters and lithographers and three special agents to make a last desperate stand. For two weeks, they worked against Pawnee Bill. They "smothered" his billboard displays until the whole city blossomed with gaudy papers calling attention to the features of the Barnum & Bailey shows.

This produced strained conditions. Pawnee Bill asked the District Attorney of New York to investigate the Circus Trust operations. Within a week, Louis E. Cooke, general contracting agent for Barnum & Bailey, arrived to confer with Pawnee Bill. Afterwards, he went to St. Louis and held a conference with Edward Arlington and John Ringling.

How their differences were patched up is not known. It was rumored that there had been a break between Ringling Brothers and the Barnum & Bailey enterprises, but before leaving St. Louis, Ringling declared there was no truth in it. At the same time, however, he remarked that other circuses would appear at Madison Square Garden and the so-called Circus Trust would be dissolved. Probably the Bailey interests found themselves more troubled with the financial pains they were undergoing with the Buffalo Bill show.

Buffalo Bill had made no secret of his drinking during his show years. He had given newspaper reporters stories about himself that in those days were considered humorous. At the World's Columbian Exposition in Chicago in 1893, he had made a million dollars. The receipts of his Wild West show swelled in the next few years, and so did his schemes for scattering money, until he became uncomfortably aware that there were limitations to the spending of even a millionaire showman.

He gave away funds, set relatives and friends up in business, invested in Arizona mines, bought forty acres in the foothills below Carter Mountain in the Big Horn Basin, Wyoming, and organized the Shoshone Land and Irrigation Company. He started a large cattle ranch called the TE, plotted a town named Cody, that had a population of nearly one thousand by 1900, and built there the Irma Hotel, the largest in the state.

With so many outlets for his money, Cody cast about for new capital. He decided to sell half interest in his show, which was bought by James A. Bailey, a tough fighter and the "little Napoleon in show business." A Michigan hotel bellboy, he had run away with a circus, and by 1880, forced a partnership on Barnum. He knew how to handle Cody, and for eight years kept his show on the profit side of the ledger.

But Cody kept on drinking and spending, and neither his partner, Nate Salsbury, nor his two closest friends, John Burke and Johnny Baker, could do anything to stop him. At one time he was connected with eleven different enterprises, was president of five of them, and had lost a half-dozen fortunes in bad business ventures. He put a show on the road exhibiting Negro life and character called "Black America" that lasted one season. In 1897, he tried "An Ethnological, Anthropological and Etymological Congress—Greatest since Adam," and lost another fortune.

He sank deeper in drink and debt. He owed Nate Salsbury one hundred thousand dollars, and asked for more. Salsbury threatened to dissolve their partnership. Cody promised to mend his ways, and they were reconciled. For a while he cut himself to four drinks daily, but was soon back to his old routine.

Differences began to grow between Cody and his wife Louisa. He was seldom at home except when the show was in winter quarters. Even then he brought guests to stay, so that she saw little of him. She cooked for them, and often lay awake into the night listening to the clink of whiskey bottle and glasses and the loud talk and laughter. In time, rumors reached her of Cody's infidelities. She tried to persuade him to adopt a life that would not keep him away from his home and family. This galled Cody. In New York, the winter of 1901, he went to his attorneys and filed for divorce on grounds of incompatibility.

He opened the 1902 season with an advance paid him by Bailey. His thin hair and goatee were almost white. In October, his show train crashed head-on with a freight near Lexington, Virginia. Many of the animals were killed, or had to be destroyed because of their injuries. Annie Oakley suffered internal injuries that finally led to her retirement. Cody was unable to return the advance made him by Bailey, and failed to meet the interest payments. At the end of the season, he took his Wild West back to England, where he opened in London. Early one morning he received the news that Nate Salsbury had died at his home in New Jersey on Christmas Eve.

It was an awful blow to Cody. For almost twenty years, Salsbury had been his gallant backer and adviser. He could never be replaced.

Cody would have closed his show, returned to America and retired. But he was too heavily in debt to Bailey, and Bailey insisted on keeping the show in Europe and out of competition with his own circus at home. He took over Salsbury's stock, practically controlling the show, first as Cody's partner, then with a lien on Cody's interest and his note for borrowed money.

Against his better judgment Cody dragged through Europe four years with heavy losses. He always claimed that Bailey had made an oral promise to assume full responsibility, but when Bailey died in 1906, the executors of his estate insisted that Cody pay his share.

Cody's position was not improved by his affair with the English actress Katherine Clemmons, with whom he fell in love at the age of 56. She became an expensive friend. When Cody's divorce trial came up in New York in 1905, the court decided in favor of Louisa, and the case was dismissed. When Cody returned to report his failure to Katherine, she promptly married the millionaire, Howard Gould, though she continued to see Cody. Gould learned of their clandestine meetings and divorced her. Cody never saw her again.

In 1907, he was back in America, riding in Madison Square Garden. It was a fairly successful season, but the strenuous life had begun to tell on him. He was now 61, tired easily and the burden of his responsibilities was almost more than he could endure. More money was needed for the exploitation of the Big Horn Basin property, his mining interests in Arizona and other enterprises needed more cash, and the Bailey estate now gave him six months to repay his notes.

In 1908, Pawnee Bill was playing an all-summer engagement in Boston. He made a sudden trip to New York, and following a conference with Colonel Cody, announced the largest merger ever consummated in the amusement field.

He had purchased the Bailey interest in Cody's Wild West show. It was combined with his Great Far East, and became popularly known as the "Two Bills" show. Their first joint season opened in Madison Square Garden in 1909.

13.   Combination with Buffalo Bill

BUFFALO BILL'S BIOGRAPHERS believe it was chiefly sentiment that shaped the deal and caused Lillie to restore to Cody his
half-ownership of all the show's earnings. They make sketchy refer-
ence to Cody's objections to the dilution of his Wild West and
Congress of Rough Riders with the spectacle of the Far East, and
how, when the first season produced a profit of more than one hundred thousand dollars, his spirits rose with all their old buoyancy
and he decided it was a "pretty good old show to tie to."

In his unpublished manuscript written in 1937, Lillie set down
the details:

I was appearing in Wonderland Park, Boston, in 1908, when I
received a message from A. A. Stewart, administrator of the Bailey
estate, asking me to come to New York at once. He had a proposition for me.

On my first visit I left with the feeling that there was no chance
of a combination of the two shows. At the death of Mr. Bailey, Mrs.
Bailey wished to dispose of both the Barnum & Bailey and Buffalo
Bill shows, and had picked on me to run the Buffalo Bill show,
Ringlings having bought the Barnum & Bailey show that spring.

The latter part of June, I had another wire from Mr. Stewart
asking me to meet the Buffalo Bill show at Keene, New Hampshire, for a conference with Colonel Cody. I arrived just as the show
was over, and watched the crowd leave. It was very light.

Then I went to Colonel Cody's private tent. He greeted me cor-
dially, and asked if I had seen the show. I replied, "No, Colonel, I
came in as you were making your final bow." We conversed about
combining the two shows and I asked him under what title the
combined shows would operate.

"Buffalo Bill's Wild West and Congress of Rough Riders of the World," he replied. "She has run under that title for over thirty years, and there has never been an atom added to nor taken from it."

"Well, Colonel," I said, "if I were in your place, I suppose I should act just as you have about it. But unless I can have the title of my show embodied in the title of the combined show, I will not be interested."

He invited me to dinner with him, but I had to refuse as I wanted to get back to my show.

As I started to leave, the Colonel said, "Did you notice the crowd? What did you think?"

"I thought it very light for your show."

The Colonel asked, "Can you tell me why our business is not better through New England?"

"Yes," I replied. "You are down here too late. I never could get any money in New England after the 20th of June."

"Why, I never heard of such a thing," he commented. "I am quite sure I have played New England this late and later, and always made money."

"Well," I returned, "maybe you can with your show, but I never could with mine. I always managed to be out by the 20th of June."

"We go into New York State next, what will I do there?" he asked.

"A lot better, but you are in the edge of haying, which will hurt you some," I answered.

"From there we will go to Michigan, what will we be able to do there?"

"Put in your 'extra' seats every day, and you will do all you can hold."

"Well, Gordon," he said, "I am going to watch and see how your prophecy comes out." He waved his hand as I hurried to catch the train. He seemed awfully convinced that the combination of the two shows was a closed incident.

When his show got into New York, I received a very friendly letter from the Colonel saying they had made no money in New England, but the moment they crossed the line business had improved. When they reached Michigan, he could not wait to write, but wired me: "First town in Michigan. Got all the 'extra' seats in. Turning people away in the rain."

On receiving a wire from Mr. Stewart, I again went to New York. He greeted me with, "What have you done to Colonel Cody? He thinks you're a superman. He is now willing to make any changes in the title you choose. And he's stronger for you than horseradish."

After another conference with Colonel Cody, we decided on the title, "Buffalo Bill's Wild West and Pawnee Bill's Great Far East," under which it operated for five years. After the deal was completed, I met the Buffalo Bill show in New Orleans. It had but three weeks to run and was to close in Memphis the middle of November.

My reception was anything but a glorious affair. Colonel Cody received me in a most cordial manner, and I knew he was glad to have me there. For his faith in the handling of the show by the administrator was gone. Since the death of Mr. Bailey, there had been several serious clashes between Cody and the assistant manager (Louis Cooke). In one of these, Cody had knocked down the manager. Orders had come from headquarters in New York: "unless Cody apologizes and begs Cooke's pardon, close the show at once and ship it back to winter quarters at Bridgeport, Connecticut." Cody held out to the last moment, refusing to so humble himself. But when he saw them making actual preparation to close the show, he apologized. This had so wrought up the Colonel that there was no friendly sentiment left in him. It was a cold dollar-and-cent-proposition, and a change in management was welcome.

When I say Colonel Cody welcomed me, that about ended it. There were 619 other people in the show—laborers, actresses and actors. They received me in a respectful manner, but as much as to say, "I am against him, but he is the 'Big Boss' now and I will have to be nice to him in order to hold my job."

I knew from my experiences with Cody as a boy that he was temperamental. I made up my mind before I handed my money to the administrator that I would get along with him. Nothing he could do would cause me to fall out with him. Now that I had met the rest of the family, I saw they were against me, and I was more determined in this resolve than ever.

I had been with the show only two days when a business matter came up that compelled me to return to my ranch at Pawnee, so that I barely reached the show in Memphis the closing day and went to Bridgeport with the trains that carried the performers. Almost everyone in the show, including Cody, left for their homes in the West. The treasurer, auditor, all the main bosses, enough working-men to pack the show away, and myself went into winter quarters with the two trains. Within two weeks we had the show stored in the building of Barnum.

When the Ringling Brothers had purchased the big Barnum show from the Bailey estate, the plant of the Buffalo Bill show went with it. The plant consisted of all the equipment used in building the structure in which the performance was given, and the contract existing between the Buffalo Bill owners and owners of the plant was very similar to the theatrical contract under which Colonel Cody had been operating his opera house shows. Mr. Bailey furnished all the property in connection with the structure in which the performance was given; Colonel Cody furnished the personnel and physical property necessary to give the performance. Mr. Bailey received a rental on this of $25,000 a year—$1000 each week on the road the first twenty-five weeks, then nothing the balance of the season.

May Lillie was bitterly against combining the two shows. She and the Major had made plenty of money with Pawnee Bill's Wild West, and could continue to do so. Their name was so well established they asked no favors from anyone. May contended, and the Major agreed, that handling the Pawnee Bill show was much easier than handling Buffalo Bill's Wild West. But the Major was persistent.

The argument went on from day to day. When May had exhausted her most favorable points, she declared: "If you go into this deal, I will never travel with the combined show. I think this is the craziest idea you have ever had.

"We have worked twenty years, fifteen of them on a shoestring, and now that you have your own show on a solid foundation, where you can make more money than you will ever need, you want to take it away from the public that has learned to appreciate your efforts in giving them a real Wild West.

"You're tearing down your whole life's work! Tell me, if you can, one good reason why you are justified in considering such a deal? Just one!"

Major Lillie had one, and no more. "May, we have worked almost night and day and have made a wonderful success. Our show is now the third best paying, and the most attractive show property, in the United States.

"You also know that during all this time the Buffalo Bill people did all in their power to stop us, even to hiring our best performers and trying to keep us from getting a permit from Washington to legally take the Indians off their reservations.

"At every opportunity they would go thirty to fifty miles out of their way to cover our advertising with theirs, reading, 'Coming Soon,' when they had no intention of playing the town. And the people would pass us up and wait for Buffalo Bill, who never came. I remember how they all threw their hats in the air and hurrahed with delight when our show failed in Maryland.

"Well, here is my reason—the only one I have: I want this combination of the two biggest Wild West shows in the world to take place, with myself as owner and general manager, so that these same people, who threw their hats in the air, and worked so hard to down me, will have to come to me and receive their check from my hand."

"Oh, Bosh!" May replied. "All those things are dead and buried long ago. Let them rest in peace. Why resurrect them at this late day?"

The wounds had healed, but the scars remained. The Circus Trust fight the year before Pawnee Bill had taken in stride and considered sport. The hard knocks had come when he was down and struggling to get up; when his purse was empty, and when money was hard to get; when the price of admittance was only ten and twenty-five cents. He never forgot it!

And the profession lost one of its most popular celebrities, a most winsome lady who had won fame and favor in many lands, and whose true womanly qualities had endeared her to a legion of close personal friends who would ever cherish her memory.

After the news went out of the combination of the two shows, Lillie received discouragement from other sources. One night as he was retiring in his hotel at Bridgeport, his phone rang. It was John Ringling. He and his brother Otto had come to talk over things in general, and the combination of the shows in particular.

During the conversation, Lillie mentioned that he was surprised they had not bought the Buffalo Bill show, since they already owned the Buffalo Bill plant and provided room for it during the winter in their Barnum quarters. He added that it was a show they could have easily handled, as it would have drawn money either ahead of, or behind, the Barnum show.

"Well, Major, I'll tell you," said John Ringling. "We did consider it, but we knew Colonel Cody is awful hard to get along with. No one can handle him without trouble. He had that Wild West bunch lined up against the Bailey end of the show. Those cowboys, Indians, Mexicans, with all those guns, tomahawks, and war clubs, kept the Bailey end of the show in dread all the time. Wait till you open and are out on the road. You'll have trouble. They'll about scalp you."

Lillie smiled. "No, John. You fail to take into consideration that I am, and always have been, one of them—the same tribe you have just mentioned with their guns, tomahawks, and war clubs. I can wield them as good as they can. Furthermore, I am the boy who's going to do all the lining up of those people myself."

"Well, Major, I'll admit you are probably the best fitted person in the United States to handle them. But mark my word—you won't get away with it."

Our offices in the Bailey Building, 28th and Broadway, New York City, were very nice, consisting of a general reception room with a number of desks, and a room for Mr. Cooke, the general agent. There were also rooms for Johnny Baker, arena director, while Major Burke, general press reporter, had a desk in the reception room.

I spent most of the early part of the winter in Bridgeport, as I made a number of important changes in the equipment and general handling of the show. George W. "Buck" Connors, the famous rifle shot expert, mustang and bronco tamer, cowboy and rough rider, a government scout under Buffalo Bill and still a protege of the Colonel's, was my private secretary. His liberal use of telephone messages to me enabled him to handle the affairs of the office in my absence. On one of my weekend visits to New York, Buck confided to me that the talk around the office during my absence was that I was not "big enough" to handle the Buffalo Bill show.

The night before I had seen the play entitled "Via Wireless," given at the opera house. It was the most scenic picture I had ever seen. It was the talk of New York.

The following morning I called on the manager, complimenting him on the wonderful production, and obtained the address of the artist who had produced these wonderful effects.

He had worked exclusively for the Shuberts. I asked him if he could make me something for our show that would create a sensation equal or greater than "Via Wireless" for our opening at Madison Square Garden in March. He thought so, as he had so much more room there in which to work with lighting effects, etc.

In two weeks I called again, and he had made me a complete working model of what he could do in the way of staging effects, but when he told me the price would be $7,700, I wilted. That was a lot of money in those days. It was three times what I had figured putting into it. But it was so great, I figured it would put the show over, even if it did not create a sensation.

The day arrived for our opening in the Garden. Putting up this great scenic piece had taken two of three days alloted for rehearsals. Early on the third day, Johnny Baker was on the job. The scenery had virtually taken all the space backstage, leaving a passageway hardly big enough for three horsemen to pass.

There was no room for props, such as stagecoaches, prairie schooners, cannons, etc. All these had to be kept in the basement. The passageway on either side of the stage was only ten feet wide and very steep.

Johnny Baker worked all day and far into the night trying to plan the program so it would work. But the enormous bunch of horsemen and material would pile up in the passageway to the basement.

To make matters worse, the Far East had been added with many new acts with camels, elephants, water buffaloes, and animals that had never been with the show before. We had stabled our Far East animals with the Wild West horses purposely to let them get accustomed to them. While it had a good effect, they had not been compelled to rub sides with them, and many of the horses were frantic, causing them to injure some of the riders.

Cody sat in a box with Louis Cooke during rehearsals, and when the horses and people would pile up in the exits at the close of an act, he would "go up in the air." Later, Cooke told Lillie that three different times during the day Cody took him to the Hoffman House. He actually lay on the bed and cried. "Pawnee Bill will ruin me!" he wailed. "I never wanted this Far East thing! We have shown in the Garden many times before without all this big scenery, and the show was always a big GO. What are we going to do, Cooke? Can't you do something to straighten it out, Louis?"

Cooke tried to pacify him, but himself doubted that Lillie would ever be able to bring the show out of the chaotic condition, or that he would be able to make a real performance out of it, unless the exits were widened and a large part of the scenery was removed. This could not be done without ruining the whole effect.

Reports finally reached the front of the house where I was very busy arranging the details for the opening. As I had staged all my performances, I offered my services to Johnny Baker. He accepted with a weak heart and I took hold, first by engaging twelve strong men with a hook-rope they attached to the back end of the vehicles without slackening the speed, and with the twelve men hanging to the rope, let them down into the basement without delay. I stationed men in the exits to keep them clear and hurry the animals and vehicles down the incline. This alleviated a large part of our trouble.

Johnny did not accept my services in very good grace, so I took him aside and said, "Johnny, I am the general manager of the show, and that is all I want to be. I do not want to be arena director, but I am positive I can render you valuable aid if you will allow me. When we get these first shows over and things are running right, the sole lauding thereafter will be yours."

Johnny put his shoulder to the wheel. We worked together all that night and the following day until noon. The doors opened at one o'clock, and what we called the first dress rehearsal was given to a large crowd. It went off splendidly, with few mishaps or waits.

At the night performance, which was advertised as the formal opening, many important personages occupied the entire large circle of front boxes. General Nelson A. Miles had come from Washington with a party of prominent army officers and their ladies. The governor of New York, the governor of New Jersey, the mayor of New York, the leader of Tammany Hall, and many others well-known in those days were there.

Every seat in the house was filled. The show went off with a bang, and was wonderfully smooth for a second performance. The United Press the following day was loud in its praise, and mentioned the Far East as a "welcome added attraction."

Louis Cooke came to me and complimented me and said Colonel Cody was pleased with the success of the show. "You and Johnny Baker deserve the credit for putting on the greatest Wild West and Far East performance ever appearing in the Garden."

I stayed at the Hoffman House, but as I always got up at six o'clock and went over to the Garden, I never saw Colonel Cody, who usually arose about nine. He seldom came to the Garden until after lunch.

I purposely avoided meeting him for several days. For after the dismal tale Cooke had related to me, I thought I would give him some time to think it over and quiet down.

With the excellent press notices received, we were sure to do a big business. The matinee of the second day was light. The night house was not what I had expected, though the statement showed more money than the opening day due to the fact there were no invited guests. The following Monday there was a large crowd both afternoon and night, the night house being a complete sell-out, with many turned away.

On Tuesday, during the Far East section of the performance, Colonel Cody's valet brought me a note asking me to come back to his dressing room. As I entered, I noticed the Colonel looked very happy.

He extended his hand to me, saying, "Pard, put her there!" I grasped his hand, wondering what was coming next. With his other arm, he pulled me up to him, saying, "Major, we have the world by the tail. All my friends tell me we have the greatest show they have ever seen."

During our five years as partners, I don't think the Colonel ever said anything to me that pleased me as much.

The engagement in Madison Square Garden "ended in a blaze of glory." The last two weeks people were turned away every night, with a number turned away at the matinees—something unusual for New York.

The show moved to Brooklyn for its first opening of the season under canvas. All week the weather was damp and cold, which hurt business. To add to the discomfort, Mrs. Bailey's representative and administrator came to Lillie's office with a complaint about New York City's expense account for entertainment of the press by Major Burke and the billing of the subways by Louis Cooke.

Shortly after my connection with the show, they had suggested to me that we cut out subway advertising, to which I had agreed, since it was the first disposition to reduce cost. It had been the first request they had made of me, and I had considered it bad policy to lock horns with them.

Subway "ads" were very expensive, but Cooke argued that it was the best mode of advertising in New York outside the press, and I felt he was right. The Hippodrome, the largest theatrical house in New York City, used them to a great extent, and a number of my New York friends thought it one of the best forms of advertising for amusements in the city. So just before we started billing New York, I had told Cooke that I would run my end of the business, that he was advertising manager and to bill anything he thought practical. This was equivalent to saying, "Bill the subways."

I asked the Bailey representatives, "Don't you think it proved the thing to do? Look at the enormous business we did. More by far than the show ever done before."

"We grant you this, but it was not the subways that did it. It was the scenic back piece and addition of the Far East. We have given this matter lots of thought. You have been doing lots of talking about economy in management and reducing costs. Well, we have come to suggest you discharge both Louis E. Cooke and John M. Burke. These two men are the most extravagant in our employ and carry with them the spending of over fifty per cent of the daily expenses of the show. You can never accomplish what you desire with these two men holding these two important positions."

I would have not been more surprised had they asked for my resignation. Louis Cooke, called the Dean of General Agents, was the highest priced general agent in the United States, and justly so. Major John M. Burke, called the Dean of Press Agents, had been with Colonel Cody for over thirty years. He was the highest salaried press agent in the country. He knew more managing editors and owners of big publications, and called them by their first names, than any man who ever lived. He was considered an authority on early Western history, and his wonderful true stories of Western heroes, both red men and white, were readily accepted by the press of the country.

Now I had been requested to discharge them for no cause. "When I decided we should bill the subways, I assumed all responsibility for Cooke," I said. "As for Burke's excessive expense account, I do not believe we did half enough entertaining the press, for I never in my life saw such liberal treatment of any show, any place, as was accorded us by the press of New York City.

"And where, gentlemen, will you get capable men to take their places? All the big shows are opened, and all capable men are under contract. There is no chance in the world for us to do this. Furthermore, we have yearly contracts with both these men, and we would have to pay them whether we used them or not during the season."

Such reasoning made an impression on my listeners. I knew these two gentlemen well enough to know that they had a general knowledge of the show business, and that there was no chance for us to get along without these two important personages.

"These two men," I continued, "and Johnny Baker, are the only three remaining of the original Buffalo Bill company. Colonel Cody made special mention of this to me and requested more than once before the combination was completed that I would always keep these men in their respective positions as long as they filled them properly and wanted to remain with us. I promised him I would do so.

"So you see, I cannot go back on them. But if you want to see Colonel Cody and talk the matter over with him, I have no objection."

To which they replied, "Major Lillie, you are the general manager. Colonel Cody does not enter into these business matters. He handles the back of the show."

I agreed, "That's why I object to granting this request. It is against the best interests of the show, and is of vital concern to Colonel Cody. I will consult him, whether it is a matter in connection with the front or back of the show. He owns a third interest, and is equal owner with us."

"No, he isn't," they denied. "He owns not one iota of the show. We own outright his third, and hold a bill of sale signed by him, including the title 'Buffalo Bill's Wild West,' 'Buffalo Bill's Rough Riders of the World,' and the right to use the picture and full title of 'W. F. Cody, Buffalo Bill.' Besides this, we hold his notes for over $70,000. This makes us two-thirds owners.

"We really think you do not give us due consideration. We can see where your handling doesn't coincide with our ideas, and that you are very headstrong. You mean to handle it entirely your own way, notwithstanding we are the majority owners. The only solution we can see would be for you to buy us out. And if the show earns a sufficient amount to pay off Colonel Cody's share, you can deed back to him a third or a half, just as you and he agreed.

"As matters are going now, I can see a chance that we are heading for serious trouble. I should regret to resort to legal means, while our relations up till now have been so friendly. Major, think it over. We will be back in a few days, and will discuss the matter further."

After they had departed for New York, it gradually began to soak in: they had given me lots of "salve" to the effect that they considered me the best Wild West manager in the country to get me tied in, as an entering wedge forcing me to buy the other two-thirds interest. I had also noticed that ever since the combination had been consummated there was a disposition to find fault; and to not approve anything of importance that I did or suggested. They had not approved the ordering of the expensive scenery, claiming that it could not be carried on the road, also that it meant an added expense of $2500 per week for our three weeks at the Garden.

I quite agreed with them that we might be "heading for serious trouble," for I saw plainly it was their intention to control the majority of the show. They could object to my mode of handling; possibly they would have some restraining order issued, applying for a receiver, and in this way, take the management out of my hands.

Lillie talked it over with Cody, but Cody could do nothing to raise money. His European losses totaled over $300,000. This had compelled him to mortgage his ranches at North Platte, Nebraska, and Cody, Wyoming, and also his big modern Hotel Irma. Even this had not been sufficient, and he had been forced to give them the bill of sale and some notes for the balance.

The entire week in Brooklyn showed a loss. The show moved to Philadelphia, where the first two days were cold, with wind and rain. On Tuesday morning the Bailey representatives put in their second appearance, making veiled threats as to what they intended to do if the show was not changed.

Business being bad no doubt had a very depressing influence on them. I am sure they had left for New York the week before with the intention of putting over their deal with me, if possible, in a friendly manner. With this in mind, I explained to them that it meant a pretty big load for me, as I had paid out $50,000 cash for the one-third interest, besides my share of the wintering, repainting and repairing of the show property.

After some figuring, they made me an offer of $66,666.66 for their two-thirds interest. I was to take up the notes and mortgages, or indorse them as guarantee of payment.

There was one note for $12,000 which had been given by Colonel Cody to Bailey in London at a time the show was making plenty of money. The Colonel claimed he had paid it, saying Bailey had taken it out of his share of the profits, and had given the Colonel a receipt in full, promising the note would be sent to the Colonel the next time he visited their main office in New York, where the note was filed.

For some reason, this had never been done and Cody had misplaced his receipt. This was the way the matter stood at the death of Bailey. The estate continued to hold the note with nothing to show that it had ever been paid.

I asked the representatives: "If I could raise the cash, would you do something about the $12,000 note, also all interest then due," which was quite an amount.

"Will you give me until noon tomorrow?" I asked.

"All right, Major, we will let the matter stand until then," they replied.

All I had to do was draw a check on the Fidelity Trust Company of Philadelphia, where I had more than enough to cover the sale. But it would take nearly all my ready cash, and I wanted to talk it over with Mr. Geist, the president of the company. If we decided it was wise to buy the other two-thirds of the show, and I found myself pinched for money, I wanted to be able to borrow it from him.

The bad weather and the fact the show was losing money daily dampened my ardor. But after talking to Mr. Geist, I decided to buy. Wednesday morning when I arose, sunlight was flooding the earth and warming the chilly air, and all my nerve came back. I could hardly wait to reach the trust company to complete the deal.

All bills of sales for property, notes and titles, were transferred to Lillie, with a deed to the Bailey two-thirds interest. Cody's $12,000 note was endorsed and returned to the Major.

Lillie's check for the full amount was passed to the Bailey representatives, and he was then sole owner of the "Buffalo Bill's Wild West" and "Pawnee Bill's Great Far East" combined shows.

When I left the trust company, I felt like an inmate who had stepped away from jail forever. I was free again.

It was about six o'clock when I reached the show lot. I found Cody in the private car at dinner. I took my place across the table and threw down the London note before him.

"Have you ever seen that before?" I asked.

"You bet!" he exclaimed. "Where and how did you get it?"

"By buying out the Baileys—lock, stock and barrel. We are now sole and equal owners of the show, your half interest to rest in my name until the show makes enough that your half of the profits will pay off all you owe me. Then I will deed back a half interest to you."

"How about this $12,000 note?" the Colonel asked.

"I made them throw it in, and they knocked off the interest on the other notes. So you are through paying interest. I will collect no interest on your notes."

"That's bully, Major!" he said joyfully. "You have made me as happy as a man with a pair of twins."

The matinee that day was great. Everybody was pleased. The rest of the Philadelphia engagement we drew immense crowds. The last three nights, persons were turned away, with large matinee showings. The gross receipts totaled over $60,000.

The following week, the show played Wilmington, Delaware, Baltimore and Washington. In the capital, they were honored by the presence of President William Howard Taft; General Miles, who visited them again; and a great many ambassadors and dignitaries of foreign countries.

The boxes looked as if the "far east" had come to the Far East, as the bright flashy costumes of the foreign legations, such as those of China, Japan and India, almost outshone the bright colors and costumes of the Far East section of the show.

Later in the season, the show played a small town in the Dakotas, giving only one performance:

As we had a long run to our next stopping place, we loaded the train after the matinee, and by seven o'clock we were entering the Badlands. I had never seen them, but had heard much about them from the Sioux. The Colonel suggested that we not turn the lights on in our car, as it was a bright moonlight night and would give a better chance to observe these freak formations of Nature.

We sat up till nearly midnight, enjoying the scenery and reminiscing of the early days. The Colonel finally ran the conversation to gold mining. He said that all his life he had wanted to own a gold mine.

"I have one now near Orical [Oracle], Arizona, up in the mountains about fifty-seven miles from Tucson. Tucson is the closest railway point and everything is hauled by freight wagon, making it an expensive operation. But according to my partner, who is an expert on mining and an engineer, we have an inexhaustible supply of rich ore, some of it testing over $100 per ton.

"Major, wouldn't it be great if a fellow had a gold mine? Whenever he needed money, all he would have to do would be send a miner down and bring it up."

"Yes, Colonel," I said, "that would be great, but I think the Lord has always been pretty good to you. In fact, you have had a gold mine ever since I have known you."

"What do you mean?" he asked.

"This old mine," I said, "we are riding on right now. She is the biggest and best gold mine you should ever hope for. She has given you your ranches, your hotel, everything you have."

"Yes," returned the Colonel, "she has always been a pretty good old mine, hasn't she?"

As the years went by, my prophecy proved true, for he derived as high as $5000 every month or so from the show.

The finish of Cody's Arizona mine came some three years later when he discovered his partner had been doubling prices on everything purchased, taking the half for himself. He told Cody the big vein of ore he had struck on their property ran directly under ten other claims, and said he could buy all ten, if taken at once, at $3000 per claim. Later he wired that he had succeeded in closing the deal for the ten claims for $25,000. He wanted Cody to wire him $5000 to bind the bargain at once, which Cody did. Then Cody learned that he had bought the claims for $250 each, making off with from 300 to 1000 per cent profit. Cody's attorney in Tucson finally wrote him, saying it was going to be difficult to make their case stick. As his partner had such a nice family, the attorney suggested withdrawing the suit. And that is what Cody did, the deal costing him between $125,000 and $150,000, "and no salvage."

This was only one of the many things that kept the Colonel's bank account down. But apparently it never made him any wiser, for he was not more than out of one, until he was in another.

It was his trusting nature. If he was for you at all, nothing ever excited his suspicion against you. In his business dealings, he was like a child. He apparently cared nothing for money, except when he wanted or needed to spend it. Then, if he did not have, or could not borrow it, it made him sick—actually sick, so that he would have to go to bed. I was to witness this myself, more than once.

During the Brooklyn engagement, a well-known actor of the time called on Lillie and presented a note for $5000 past due, given by Cody, and demanded instant payment. Lillie took him to Cody's tent. Cody acknowledged the transaction, and asked Lillie to pay it, charging it to his personal account.

I told him his account was overdrawn to the extent of his four weeks' bills at the Waldorf. Furthermore, I had made a large remittance to several of our printers, which had depleted the cash account, and due to the bad weather, we had added nothing to our surplus. I did not see how it was possible for us to pay this note before the latter part of the Philadelphia engagement the following week.

With this, I left the Colonel and his friend and went back to the front of the show. It was fully an hour before his friend made his appearance at the front of the show. He was very excited and made it plain to me that he had come over to collect on this note, and was going to do it.

I explained to him again that we could not pay at this time and why. "This is an entirely personal obligation of Colonel Cody's. The show company and myself are in no way responsible, but if you will wait until next week, I am willing to guarantee it personally and also by and for the company as its general manager."

This did not satisfy him. "I am not going to leave until it is paid," he said. "Unless you pay it at once, I am going to attach the show property."

This began to sound serious. I had no idea he would go this far; he and the Colonel had been close friends for years. But from his positive manner, I could see he meant what he said, so I went back to see Cody.

I stopped at the treasure wagon, and found we had only $12,000 in the safe. Cody's bills amounted to $1422.40.

I found the Colonel in bed. He said he was sick.

"Where are you sick?" I asked.

"All over," he replied, "it's my nerves, they always go back on me when anyone threatens to attach the show. Did you fix it up with him? What did he say?"

"He's going to attach the show."

"I can't understand him. He has loaned me money before and always been lenient with me. Can't you do something to fix it up? Something must be done to get it off my mind, or I will never be able to go into the performance tonight."

"We have only $12,000 in the treasury of the show, Colonel. Paying $5000 and interest would bring us down to less than $7000, which could easily wipe us out with two days rain."

"Major, please pay this note. We will get along even if it rains. I have lots of friends in New York that I can get $5000 from on a plain note. We are sure to have some good weather. We have had bad weather for over a week. I look for good weather tomorrow, and business will pick up right now."

I saw the Colonel was in a bad way. I had never before seen him in such a condition. I felt sorry for him, and wanted to relieve his anxiety. "All right, Colonel, we will pay it, and charge it to your account."

This I did, and took the note back and turned it over to the Colonel. He was like a child expressing his joy and gratitude. He grabbed me by the hand, and leaping from his bed, embraced me and kept saying, "I thank you! I thank you! I will never forget you for this—you have greatly relieved my mind."

The matter put Lillie to thinking. He wondered if Cody could not have quite a number of these notes out among his friends.

When B. M. Bickerstaff, manager of the United States Printing and Lithographing Company, came to the show to consult the Major about making their paper for the coming year, Lillie related to him the whole story of what had occurred in Brooklyn at the very worst part of the season.

"What I am afraid of, Bick, is that a note would come up like this for $20,000, or even more, when we were in Arkansas, Kalamazoo, or Oshkosh—away from our friends—and this thing would come at a time when business was slack or after a siege of rainy weather when our treasury was low. It would cause a lot of trouble. You know what it would mean—big headlines in the papers all over the country—Buffalo Bill and Pawnee Bill Attached!"

"Why don't you incorporate the show?" suggested Bickerstaff. "This would protect all your property outside of the incorporated company's property."

"This is a fine idea, Bick. I will take it up with the Colonel, and if he is agreeable, we will come to New York at the close of the season and have it fixed up."

The show closed November 20 at Richmond, Virginia, and the Pennsylvania Railroad ran a special pullman into New York to carry its people. The Far East personnel sailed from there to the various foreign countries, and nearly all the business staff lived in New York. The B & O Railroad ran a special from Richmond to Chicago, carrying Mexicans, Indians and cowboys. A private car took the Indians to Gordon, Nebraska, and they were conveyed from there to the Brulé Sioux reservation by wagons.

There were always many an affecting scene at the closing of our show. I have seen a big Indian chief holding the hand of a Russian Cossack, or perhaps an Arab dancing girl, each looking the other straight in the eye with an expression of regret, neither being able to even say good-bye in a language common to both.

Many peculiar and strange attachments, even unions, were made. Our show physician was a graduate of our best medical colleges and from one of the finest families of Virginia. His father was an army officer of note, in the class of Custer and General Miles as an Indian fighter. He married the prettiest little Russian dancing girl, who could not speak a word of English.

Years afterward I heard from them in Maryland. The doctor was practicing medicine and they had a fine family of two beautiful girls and a boy. Generally a marriage with the show meant the exit of the pair from show life forever.

Lillie and Cody, with Bickerstaff as legal adviser, went from New York to Trenton, where the "Buffalo Bill's Wild West" and "Pawnee Bill's Great Far East" were incorporated.

Cody was elected president; Lillie, vice-president and general manager; Charles Meitus, treasurer, and Harry Stratton, secretary and attorney for the company. The company was licensed under the laws of the state of New Jersey, with offices at Bromley Inn, in charge of Stratton, as provided by Jersey law. They caught the show train as it went through Jersey City, and went on to Bridgeport, Connecticut, their winter quarters.

After storing everything and putting the mechanics to work repairing and repainting the two train loads of equipment, including the two trains of fifty cars, Lillie reviewed, approved and ordered many changes and improvements in the program, the executive staff, their advance brigade, and their route for the coming year. By December 10, he was ready for his annual visit to Pawnee.

Cody had caught the first train west for Wyoming and his famous hunting lodge in the Rocky Mountains, called Pahaska Tepee.

As he bade Lillie good-bye, he said, "You know, Major, by the time the season closes, I am just about all in. The constant noise and turmoil, both day and night, wears on a fellow. I can hardly wait till I reach my hunting lodge. I take a bunch of congenial friends, a good cook, and plenty of good stuff to eat and drink. We go up there to hunt, play cards, relax and rest for three or four weeks, and it brings back my old self—Billy Cody again."

His fear of growing old was heightened by the announcement that his granddaughter was being married. That winter, he received a telegram from his grandson, begging him to come to North Platte for the holidays. Here he was greeted by his wife, after nine years of estrangement. The family left them in a room together. When they came out, they were arm-in-arm. The past had been forgotten and forgiven. Two hundred and fifty neighbors and friends assembled at Scout's Rest Ranch to celebrate the reunion, and Louisa went north with her husband to the Wyoming ranch, where she had never before been welcome.

Before Lillie could leave Bridgeport for Oklahoma, he was contacted by Otto Ringling, manager of the Barnum & Bailey circus and the Buffalo Bill plant. Otto was considered the "hub" of the Ringling Brothers in financial matters. He was called the "King." He was a bachelor, forty-five years old, rather morose, and had the reputation of being very close in business matters. This held true in small matters. But in large transactions, Lillie described him as "the biggest man I ever dealt with."

Otto said to me, "Wintering the two shows here in the same quarters crowds us too much, makes it unpleasant for both shows. I thought I might be able to sell you the Buffalo Bill plant. Then you could establish your own winter quarters, and be independent."

"Mr. Ringling, I was forced to buy out the interests of the Bailey estate, which included Cody's interest. The Colonel and I are now equal owners, but at present I am carrying the whole load. He owes so much to his friends, he was unable to pay me anything on his half interest this season. And it will be up to me to supply the money to winter, repair, and put the show on the road next spring. But if we have as good a season next year, I might consider it next fall when we come in."

"But, Major, I will name you a price that is so low it will be almost like paying rent. We really need all the room here for the Barnum show, or it would make no difference. It's a shame to have to leave the parade wagons in the lot exposed to winter weather, which we have to do to make room for you. If you can raise $50,000 cash, when I meet my brothers in Baraboo, Wisconsin, I think I can show them where it will be to our interest to sell the property at this low figure."

This was almost like finding it. There were fifty railroad cars, 168 head of baggage horses, and 80 baggage wagons, besides seats, harness, lights, grandstand, and hundreds of smaller items. I said, "Otto, when I return from my visit to Oklahoma, I will see what I can do."

"No—I'll tell you what you do," returned Otto. "Wire me by Christmas at Baraboo. My brothers will all be there. We are having a kind of reunion Christmas. Your wire and offer of $50,000 may be the influence I need to help put it over—for I am sure some of the brothers will object to such a low price."

I wired Thomas Smith, a fine young man who lived at Beaver Falls, Pennsylvania. He had fallen heir to a fortune, and had tried to purchase an interest from me in the Buffalo Bill and Pawnee Bill shows. I told him to meet me in Pittsburgh.

There was never a time that his conversation didn't run or refer in some manner to horses. One day he said to me, "Major, I was introduced today to what I think is the finest and prettiest woman I ever seen."

"Is that so, Tom, what did she look like?" I asked.

"You never saw a three-year-old filly in your life that compared to her. Head in the air, neck set just right, eyes that needed no blinders, and travel—I bet she could run a 2:40 down a plant road and never wheeze."

Because of his wonderful knowledge of horses, I believed he would make a valuable addition to my staff. "Tom," I told him, "I'll give you a letter so you can get into quarters. That place is run like a military camp since the Ringlings got half of it."

Tom went to Bridgeport, and after a thorough investigation wrote me that he considered it a good deal. He said, "Suppose you offer them $40,000. In a deal of this kind we can raise it a lot easier than we can lower it."

I wired Otto in Wisconsin: "Will you take $40,000 for the plant? Twenty down; twenty before we leave in the spring." I doubted they would accept this offer, and expected a counter offer of $45,-000, splitting the difference between us. This I would have accepted, I am sure—but the reply came back the same day: "We accept your offer. The Ringling Brothers." So I wrote Tom, made him an offer to go in half with me, and we bought the plant. After all costs of operation was deducted, we would divide the profits. He would be general manager and in possession of the plant at all times. He was to receive and pay out all monies.

14.

The Denver Debacle

THE SEASON OF 1910, Major John Burke, growing fat, gray haired and worried, but remaining as industrious as ever, dreamed up one of the most successful publicity schemes of his career. Buffalo Bill was "nearing the three score and ten limit"; the years were "lurking in ambush" for him; he "must prepare to retire in good order from the arena, or take the chances of being left to lag superfluous on the state." They would announce Buffalo Bill's farewell to the public, a three-year route that would take him to every corner of the country without appearing twice in the same place, so he could say, as he did in his valedictory, "Few remain of the great leaders in war and peace, many of whom came out of the West—the West of the old pioneer days—the Wild West, with which all my life has been so closely interwoven. Time beats us all at last. Time has come for parting words to the friends of my life time and my best patron, the American public. . . . On my honor as Buffalo Bill, my present visit will positively be my last hail and farewell in the saddle to you all."

People took Cody at his word and packed every performance to see him for the last time. Buffalo Bill and Pawnee Bill joined forces in a tremendous exhibition. Nothing like it had ever been seen before. A million dollars poured into their pay wagons; their profits amounted to more than four hundred thousand dollars. Cody poured every dollar into the Big Horn Basin and his Arizona mines. Pawnee Bill deposited $100,000 to his personal account, and put another $100,000 into his new home on Blue Hawk Peak.

After retiring from the show, May Lillie had operated the Buffalo Ranch at Pawnee, living in the modest log house built by the Major's own hands. It continued to stand as a memento of their hard work and untiring efforts to rung the ladder of success. But, in 1909, when Gordon returned from Bridgeport for the winter, they planned the house of which they had been dreaming for twenty-four years. It was to be built on the highest point of Blue Hawk Peak. Pawnee Bill sent for James Hamilton, his architect friend, of Chester, Pennsylvania, entrusted the building to him, and went back on the road with his show in the spring of 1910.

Twice that season Hamilton wired me to come back and reason with him. The first time it was about the den, which was divided from the entrance hall only by solid mahogany pillars. He told me it wasn't private enough, that tobacco smoke would get into the rest of the house.

The second wire was about the dining room. I wanted it with the whole west side a half circle of windows looking out over my favorite view. Hamilton said, "Nobody is building houses that way any more." But I told him, "Once when my show was playing a little town in Pennsylvania, I was walking down the street, and I was hungry. I smelled food cooking in a little German hotel, and I said to myself, 'I bet they'll have good food in there.' They did. That hotel dining room had a round window, and I made up my mind then that I would have a round window in the dining room of my house."

He also had built-in cupboards along the east walls after the fashion of an old southern mansion where he had once been entertained, and ordered tapestry-covered walls, because he "was taken with tapestry" the first time he saw it as a guest in a castle in Antwerp, Belgium.

The house was a huge bungalow of rough, buff-colored stone quarried from Blue Hawk Peak, held together with red cement the color of Oklahoma soil, and roofed with red tile. Its hardwood interior, selected from the rarest and most expensive mahogany, was arranged so that the spacious rooms were thrown together with nothing but open arches, pillars, fretwork and portieres to obstruct the vision. Windows, with glass of the finest imported bevel plate, reached to the floor and were hung as half-doors.

Contemporary reports described its interior as "a spread of refined lavishness." Entering through massive stone arches, one twisted the knob and stood beneath the head of a buffalo Pawnee Bill had shot when a boy. The living room was "rugged with Oriental weavings, with here and there a monster bear, buffalo, lion skin or highly-colored Navajo blanket; the furniture is leathered in red and brown to harmonize with the dark and precious woods; a monster open fireplace with solid bronze andirons, surmounted with a mantel of special design, extends a merry glow of warmth and hospitality; drop chandeliers of diamond cut glass radiate a dazzle of electricity, and gold stained burlap frieze creep up to an old Dutch ceiling. . . . The walls are decorated with the most artistic and appropriate hangings and paintings, every niche and corner having something specially designed; and more rare and unique is a series of original Western scenes by such renowned artists as Schreyvogel, Stephens, Demming, Cross, and Emil W. Lenders, who lived at the ranch and trailed the Major's buffalo herd for days in a buckboard to get his sketches.

"Just beyond the living room is the spacious dining room. The walls carry tapestries made in the 17th Century, while closets glitter with crystal and china of rarest design, and the sideboards are laden with magnificent silver services made to order in different parts of Europe. On one side is a bay window with plate glass, nearly twenty feet long, above a leather covered window seat; a seven foot diamond cut glass chandelier drops to within a few feet of the table that will seat fifty guests.

"To the left is a cozy little den, tiled with red and white stone, furniture in weathered oak, another open fireplace, and walls hung with pictures and trophies of early pioneer days and the chase. . . . A cheerful hall and broad staircase lead to spacious bedrooms above. The bedrooms are in various tints and furnishings; here and there are scattered huge rugs of buffalo, bear, or lion, and the walls are hung with oils of the finest masters.

"As the visitor leaves, he crosses a porch with massive stone arches onto a terrace inset with tile showing buffalo against green grass and blue sky. A bit further on is the garage and stable, an elegant combination of native stone and hardwood in keeping with the general exterior finish scheme of the bungalow. Below is the Major's magnificent garden, and beyond, stretching so far its owner can ride as far as he likes without getting off his own range, the ranch.

"Here roams one of the few remaining buffalo herds in the country. Here also is a herd of calico Indian ponies, a sod house and old settler's cabin of cedar logs, and a Pawnee Indian council house covered with earth and sod three feet deep, all under the supervision of the Major's ranch foreman and devoted companion, Mexican Joe. In the background is a level mesa, where several lodges and tepees of the Pawnees lend the remaining touches of pioneer color needed.

"Circling along a sloping knoll, following a newly macadamed roadway shaded with trees and vines, one leaves the ranch through a massive stone gateway, standing like a citadel, ornamented with the words 'Buffalo Ranch' in raised metal letters over the arch, and the gilded steel initials 'P. B.' made from the barrel of a rifle once carried by his great friend, Major Frank North."

The house was finished by December, 1910. On December 6, Lillie added twenty-seven buffaloes to his herd, purchased from the Austin Corbin ranch at Newport, New Hampshire. Joe Barrera had charge of the car in which they were shipped at the expense of $525. All were young animals less than four years old, and together with those the Major had, gave him the largest privately owned herd of pure-blood buffalo in the United States.

On December 10, some fifty invited guests, many from the elite centers of Europe and America, journeyed to the prairie, and the citizens of Pawnee and surrounding towns turned out en masse to celebrate the homecoming of the beloved and esteemed Pawnee Bill and do him homage.

Cowboy boots and the patent leathers of artists, writers and men famous in many professions toed each other under the Major's hospitable table. Among his guests were Childs Schreyvogel of New York, who painted "My Bunkie" and created a stir in the art circles of Paris in 1909; H. H. Cross, the Chicago artist; D. E. W. Demming and Emil W. Lenders of New York; James Hamilton; Michael Russell of the Russell Stage Company of Montana; Charles Meitus, treasurer of the Wild West show; Major John M. Burke; Johnny Baker, the arena director and fancy shooter; Louis E. Cooke; Joe Miller of the 101 Ranch of Bliss, Oklahoma; Mark L. Stone of Paris; Henry Valliers of Vienna; and Lee Cruce, governor-elect of Oklahoma.

Louis E. Cooke wrote: "With such environments, feasting at a bountiful table supplied with every delicacy of the land, and

Colonel William F. Cody as the guest of honor, it is doubtful if ever a more cheerful, vivacious group foregathered from so many different sources or represented a greater variety of art, intellect and ability to entertain or be entertained with song, story, sight-seeing and recounture of daring deeds, diversions and discussions of almost every interesting subject.

"Frequent tours, hunts, feasts and cross-country riding were some of the surprises furnished by the worthy hosts, and the happy occasion will lurk in the minds of all concerned so long as memory shall last."

An unruly old buffalo bull had been mistreating the other animals in the herd. During a tour of the ranch, the shaggy former king of the plains knocked down James Hamilton with a heavy thrust of his powerful shoulders. Major Lillie decided that the ill-tempered brute should die. He chose Colonel Cody to do the honors.

Cody was accompanied to the scene by the entire party, together with a band of Pawnees, led by old Eagle Chief. Mounting a cow pony, and armed with his repeating rifle, Buffalo Bill started the hunt. The buffalo was given every chance, but at last fell from a single shot fired from Cody's rifle. The incident was so impressive that Major Burke wrote the following poem to commemorate the occasion of the great scout having killed probably his last buffalo, and the first one in almost half a century:

> Condemned for cruelty to his fellows,
> Snorting challenges in fierce bellows,
> Pawing earth, shaking in temper riled,
> The Last Bison Monarch stood defiant—wild,
>
> His czar-like rule voted out of tune,
> And he from penalty not immune.
> A stately, well-armed cavalier
> And prancing charger o'er hill appear.
>
> A deadly dual charge was made
> An angry brute quick and low is laid.
> A victim of the unerring skill
> Of that prince of hunters, Buffalo Bill.

A memorial tablet will mark the spot
As the Buffalo's Last Stand and Bill's Last Shot.

A barbecue of buffalo meat and an old-time council and dance by the Pawnee Indians was a striking climax to the festivities. The many speeches followed the theme of "delight that Pawnee had shown such an example of possibilities in comfort and luxury without ostentatious display." Colonel Cody paid tribute to the progressive spirit of Oklahoma and the success of his partner, Pawnee Bill. Major Lillie thanked the assemblage for the honor they had extended him and the interest they had displayed during the building's progress. Judge McNeill responded with an eloquent eulogy of the personal standing, business probity and executive ability of Major Lillie as a ranchman, showman and banker, which was highly endorsed by a score of fellow citizens, each relating some episode in the Major's career.

The Pawnee *Courier-Dispatch* of December 15 commented: "Writers of poetry, history and romance have valued highly the love of the homeland as a sentimental virtue. The Frenchman's love of La Patrie; the Englishman's steadfast affection for the green fields of merry England; the Irishman's love for the old sod of the Green Isle; the Polish exile's mourning for his shattered patrimony; the Teuton's fidelity to the Fatherland have been for ages the theme of song and story. Such feeling has been actuating races and nations of all times, but in no case does this sentiment appear stronger than among the American Indians, who reverently look upon the land from which they have sprung as the 'Great Mother.'

"This fidelity and steadfast devotion to the home of their youth is exemplified by the loyalty of Buffalo Bill and Pawnee Bill to the sections where their adventurous early lives were spent and their continued efforts during all their wanderings and with their surplus accumulations lavishly used to assist in the development of their beloved Old West.

"In youth they saw it in its primitive condition, and with a loyalty unbounded have stuck through trials and tribulations with a faith to be admired in a destiny now fructifying and repaying them by grandeur of progressive conditions even exceeding their fondest dreams. Chapters could be written upon the years' patience,

toil and investment that through thick and thin they have practically shown in their confidence in the happy results to come.

"Major Lillie can be heartily congratulated on the completion
of his interesting home and can take pride and pleasure in looking
back to his early associations and his present fortunate position in
the phenomenal state of Oklahoma."

Buffalo Bill returned to his Scout's Rest Ranch on December 31,
1910. In January, he made a trip to Arizona to look after his mining
interests, returning before the month ended, and remained at
Scout's Rest until the show season opened. His health was still
troubling him, and two tours, one east and one west, in 1911 and
1912, were advertised as "farewell tours."

The Sells-Floto circus, owned by Harry H. Tammen and Frederick G. Bonfils of the Denver *Post,* was still at war with Barnum
& Bailey and Ringling Brothers. The bitter competition, beginning
in 1908, had resulted in torn-down billboards, wrecked trains and
cracked heads. Pawnee Bill and Buffalo Bill had the only Wild West
show of any consequence in the world. With no competition, they
could make money either ahead of or behind the circuses.

Cody continued to get rid of his share of the profits as fast as he
received them. About this time his mining venture in Arizona blew
up. His ranches and hotel took much more of his money, but, by
1911, he had reduced his debt to Lillie to $30,000. He offered to
sell Lillie the Scout's Rest Ranch for $100,000. The Major entered
into negotiations with Mrs. Cody, in whose name the ranch was
deeded. He agreed to pay $100,000, provided Cody let the $30,000
debt go as part payment. Mrs. Cody, more prudent than her husband, would not agree to more than $20,000 of the debt being used.
Lillie accepted these terms, giving her $80,000. A $10,000 loan
against the Irma Hotel was practically forced upon him by Cody.
He told the Major he wanted him to take the mortgage "to fore-
stall unfriendly litigation."

Despite these deals, Buffalo Bill was in better financial condition
in 1911 than in any year previous. His partnership with Pawnee
Bill had enabled him to reduce his indebtedness to the Bailey estate
from $250,000 to $70,000, and he owned a clear half interest in the
combined shows. There "wasn't a cloud in the Two Bills' horizon"
in 1911, nor the early part of the 1912 season. Buffalo Bill's health

apparently was mending, and he insisted on taking the show out again in 1913.

The 1910 and 1911 seasons had been successful, because the crowds believed this was a genuine farewell. Business fell off in 1912. There were profits, but hardly enough to keep Buffalo Bill ahead of his creditors.

Wintering the combined shows amounted to nearly $40,000. Every season, Lillie had been advancing all wintering funds, taking Cody's share from his next season's drawing account. At the end of the 1912 season, he asked Cody for his half of the wintering funds in advance:

> Cody replied that he would have to go to North Platte to get the money. Along in January, 1913, he sent me a check for $15,000, saying he would send the remainder later. About this time I read that the Colonel had been visiting Harry Tammen in Denver.

On February 3, 1913, the Denver *Post* announced "the most important deal ever consummated in American amusement enterprise . . . the strongest combination ever formed in the history of American amusements, if not in the world." Buffalo Bill's Wild West would be "preserved" with the Sells-Floto circus of Tammen and Bonfils. When Lillie asked for details, Cody sent him a telegram: "Pay no attention to press reports; I have done nothing that will interfere with our shows."

The facts were that early in 1913, while visiting his sister in Denver, Cody had met Harry Tammen. Tammen had appeared friendly, and when Cody told him he needed $20,000 to pay his part of wintering the combined shows, the newspaper proprietor was quick to oblige, taking a six months' note on the show property as collateral, and obtaining an agreement from Cody that he would leave Pawnee Bill at the end of the season and appear with the Sells-Floto circus in 1914.

Buffalo Bill did not realize that he had involved himself with a man who wanted a big circus that could compete with Ringling Brothers. All his life Harry Tammen had played with expensive toys. When he decided he wanted a circus, Bonfils had advised him to study nature. There were, for instance, 405 species of birds in

Colorado. "Birds hell!" Tammen said. "I want elephants." So he got elephants.

He had started with the Floto Dog and Pony Show. Floto was the name of the sports editor of the Denver *Post,* who never owned a single share in the show. But Tammen liked the name, and took it. As his circus grew, he cast about for another name to add to the title. He hired a relative of the Sells family and called it Sells-Floto.

Ringling Brothers objected to the use of the Sells name, because they had bought the Sells Brothers circus. They filed suit. In 1913, Sells-Floto was in the hottest part of its long, bitter fight with Barnum & Bailey and Ringling Brothers shows, and Tammen was grabbing any possible attraction that would give him an edge over the trust. In the midst of his grabbing, Cody walked into his office and naively asked to borrow $20,000. The idea of seizing Buffalo Bill's Wild West sprang into Tammen's mind, and from that moment he seemed determined to make Cody his personal property. The $20,000 became the shackle that was to reduce the once proud plainsman to humiliation, and wreck what was left of his career, for it lost him the support of Pawnee Bill.

The combined shows went on the road as usual in the spring of 1913. It was against Lillie's better judgment to foist another farewell tour upon the public. Small audiences and bad weather left them owing everybody. Feed bills mounted, and they owed the United States Printing and Lithographing Company $60,000 for posters.

Cody had paid nothing on the note he had given Harry Tammen, which was due in July. By now, Pawnee Bill had learned the whole story, and he found it hard to take. Sixty-nine thousand dollars would have squared the show with its creditors, and Lillie might again have been willing to foot the bill. He had rescued Cody when he needed money and given him back half the show. Cody not only had mortgaged the property, but had agreed to leave his friend and benefactor for a rival. Lillie refused to use a cent of his personal funds.

For weeks the two men hardly spoke to each other. Cody became ill and complained that Pawnee Bill's sour disposition had upset him. Lillie ignored him.

The tour would take them to Denver in July. While the show was playing Chicago, Lillie's old friend Bickerstaff, of the printing and lithographing company, came to his private car.

"If you go to Denver, you'll never get out with your show," he told Lillie. "Tammen and Bonfils are waiting for you. They are going to wreck your show and take Buffalo Bill."

Bick had come all the way from New York to tell me this and also to tell me that his company had been forced into the deal by Tammen and Bonfils. Yet, I knew he must be mistaken. I reasoned that if they wanted Buffalo Bill they wouldn't ruin our show to get him, because that would detract from his drawing power.

Years later, Lillie said:

It was good reasoning, but it was based on the premise that Tammen and Bonfils were showmen. That's where I was wrong. They . . . always used desperate methods as the shortest cut to whatever they wanted.

The show opened in Denver on July 20, as scheduled. At two previous engagements there, Tammen and Bonfils had been honored guests. Neither appeared at the 1913 opening.

On the second day, during the matinee performance, while Lillie was watching the grand entry, six deputy sheriffs, one armed with a writ, entered the show grounds and informed him that the entire property of the Wild West and the Far East show had been attached, including the ticket wagon with all its private papers and business records and $6,000 in cash.

The proceedings had been brought by Bickerstaff's company for its printing bills, despite the fact that the season was only half over and it was customary to settle such accounts when the season was finished. Louis De Montouzin, general sales-manager for the company, told Lillie he had come to Denver two weeks before and signed the application for the writ at the insistence of Tammen and Bonfils, with *Post* attorneys handling the legal proceedings for his company. He agreed that a sizeable payment made to his company might prevent the show properties going under the auctioneer's hammer. Cody tried to raise the cash among old friends in Denver, some of them bankers; but he found no help there. The afternoon performance of July 21, 1913, was the last given of this greatest Wild West show on earth.

Old friendships were cracking under the pressure of Tammen and Bonfils. The *Post* accused Lillie of obtaining Scout's Rest Ranch from Buffalo Bill "under dubious circumstances," and gaining control of the hotel property by means "not laudable." Cody, in wild legal confusion, charged Lillie with obtaining money under false pretenses and demanded a complete accounting of all their transactions. The case never came to trial.

With legal arrows flying thick and fast, only Major Lillie knew exactly what happened. Tammen and Bonfils didn't know that there were two companies involved in the combined shows. The show itself was owned by Buffalo Bill and Pawnee Bill, but the plant, which included all rolling stock and transportation equipment was owned by Pawnee Bill and Thomas Smith of Beaver Falls, Pennsylvania.

Lillie's first move was to sign over his share of the plant to Smith. Smith, in turn, mortgaged the entire plant to the Federal Title and Trust Company, thus complicating matters to a point that prospective buyers became wary, and the *Post,* fuming at the delay, through its columns "brought thunders of invective down on Major Lillie's head."

These new legal entanglements forced Tammen and Bonfils into the open. They were supposed to have nothing to do with the entire affair; it was the Two Bills show versus the lithographing company. They charged that Major Lillie had fraudulently sold attached property. His hotel was watched, his every move reported.

Finally, he slipped out of Denver and went to Trenton, New Jersey, where he had the whole show thrown into voluntary bankruptcy, and an injunction stopping the auction wired to Denver. Despite this injunction, the sale proceeded, but was set aside later. In September, 1913, a final sale was held, and Major Lillie returned to Pawnee with a trunk and his saddle—all that he got out of his show.

Thus, Buffalo Bill's Wild West and Pawnee Bill's Far East died ingloriously. Buffalo Bill went to North Platte to be comforted by Louisa. With two ranches, a hotel, mines and thousands of acres

of land, nothing paying a profit and debts pressing, he told his wife:
"I can't quit. I have to start life over again, with no capital."

He secured a one-third interest in a motion picture company,
producing a historical film of the last Indian war, and made some
money. But in the spring of 1914, he was forced to fulfill his contract with Tammen. He borrowed $2000 from a Denver bank for
expenses, Tammen endorsing the note, and set out with the Sells-
Floto circus—a poor affair, with drab sideshows, sword swallowers
and freaks. In 1915, he was out with Sells-Floto again when he
should have been under a doctor's care. It was a pretty rotten show,
and Cody declared open warfare with Tammen. Tammen lost his
temper and demanded payment in full on all the money he had
ever advanced Cody, the $2000 note and $20,000 loaned him while
with Pawnee Bill. Cody thought the sale of his show had covered
this, but Tammen said not, and ordered the circus cashier to with-
hold fifty dollars a day from sums due Cody until his debts were
paid.

It was a sorry business. Cody grew frantic. In September, when
Tammen came to his tent to discuss the matter again, he saw a look
in Cody's eyes that caused him to agree to drop the deductions. Perhaps Tammen had a better reason, for Cody had written a friend
who possibly had passed the word to Tammen: "This man is driving me crazy. I can easily kill him, but as I have avoided killing in
the bad days, I don't want to kill him. But if there is no justice left
—by heaven, I will!"

When the season ended, there were no further contracts between
Tammen and Cody. Cody was free again. He still thought another
fortune could be made and sent Major Burke and Johnny Baker
in search of capital. He found an opening with the 101 Ranch Wild
West Show of Oklahoma, appearing in 1916 with twenty soldiers
in a Pageant of Preparedness, a recruiting stunt—still signing away
his prospective profits for ready cash, and paying expenses of several
lawsuits he had started, including one against Tammen.

When the show closed at Portsmouth, Virginia, November 11, he
set out for Chicago with hopes of raising $100,000 to finance a new
Wild West. Despairing finally of his rich friends, he found a professional money raiser, who agreed to sell stock to the general public

through newspaper advertising on ten per cent commission, but Cody's state of health made it impossible to complete negotiations. His chest was congested with a cold. Doctors suggested he go to Glenwood Springs for mineral baths, and see Dr. W. W. Crook, who could help him. But uremia had already set in. At Glenwood Springs, he collapsed. He was taken to the home of his sister at Denver. On January 10, 1917, he died.

His body lay in state in Denver, while the whole nation mourned his death. He left everything to Louisa, but his estate was so involved in mortgages and complications that she realized only a small income during the four remaining years of her life. She died in 1921, and was buried beside Cody.

Major Lillie wrote:

Time smoothes everything. Buffalo Bill died my friend. He was just an irresponsible boy.

15.   Blue Hawk Peak

PAWNEE BILL saw the doom of the tent show business in the brisk new amusement called "motion pictures," that had given their first warning flicker in the peep-show machines twenty years before and now "flaunted their silver screens in every village." Glad to retire to his quiet ranch in Oklahoma, he quit the Wild West show life for good.

He believed in the future of his state and invested heavily in real estate, oil and livestock. A part of his vast ranch he placed under cultivation to raise feed for the various animals, but most of it was retained in its primitive wildness for use of his ever-increasing buffalo herd. The ranch operations were under the supervision of his trusted foreman José Barrera, and José's daughter, Mary, was Pawnee Bill's secretary.

He had thousands of close friends all over the world and plenty of money to keep him in comfort the rest of his days. He owned part or all of many businesses, and was still vice president of the Arkansas Valley National Bank. All he had to do was "sign his name to a lot of paper money."

He had lived through some "wild and woolly" times, and could match stories of the old days and their heroes with the best of them. He had known them all, and done everything a boy of his generation had dreamed of doing. He had befriended the Pawnee Indians and had been made White Chief of the tribe, and had taught them the way of the white man. He had hunted buffalo, trapped, driven cattle up the Chisholm Trail, shot it out with rustlers and trailed bank robbers; he had known such Robin Hoods of the day as the James boys and the Daltons; he had led the boomers into Oklahoma, and had been a great showman "with long hair and a sure aim."

His close friends had been Dave Payne, Captain Couch and Sidney Clark, the great trio of original boomers who had devoted their lives to the opening of the last frontier, and Marsh Murdock of the Wichita *Eagle,* who had rendered them generous assistance. He had been with Doc Carver, John Burke and Major Frank North as a member of Buffalo Bill's original Wild West. As long as he lived, these men would "ride their phantom horses across his memory." Most of them already had gone to the eternal West beyond the setting sun. Pawnee Bill, almost alone, remained to tell their glorious tales.

He was just the picturesque character around which one could build a fairy story, using him for the hero prince. Blue Hawk Peak was indeed a place of enchantment, with its famous paintings and tapestries, rare old books, Indian curios, frontier relics, and fine objects of art given him by princes, presidents and notables everywhere. In the twilight of a crowded, colorful career, he needed only to "sit back on Buffalo Ranch with these memories and watch the world build cities on the prairies that a half-century before he had seen swarming with buffaloes and redmen."

But the Major was not ready to settle down in any such notable manner. His showmanship was only one side of Lillie's character. His chief interest was in perpetuating the life he had grown to love. For twenty-five years he had done it with a Wild West show. Now he turned to exploiting his Buffalo Ranch and Blue Hawk Peak home as a show place that annually attracted thousands.

The buffalo on his ranch, while kept mainly for show and to preserve the breed, were occasionally used to furnish meat for banquets and barbecues at big Indian powwows. Excellent saddle horses, Indian villages with genuine decorated tepees, a lake abounding with wild duck and greese, frontier cabins, dugouts, old stagecoaches, prairie schooners, and other relics added interest for the visitors.

In their home, Gordon and May Lillie entertained famous people from every walk of life. Countess Anna de Lozina, who presented stirring lectures on her personal experiences in Russia during World War I and gained an international reputation as a versatile entertainer, came to Pawnee for a brief stay at Blue Hawk Peak. Robert Lindneux, famous landscape and portrait artist of

Denver, who did the life-size painting of Colonel Cody that stands
in the center of the Cody memorial on the crest of Lookout Mountain, came to visit his old friend Major Lillie and to make some
sketches of the scenic beauties peculiar to Blue Hawk Peak before
proceeding to San Antonio to paint for General John J. Pershing
a war picture titled "The New Era." Blue Hawk Peak was headquarters for eminent newspapermen and editors such as Ray Long
of *Cosmopolitan,* and such distinguished writers as Rex Beach and
Irvin S. Cobb. The ranch celebrations and powwows attracted such
personages as Leonard Stroud, who gave an exact repetition of the
riding which had won him the title "Champion of the World."

Pawnee Bill's annual buffalo hunt to eliminate surplus bulls in
his herd furnished some real frontier sport as well as a rare treat
of buffalo meat for those fortunate enough to secure it. This occurred early in December each year, when the buffalo were in best
condition. It was a gala occasion at Buffalo Ranch, and arrangements were always made to make each one excel all previous hunts.
The animals were killed by famous Indians and noted hunters
of the West, or by some distinguished statesman or celebrated
personality.

One winter the hunt was staged in honor of Courtney Ryley
Cooper, an intimate friend of the Major's, who stayed at the ranch
while gathering material for his novel, *Oklahoma.* He was accompanied by several cowboys from the ranch and fifty Indians from
the Pawnee reservation.

In 1916, Lillie wrote:

> The herd is what I believe to be on a permanent basis, and I feel
> no uneasiness about them. They will continue to thrive and multi-
> ply as time passes, although the demand for them as beeves is a
> tempting one.

"It is true," said the Pawnee *Courier-Dispatch.* "The demand for
buffalo roasts and steaks cannot be supplied, or rather will not be
supplied, by the owner of Buffalo Ranch, for the reason that he
will not slaughter one which might jeopardize the life of his herd.
Usually, in the fall, two or three are slaughtered and choice cuts
sent to the President of the United States, other prominent men,

and friends of Lillie's. Such parts of these animals not given away are sold to cafes in Chicago, Philadelphia and New York at prices which would seem to make buffalo meat the most expensive on the markct."

That fall, Lillie mailed a circular letter to twenty restaurants over the country, offering six fine buffalo, dressed and packed for shipment—"the rarest, gamiest meat of all the big American game." No order for less than twenty pounds would be accepted. The buffalo would be slaughtered December 14 and shipped on the 20th.

Orders came thick and fast. Buffalo meat became a part of the delicious Christmas menus of the New Astor House in New York, the Clay Pool Hotel at Indianapolis, and the Café L'Aiglon in Philadelphia. Even the country's most fashionable divorcees were supplied, as the rarest morsel on the Riverside Hotel menu at Reno, Nevada, that Christmas, was roast buffalo from Pawnee Bill's famous ranch.

One entire carcass went to the Highland Hotel at Springfield, Massachusetts; another to the Seelbach at Louisville, Kentucky; and the famous hostelry, The Continental, at Newark, New Jersey, served roast buffalo at Christmas and New Year's. Soon the supply

A Christmas Dinner

PRIME BUFFALO MEAT FOR SALE

THE MONARCH
OF THE PLAINS

THE INDIAN'S
STORE HOUSE

THE RAREST, GAMIEST MEAT OF ALL THE BIG AMERICAN GAME

I AM OFFERING THIS YEAR SIX FINE FAT BUFFALO--DRESSED AND PACKED READY FOR SHIPMENT--AS FOLLOWS:

Hump Roast, per pound	60c
Prime Rib Roast, per pound	50c
Porter House, per pound	60c
Sirloin Steak, per pound	50c
Round Steak, per pound	40c
Brisket and Plate, per pound	30c
Heart and Tongue, each	$3.00

NO ORDER ACCEPTED FOR LESS THAN 20 POUNDS

THE BUFFALO WILL BE SLAUGHTERED ON THE 14TH AND SHIPPED OUT ON DEC. 20TH

was exhausted and to have shipped the unfilled orders would have wiped out the herd.

"There is no danger of this," said the *Courier-Dispatch*. "No one will be permitted to rob this country of its native buffalo during the lifetime of Pawnee Bill."

In June, 1916, Pawnee Bill announced that he had developed a peculiar breed of swine. Near Hunnewell, Kansas, he had noticed a number of boars with glossy black bodies and almost perfectly white faces, which made them conspicuous in a neighborhood of Poland-Chinas. He observed that their markings were as uniform as those of Hereford cattle, and that they responded to feed quicker than other breeds. He managed to obtain one. He crossed it with a number of Poland-China sows, and the result was thirty pigs which were marked with the white face "as uniformly as so many black-eyed peas."

They are only pigs yet, but thriftier than anything in the hog line I have ever seen. You can almost see them grow. Registered? No, there is no society of the breed. If I am successful in getting another boar of the same marks, it is my intention to establish the new breed—make a permanent thing of it—and organize a registration society.

"Of what name?" he was asked.

"How would the Hereford Swine Breeders Association suit?" he queried.

"Better go one better and christen it the Pawnee Bill Hereford Swine Breeders Association of the United States of America," was suggested.

"Too much of a handicap for a new breed of hogs," decided Lillie.

For years, white-faced hogs monopolized the Major's attention. In 1924, he proved that his active life was still at its zenith by raising purebred cattle, specializing in Scotch Shorthorns, an extremely popular breed in Great Britain and Canada.

That summer, while visiting Guy Weadick, producer of the Calgary Stampede (Canada's official championship cowboy contest and frontier day celebration), whose T. S. Ranch joined the E. P. Ranch owned by the Prince of Wales, near High River, Alberta, Pawnee Bill attended the first annual sale of some of the best specimens of the Prince of Wales' famous Scotch Shorthorn herd. After much spirited bidding, Lillie purchased "Princeton Enthusiast," a fine young bull, bred on the ranch, and shown at the ranch for first place in four Canadian shows that year. He was the best bull offered for sale, and Lillie gave the highest price paid for any animal sold. The Prince was delighted that his best animal was going to the United States to represent his ranch and shorthorn herd in the Southwest.

Major Lillie exhibited his purchase, together with the other show stock of His Royal Highness, at the Toronto Royal Winter Fair and the International Livestock Exposition at Chicago, where the animal won two additional ribbons, before being shipped to Buffalo Ranch in December. During the next two years, Lillie purchased several of the best shorthorn females he could secure. From this foundation, he developed a herd of seventy-five, the most important herd in the Southwest, and the largest in the United States.

In 1926, on Blue Hawk Peak, Lillie constructed a basement-type barn, the largest to be found in that part of the country. The basement was used for his horses, the second floor to shelter his pure-bred cattle, and the third floor for storage of tons of alfalfa and other feed crops grown on the ranch. The structure was of native stone and cement reinforced with steel. Steel beams supported the upper floor and a roof of red tile. The rapid growth of the Major's herd had made this huge barn a necessity.

Many farmers in Oklahoma became interested in the breed. In February, 1926, Lillie sold his first high-grade purebred animal, a male thirteen months old out of Avendale heir, grandson of Evolution and imported Proud Emlein, to Clarence Dilley, a young man with a wide knowledge of fine cattle, who had twenty-seven registered shorthorns on his farm northeast of Pawnee. In 1929, farmers and cattlemen from Kansas, Texas, Missouri and Arkansas, came to Blue Hawk Peak to attend the shorthorn dispersion sale, at which Pawnee Bill offered seventy head, consisting of twenty-eight bulls and forty-two females, as "seed" stock.

In his open invitation to "everyone interested in better breeding of cattle," Lillie wrote:

It is an opportunity to Shorthorn breeders and farmers of Oklahoma to add good foundation stock to their herds. It is also an opportunity for younger breeders to secure foundation females of
proven worth and tested breeding ability . . . . My chief object in
establishing this herd was to develop some cattle that would go on
and improve the livestock of this state.

John C. Burns, president of the American Shorthorn Association,
was at the ranch to assist with the sale, as were Ralph Dawson of
the Kansas City *Daily Telegram,* and A. C. Hartenbower of the
Oklahoma *Livestock News.* An Indian powwow was one of the featured entertainments for the visitors.

In 1916, a deal had been closed by which the Arkansas Valley
National Bank of Pawnee passed into the hands of C. H. Stratton
and C. S. Schmelzel of Tulsa, and E. W. Beeson of Okmulgee, all
men with long experience in the banking business. In July, 1917,
the Arkansas Valley National was superseded by the Security State
Bank, and Pawnee Bill invested his money in oil.

In 1918, Lillie and associates opened the Pawnee Bill Refinery at
Yale, Oklahoma, in true circus fashion—with flags flying, bands
playing and a buffalo barbecue as a free side show. A more cosmopolitan crowd had never been brought together—millionaire oil
refiners and oil producers rubbed elbows with the workers, drillers,
farmers and ranchers. Over seven hundred were there to "break
bread" with Lillie and fill up on his buffalo meat, camp coffee and
other delicacies.

The plant had a capacity of 2000 barrels per day, and held the
crude contracts of the Hake, Prowant and Jones productions. Pawnee Bill was as proud of the refinery as of any of his show successes.
In 1921, he leased to the Buffalo Refining Company of Tulsa. For
years, the company had contracts for all the fuel oil and refined
products the plant could turn out, working full capacity.

Pawnee Bill took time out for civic and lodge work. He was an
active member of Pawnee Lodge No. 82, A. F. & A. M.; the Old
Time Cherokee Strip Cow Punchers Association; Range Riders of
the West Association; B. P. O. Elks Lodge No. 654; Council Member and Honorary Commissioner of the Cimarron Valley Council
of the Boy Scouts of America; Life Member Oklahoma Consistory

at Guthrie, 32nd degree Mason; and member of the Akdar Temple, Mystic Shrine, at Tulsa.

In June, 1923, Pawnee Bill and the Miller brothers, of the 101 Ranch, put on one of the country's famous rodeos in Washington in connection with the session of the Imperial Council of the Shrine.

Lillie was a firm friend of the Boy Scout movement and strongly supported its traditional "guidance of boys to manhood." The first troop in Oklahoma, and possibly the first in America, was organized at nearby Pawhuska in 1910. Its small charter was the spark of a registration which spiraled to 16,095 by 1938, and to 29,378 ten years later. In 1954, the count was a record 40,033 Cubs, Scouts and Explorers. Pawnee Bill's interest was greatly stimulated by a Scout leadership training course conducted at Pawnee for thirty-six leaders of Indian Boy Scouts. To express his gratitude for the work done among Indian boys, in November, 1930, he donated a quarter-section site on Buffalo Ranch adjacent to his Indian village, not only as a camp for local Boy Scouts, but also for Scouts from all over the nation.

With Vern H. Vandever, wealthy Tulsa department store owner, and Alf C. Ellis and Raymond Cook, Pawnee Bill founded the Mounted Troops of America, a riding organization of hundreds of young boys and girls that functioned much as did the Boy Scouts of America, except that their activities were on horseback. Its purpose was to combine natural love for animal companionship with horsemanship activities. All the boys and girls were taught the care and management of their mounts, manual training, calisthenics and equestrian acrobatics. Many became so proficient that they were the equal of any grown cowboy, and were invited to participate in parades and rodeos across the country. In 1927, Lillie became national commander, and saw patrols organized in cities throughout Oklahoma, Texas, Louisiana, Missouri, and Arkansas.

Making her home at the ranch since her retirement from the road, May Lillie became active in church and community service. A well-known figure throughout Oklahoma and the Southwest, she made a charming hostess for the frequent entertainments at Blue Hawk Peak. Her father had been a Union soldier during the Civil War, and she became keenly interested in the work of the Women's Relief Corps, the Grand Army of the Republic auxiliary.

The last week in December, 1916, she and the Major made a trip to Kansas City and returned with a bright-eyed, adopted baby boy, four weeks old, whom they named Billy. For years, May Lillie had the satisfaction of being a mother to a wonderful child. But in 1925, he was killed in an accident at the ranch. It was the second such tragedy in her life.

She kept busy with the ranch and its buffalo. Besides the hogs and shorthorns, there were horses, mules, colts and chickens, and two thousand acres of native pasture and feed crops to occupy her attention. After an early breakfast each morning, she would saddle up and ride with the Major on his rounds, and there was nothing on the place they failed to inspect.

"Both enjoy their present existence immensely," wrote a correspondent in 1926. "It is easy to see they are still sweethearts. On the occasion of a visit made to the ranch, the graphonola was started, and Mrs. Lillie glided about the floor with all the enthusiasm of a school girl.

"After dinner, as I sat with the Major on the veranda, listening to the tales of the early days, I could not help thinking of the contrast between the early bunking places of Pawnee Bill and the excellently furnished $100,000 residence which affords every possible convenience and comfort to the Lillie twain today.

"Margaret McLoughlin, author of 'Barnett's Bubbles,' once said that the contrast between the tranquil beauty of the Palisades, on the New Jersey side of the Hudson River, and the busy scenes of a New York department store on bargain day, suggested the poem. If she could spend an evening on the veranda of the bungalow at Buffalo Ranch, after having viewed the Indian village, the Council House, the buffaloes, the pioneer cabin, and miles upon miles of beautiful hills and valleys undulating as far as the eye can see; if she could view the sun cutting fantastic capers with the billows of crimson and gold in the clear, blue sky as it sets behind a gently sloping horizon in the west, and the baffling transformation of the surrounding landscape while the tints and hues of green are darkened by the twilight; if she could sit with these surroundings and see the sweet, cool evening breeze gently stirring the gray locks of the great White Chief as he relates his glorious achievements among the Indian and buffalo of our early West, and witness the expression of perfect contentment when he speaks in dearest terms of his home life—if she could do this, the contrast of such environments with the dust, dirt and soot of a broiling metropolitan city would, indeed, be an inspiration for a noteworthy theme."

Nothing much in these years disturbed Lillie's rather peaceful existence. But when he received an invitation in 1926 to join the "last big buffalo hunt" to exterminate three hundred head of buffalo on the 33,000-acre Antelope Island in the Great Salt Lake of Utah, he became enraged. In reply to A. H. Leonard of Fort Pierre, South Dakota, owner of Antelope Island, who proposed the slaughter because the animals were "too troublesome to move to his ranch," Lillie wrote:

I have probably done more for the preservation of buffalo than any other man now living. Now comes an invitation to attend the last great buffalo hunt at which three hundred fine specimens of the American buffalo as I have ever seen are to be slaughtered by rich men who call themselves sportsmen. . . . How a modern city like Salt Lake can sit idly by and allow such an outrage at her very doors is something I cannot understand.

Will the multitude of American sportsmen, who match their skill against the cunning and wariness of wild game, permit the butchering of tame buffalo with bullets of gold? I protest and ask every sportsman to take hold and save the remaining buffalo. Years ago fifteen million were slaughtered, to our everlasting disgrace. We must not heap more shame upon ourselves by killing, for pay, the few buffalo we have left!

Bitterly he attacked the proposal, dispatching copies of his reply to leading newspapers of the country. In accompanying letters to the editors, he said:

Three-hundred buffalo are to be slaughtered in November to make a pleasant holiday for any "sport lover" who has the price, and the price is several hundred dollars. . . . Gentlemen armed with rifles will ride over the island and have a lot of fun. Will the buffaloes—almost the last of fifteen million that once ranged the Great Plains—have fun, too?

Not until 1906, when I, through the good offices of Bird S. Mc-
Guire, congressman from Oklahoma, got a bill passed setting aside
the timber preserve in the Wichita Mountains of Oklahoma, was
any concerted sentiment and effort put forth to protect and preserve
the buffalo. Our success was due largely to the good offices of the
press of the large cities in the country, without which the buffalo
would now be entirely extinct. Again I solicit their support to prevent the slaughter of buffalo on Antelope Island.

The Chicago *Herald and Examiner* blazoned his protest, publishing the full text of his letters. John Sturgis Codman, vice-
president of the Anti-Vivisection Society of New England and a
well-known writer on subjects pertaining to animal welfare, declared: "Experience has proved that the buffalo will become extinct
in a very short time unless every precaution for its welfare is taken.
The present herds were raised only after the expenditure of enormous effort and money."

Across the country, animal lovers and game hunters who believed
in real sportsmanship entered the fight. The Los Angeles *Examiner*
of October 20 reported: "Vigorous protests from Southern California sportsmen and public officials were aroused when Pawnee
Bill's statement was published in the *Examiner* yesterday. The
question proved to be one of burning interest here where game
conservation has made such strides. Today they joined Pawnee Bill
and with one accord branded the projected 'hunt' as 'utterly un-
sportsmanlike, savage and unthinkable.' "

The San Francisco *Call-Post* of the same date reported that "San
Francisco clubmen and sportsmen have registered a storm of protest against the proposed slaughter," and labeled it an "insult to
all true hunters." Its issue of October 26 stated: "Once buffalo
swarmed as numerous as flies around a molasses jug and real men
were needed to head them off and kill them for army meat. In those
days a fearless man was chosen by the frontier population to negotiate with the then savage redmen for rights to hunt the buffalo.
Uncle Sam could easily make a spectacle of himself snubbing the
lonely remnant of the herd while dudes knocked it in the head."

The Charleston (South Carolina) *Evening Post* published this
commentary: "There are plenty of men in this country willing to

pay the sum of $1000 or more to be able to say that they shot and killed a buffalo, even though the animal is penned up on an island, where it has no show to escape. A number of such men have banded together to slaughter without mercy the last emblem of the mammoth herds which once stretched from the Mexican gulf to the Canadian line, and from the Alleghenies to the Pacific slope. The large sporting publications have been predicting for years that one day this herd would be destroyed in one fell swoop by a few human vultures, and now their predictions seem scheduled to come true, unless the public is aroused in time. Every honest man in America who learned of this atrocious attempt to butcher a few hundred head of buffalo going under the head of 'wild', but still tame animals which will advance in a body to accept morsels of food from willing hands of passing travelers, and who wishes to aid in preserving them to posterity, will be doing a humane act if they will protest in every way possible."

Outdoor Life and the *Hunter-Trader-Trapper* printed Lillie's appeal to their readers. Edmund Seymour, president of the American Bison Society, said, "None but poor sportsmen would join in such a hunt," and like expressions came from George Bird Grinnell, famed Indian authority and president of the Boone and Crockett Club. Dr. William T. Hornaday, of the New York Zoological Gardens, believed that "American men who know enough to shoot a rifle and ride a horse will have little stomach for playing at hunting with buffalo that are too wild to catch and too tame to kill."

Georgia newspapers printed Lillie's plea with emphasis: "It deals with a topic that we Americans are prone to treat lightly—and yet, it is something that should challenge the pride, the humanity and even the patriotism of all." The Buffalo *Times* said: "Pawnee Bill's appeal merits the careful perusal of every citizen whose heart and conscience rise up in protest against the careless, wanton and callous extermination of animals which are exclusively the typical fauna of the North American continent," and the Milwaukee *News* called it "no less than a bloody spree that cuts down the standing of the human race, and should be stopped."

The controversy gave the state of Utah a black eye in every section of the country. Following an attack upon Utah authorities by prominent clergymen, citizens and numerous organizations of Boston, Governor George H. Dern declared: "Utah has done everything possible to save the buffalo herd at Antelope Island. Easterners evidently believe the animals belong to the state. Both the island and the buffalo are privately owned, and the state hasn't the money to purchase the buffalo or the island. We have protested against the destruction of the animals, but there is little else we can do."

Governor A. T. Fuller of Massachusetts inquired if there was some way that the herd might be turned over to the city of Boston, which wanted them and would care for them. Governor Dern replied: "About the only way the animals can be saved is by some philanthropist or group of individuals donating the money with which to purchase them." He suggested that if the people of the United States in general were sufficiently interested, the island and animals might be purchased and the island converted into a national park. "There is an excellent beach here, and should such a resort be established, the animals would prove an asset."

At Fort Pierre, A. H. Leonard, who had received an avalanche of protests, stated that he was "willing to call the whole thing off and wire every hunter that intends to participate to that effect" if the governor of Massachusetts, state of Massachusetts, or any person or group of persons wished to purchase the buffalo. "I am willing to sacrifice a $25,000 profit that I will make should I carry the hunt through. However, if easterners wish to act, they must act soon." He refused to give the names of 106 hunters who had accepted his invitation to participate in the extermination.

Other governors joined Governor Fuller in an effort to bring the buffalo to New England. An organization was formed to raise funds with which to buy the herd and move it there, and Major Lillie left for Boston at once. On December 14, he was back home on Blue Hawk Peak, "assured that the Utah herd would be preserved."

In June, 1927, he was invited to Norfolk, Nebraska, as guest speaker before the National Convention of American Editors. It was attended also by many editors from Canada and Europe, and Lillie chose for his subject the preservation of buffalo and other wild animal life. At the close of the convention, he proceeded to South Dakota, where he was a guest of President Calvin Coolidge at the President's summer home in the Black Hills.

In 1930, Lillie was appointed by Governor William J. Holloway to go to Mexico City to attend the inauguration of the new President of Mexico, Pasqual Ortiz Rubio, as a special representative of Oklahoma. The Major had made Rubio's acquaintance during his Wild West show years, which added special interest to his visit. He was introduced to all the important officials of the Mexican government, and was not far from the entrance to the palace grounds when a would-be assassin, hidden in the immense crowd of fifty thousand people, fired upon the presidential party, wounding Rubio in the jaw.

The only time Pawnee Bill dabbled in politics was in 1928, when Senator Charles Curtis, a Kaw Indian, ran for vice-president on the Republican ticket with Herbert Hoover. It was Pawnee Bill and the Indians, whose votes were sought by the Republicans in their efforts to swing Oklahoma into the Hoover-Curtis column, that caused the Senator to pass up some of the big population centers of the country to make a visit into the heart of the Indian country at Pawnee. A powwow was given in his honor by the Kaw nation, and Pawnee Bill served buffalo meat to the visiting Indians.

From the south the Cheyennes, Arapahoes, Sac and Fox, Kiowas and Comanches came in full force. From the Five Civilized Tribes came Creeks, Seminoles, Chickasaws, Choctaws and Cherokees. Horse Chief Eagle of the Poncas led his band to mingle with these tribes. Bacon Rind, Tall Chief, Bear Track, Red Eagle, Fred Lookout and the Osage tribe moved to Pawnee that day, and thousands of white men, farmers and ranchers, who were big enough to forget partisan politics, came to hear the words of this son of the Kaws. Two Hoover-Curtis clubs were formed, one for Indians and one for whites. It was estimated that in his meetings over the state the Senator spoke directly to 200,000 people. In the general election in November, his ticket carried Pawnee County by a majority of 2,594 votes, and Oklahoma by over 150,000, in one of the greatest political landslides in the history of the republic. Pawnee Bill wrote:

The G. O. P. victory was due to the Indian. In the election Tuesday, the Indian at last came into his own. His vote put Oklahoma into the Republican column. In other western states his vote counted heavily.

For years the Indian has been a little child of the government. He was not given recognition. The government thought for him. Finally the real American was given the voting privilege. The Indian took advantage of the first recognition, gravely and sedately.

He went to the polls yesterday. He took his squaw and his boy and girl of voting age, and they cast their votes.

The Indian selected the Hoover-Curtis ticket because Senator Curtis, in whose veins the blood of the Kaw flows, told them Hoover would make a good white father.

They said, "Words of truth drip from the tongue of Uncle Charley. He is our blood brother. We will fight for him."

An Indian never goes back on his word.

They won in the battle of ballots. Today they are delighted and happy. In one day, they feel, they have grown up. They now feel they are a factor in the affairs of the nation.

This is good medicine. It places the Indian on a high hill instead of in a valley. It gives him new thoughts for the betterment of his race.

This recognition may serve to make him an asset instead of a liability to Uncle Sam.

On March 4, 1929, Pawnee and adjoining counties helped to inaugurate the men whom they had helped to elect, when a delegation of pioneers and 118 prominent Indians, representing seventeen different tribes, under the leadership of Pawnee Bill, marched down Pennsylvania Avenue in Washington in the ceremonies attendant to the installation of Herbert Hoover and Charles Curtis as President and Vice-President of the United States.

We took a special pullman train to the capitol city, and created some stir, just one ovation after another, from the time we left Pawnee until we returned. In every big city and many of the small ones, great crowds were at the station to see our train go through, and the press was very generous.

It was like being on the road with his Wild West show again.

16.

The Last Years

NOW SEVENTY, but still alert and active, Gordon Lillie searched for new adventure, new enterprise. He conceived the idea of building an Old Town and Indian Trading Post, a replica of those which dotted the frontier when they were the only contact between the westward-sweeping white race and the red hordes of the plains:

Behind this desire is but one thought—that of leaving to posterity a town with the construction and atmosphere of the days of the pioneer, who saw the country as I did in my boyhood, some fifty years ago, before the blight of the white man was upon it, before it was riddled with railroads, before the big race for money had started, when the American Indian was its ruler and master, when the cattlemen and post trader were its only merchants, and it was as restful and quiet as when God Almighty completed it and said, "It is good."

He chose a site on Buffalo Ranch two miles southwest of Pawnee on the western fringe of Black Bear forest, and on either side of Highway 64, where more than half a mile of gently rolling hills formed a natural setting for the memorial. The project was completed in 1930.

In the front open vista stood the trading post, built of split logs, standing sixteen feet in the air, with a low-pitched roof spread below their upper ends, and doors and window frames made of bark-covered strips. The building was rock-floored and sanded and covered a space of 40 by 80 feet. The interior had massive stone fireplaces, tables of tree stumps and hickory furniture. Gaping at the visitor from the rear wall stood a relic of the hard-drinking days of Old Oklahoma—the 2-John Bar, which for many years in Oklahoma City was known more to renegades and soldiers of fortune than to preachers and men of letters. Here again it had been set up, with mirror and brass rail, in mahoganic splendor, its shelf lined with de-alcoholized bottles of Johnny Walker, dry Martini, Four Roses, and Gordon's Dry Gin, reminiscent of the hectic days of its early supremacy.

If one turned his back to the bar and gazed left, he saw implements and accoutrements of another time—muzzle-loading rifles, pelts, beaded moccasins, chaparejos, broad-brimmed Mexican hats and other pieces of equipment built for utility rather than beauty which helped make the life of the pioneer possible as well as picturesque. Further along the wall stood the Major's curio collection, much of it consisting of gifts from great potentates, brought from the four corners of the world.

At the west end of the park stood a model of the mysterious ancient cliff dwellings of the Southwest, called the Tewa House. This monument at Old Town was also the museum, housing the unique collection of Indian relics and handicraft gathered by Pawnee Bill from various tribes, and it housed as well the administration and service systems of the trading post.

At the east end stood the Indian village, with the towering tepees of the Cheyennes, Comanches and Kiowas, the bark houses of the Seminoles and Pottawatomies, and the historical Pawnee Council House and mud lodges, replicas of the dwellings in the villages of the several branches of the Pawnee tribe in the Niobrara and Platte valleys, whose plans had been brought to the Pawnee reservation in '75 and '76.

Former members of Pawnee Bill's Wild West shows and his Indian friends were the sole custodians of the post. There were fifteen cabins for tourists, double bungalows made of logs to fit into the scene, but equipped with modern facilities. In the center of Old Town a big spring that had quenched the thirst of many a pioneer and marauding redman in the early days supplied an abundance of cold pure water for drinking, cooking and bathing.

And in the background grazed the buffalo.

Old Town was opened officially May 1, 1930. Governor Holloway of Oklahoma, General Sears, the old Indian fighter of Topeka, General Metcalf of the United States Army and many other prominent persons were honored guests. The Indian dances on this occasion were the most elaborate ever witnessed in Oklahoma. High school bands and other orchestras mingled modern music with the beat of the Indian tom-tom. Sight-seers, tourists, mildly curious question-makers, intensely interested students and itinerant news and feature writers made up the steady crowd of visitors that day.

One correspondent thought it "looked like something executed by a Hollywood expert in sets for moving picture productions." Another reflected: "When one ignores gasoline signs and the hum of motors, there is a strong suggestion of the purpose set forth. The soda-pop wagons and the knickered Indian daughters, however, indicate that even this will soon be gone, and that the last echoes of that great American symphony, The Winning of the West, will have been lost except to the printed page."

"It was planned not so much commercial as sentimental," observed the Arkansas City *Daily Traveler*. "It is Pawnee Bill's final contribution to the preservation of historic scenes and memories of the Great West in the making. They were rude, perhaps, but they proved powerful stepping stones, which lead to our present high state of civilization."

The opening of Old Town marked a climax to the life of showmanship and exploitation of frontier life which Lillie had begun fifty-five years before on this spot as a trapper, interpreter, teacher and White Chief of the Pawnees. On June 2, his car, painted and decorated for advertising purposes, with a large built-in calliope, left for Memphis, Tennessee, and points south and east on a mission of good will, inviting all tourists to come over Highway 64 to Pawnee and the Indian Trading Post. As the big automobile rolled down the streets, businessmen stood in their doorways and wished for it a successful journey.

For several years Old Town attracted tourists from all parts of the United States and the world. Huge crowds attended rodeos and celebrations, and prominent personages and famous Indian chiefs were always guests for the occasions. Less than a year after its completion, five hundred Boy Scouts held their annual rally at Old Town, and it became one of the outstanding events in the life of a Boy Scout, especially with Pawnee Bill as the host to all.

While the last years of his life seemed dedicated to keeping alive the traditions of the Old West, Lillie also promoted the new. He envisioned the great progress that the automobile would bring, and the highways that would traverse the West as the railroads had for many years. He helped build Highway 64 from a stagecoach road of the early days into an all-weather route from Little Rock, Arkansas, through Oklahoma to Raton, New Mexico. For three years he served as president of the Highway 64 Association, which he had helped to organize in 1927. Its headquarters were at Old Town, and the highway through Oklahoma was known as "The Pawnee Bill Route."

Shortly after, the association was rewarded with a federal marking, making it U. S. 64, and in 1933, it was extended through Tennessee and North Carolina to Raleigh and Fort Landing, with Manteo, the home of Sir Walter Raleigh's colony and the birthplace of English-speaking civilization on the American continent, as its eastern terminus. This highway also became the shortest route west to Grand Canyon and the Pacific Coast.

Major Lillie's activity in highway work brought him again into national prominence, and with the attendant publicity, various historical societies and movements and Old Timer reunions claimed his services and received his assistance.

He and May spent their summers in New Mexico at Taos among the artists. Here, on August 31, 1936, they walked down the stone-flagged path of the town plaza to the strains of the wedding march from Lohengrin, in celebration of fifty years of married life.

The simple ring ceremony which had joined a young showman and a little Quaker girl with pig-tails at Philadelphia a half-century before was repeated with Reverend James Airey of the St. Andrew's Episcopal Church of Houston officiating.

More than five hundred guests and spectators were present at the picturesque event. A simple altar was bedecked with flowers in Indian vases. Red, blue, green and purple Taos blankets draped a bandstand and hung from the courthouse balcony. Underfoot, Navajo rugs formed a pattern on the green grass.

The streets were lined with a strange mixture of old wagons and buggies and shining new automobiles. Cowboys and Spanish-American vaqueros sat astride restless ponies while stolid-faced Taos Indians in white blankets mingled with artists and tourists in modern dress.

PROCLAMATION

🙖   🙖   🙖   🙖   🙖

To the People of Taos, N. Mex.
GREETINGS:

WHEREAS, Now Gordon W. Lillie (Pawnee Bill) and his devoted wife May Manning Lillie will celebrate their Golden Wedding Anniversary in the Village of Taos, New Mexico, on Monday, August 31, 1936 at 12 o'clock, noon, by a public re-marriage ceremony, and

WHEREAS, by reason of the world wide acquaintance of these celebreties, many distingushed visitors from throughout the United States will be present, and, the Fox Movietone News is sending its sound equipment to record this momentous event, which will be shown in the motion picture theaters throughout the world, and it is a signal honor to our city, and

WHEREAS, it is deemed fitting that a holiday be declared on said day, between the hours of 12 and 2 o'clock p. m. in order that all may have an opportunity to participate in this ceremony

NOW THEREFORE, we the governing body of the Village of Taos, do hereby declare Monday August 31, 1936, between the hours of 12 and 2 o'clock p. m. a holiday and urge that all places of business be closed between said hours, and, that ALL CITIZENS ATTEND SAID CEREMONIES DRESSED IN NATIVE COSTUME.

WITNESS, our hands and the seal of said Village this 29th day of August, 1936.

John B. Sanchez. Mayor.

(Seal)

Al Pueblo de Taos, Nuevo México, SALUD:

POR CUANTO, Ahora Gordon W. Lillie (Pawnee Bill) y su devota esposa, May Manning Lillie celebrarán el Aniversario de sus Bodas de Oro en la Villa de Taos, Nuevo México, el lunes, Agosto 31 de 1936, a las 12 del día, volviéndose a re-casar en una ceremonia pública, y

POR CUANTO, y por razón del reconocimiento mundial de estos célebres, un gran número de visitantes distinguidos de todas partes de los Estados Unidos estarán presentes, y la "Fox Movietone News" va a mandar su equipo parlante para reproducir este importante evento, el cual será enseñado en los teatros del cine por todo el mundo, lo cual significa un honor para nuestra ciudad, y

POR CUANTO, se le pide a todos los ciudadanos de Taos de que demuestren su aprecio de honor atendiendo en masa y usando trajes nativos durante la ceremonia, y

POR CUANTO Se pide de que un día de fiesta sea declarado, en dicho día, entre las horas de las 12 y 2 p. m. a modo de que todos los obreros tengan oportunidad para participar en esta ceremonia,

AHORA POR LO TANTO, nosotros el cuerpo gobernante de la Villa de Taos, por estas declaramos el lunes, Agosto 31, 1936, entre las horas de las 12 y 2 p. m. un día de fiesta y pedimos de que todos los lugares de negocios sean cerrados durante dichas horas, y, de que todos los ciudadanos atiendan dichas ceremonias vestidos con trajes nativos.
TESTIFICAN, nuestras manos y el sello de dicha Villa, este día 29 de Agosto, 1936.

John B. Sanchez, Mayor.

(Sello)

The bride wore a blue gown of lace and chiffon, with a lace turban to match covering her graying hair. She carried a corsage of gardenias and roses.

Pawnee Bill was attired in a buckskin suit, gauntlets, black shirt and tan four-gallon hat, the apparel he had worn at the wedding in the little Philadelphia church.

A gold-tinted automobile was presented them by admirers.

On the night of September 13, they were returning to Pawnee from Tulsa, where they had visited a host of friends and had previewed the film of the wedding which motion picture companies had made for the newsreels. It was a time of great happiness for May Lillie and her gray-haired husband. Lillie was driving the golden automobile.

Apparently blinded by lights and confused by turns in the dark, oiled road near Cleveland, between Tulsa and Pawnee, he crashed head-on with an approaching car.

Pawnee Bill suffered a severe scalp wound. May received a concussion and fractured right knee. Throughout the night she weakened and administrations of oxygen failed to revive her. She died with her husband at her bedside.

Hundreds of friends came from afar in token of their love and esteem for this woman, once her husband's Wild West show star, who had displayed amazing feats of marksmanship from the back of a racing horse, and to speak words of sympathy to the bereaved Pawnee Bill. The procession of cars that followed the remains to the cemetery was more than a mile long, and a number of cars and one large truck were required to carry the flowers and wreaths sent by neighboring mourners, as well as by friends from all over the United States.

Pawnee Bill went back to the big ranch house on top of Blue Hawk Peak. He now ruled alone the vast frontier empire so long made cheery by his beloved wife.

He had lost his single real interest in life. The rest didn't matter:

I never stopped until May passed away. I didn't know until then that she was everything to me. There wouldn't have been any Pawnee Bill if it had not been for her. I did everything for May, and now I know that it was her approval which kept me going. We had fifty years of happy married life, and that is much more than my share. I'll just try to keep busy now.

He spent his last days driving about Buffalo Ranch and his other properties in his Pierce Arrow, with his white hair flowing, wearing his characteristic Stetson, and his unmistakable western air. At seventy-nine, he completed plans whereby his spectacular mansion with its painting, finery and handicraft, which any museum would have rejoiced to have, would go to the Boy Scouts of America, and with it his spotted Indian ponies and buffalo.

It is my hope it will be kept as a sort of reminder of an old fellow who was always interested in children—and of his wife who was a thoroughbred any way you looked at her.

He leased out the post management, which still gave employment to many Indian families. In 1939, Old Town burned, and with it went many valuable relics and objects of art.

The end was nearing. On February 3, 1942, Pawnee Bill died in bed as the residents of the ranch prepared to celebrate his eighty-second birthday. His services were conducted on Blue Hawk Peak, and he was placed beside May and little Billy in the Lillie mausoleum at Highland cemetery.

With Pawnee Bill's death, the last of the picturesque characters of the drama of the winning of the West passed into the everlastingly verdant range where the grazing buffalo will never be disturbed by the shriek of the iron horse or the crack of the pioneer rifle.

Bibliography

Adams, Zu. "Biography of John Brown Dunbar." *Kansas State Historical Society Transactions*, 1907-08, Vol. X.

Annual Reports of the Commissioner of Indian Affairs to the Secretary of Interior, 1873-94. Washington: Govt. Printing Office.

Arkansas Daily Traveler, Feb. 18, 1930.

Atlanta Constitution, Oct. 19, 1890.

Avery, Cyrus S. "Why U.S. Highway 64?" *The Tulsa Spirit,* Sept. 19, 1928.

Barber County Index (Medicine Lodge, Kans.), June 29, 1944.

The Billboard, Vol. XX, No. 32, Aug. 8, 1908.

Biscup, Walter. "Buffalo Bill—How Many Indians Did He Kill?" *Tulsa World,* Jan. 24, 1937.

Blackwell Morning Tribune (Okla.), Dec. 26, 1929.

Boston Advertiser, May 13, 1911.

Boston American, Oct. 18, 1926.

Boston Herald, May 12-13, 1911.

Boston Journal, May 13-15, 1911.

Boston Post, May 10-15, 1911.

Boston Record, May 12-13, 1911.

Boston Traveler, May 13, 1911.

Bowman, James. "The Pawnee Indians from Nebraska to Oklahoma." *Pawnee Courier-Dispatch and Times-Democrat,* May 4, 1922.

Branch, E. Douglas. *The Hunting of the Buffalo.* New York: D. Appleton & Co., 1929.

Bridwell, Arthur. "Pawnee County—the Triangle Country." *Sturm's Oklahoma Magazine,* Vol. 6, No. 4, June 1908.

Bruce, Robert. *The Fighting Norths and Pawnee Scouts; Narratives and Reminiscences of Military Service on the Old Frontier.* [Mainly from extensive correspondence with Capt. L. H. North, 1929-32.] Lincoln: Nebraska State Historical Society, 1932.

Buel, J. W. *Heroes of the Plains.* New York: Parks Brothers, 1882.

Buffalo Times (N. Y.), Oct. 27, 1926.

Burke, John M. *Buffalo Bill, from Prairie to Palace. An Authentic History of the Wild West, with Sketches, Stories of Adventure, and Anecdotes of Buffalo Bill, the Hero of the Plains.* Chicago: Rand McNally & Co., 1893.

Burnham, J. H. *History of Bloomington and Normal, in McLean County, Illinois.* Bloomington: J. H. Burnham, 1879.

Caldwell News (Kans.), Feb. 1, 15, 1888.

Caldwell Standard (Kans.), May 8-9, 1884.

"The Centennial Celebration at Pike's Pawnee Village." *Kansas State Historical Society Transactions,* 1907-08, Vol. X.

Certain Lands in the Indian Territory. Senate Exec. Doc. No. 50, 48th Congress, 2d session.

Chicago Herald and Examiner, Oct. 20, 1926.

Chicago Journal, May 23-24, 1907.

Chicago Post, May 23-24, 1907, Jan. 4, 1911.

Chicago Tribune, May 21, 1911.

Clancy, Foghorn. *My Fifty Years in Rodeo, Living with Cowboys, Horses and Danger.* San Antonio: Naylor Co., 1952.

Clark, J. S. "A Pawnee Buffalo Hunt." *Chronicles of Oklahoma,* Vol. XX, No. 4, Dec. 1942.

Cleveland American (Okla.), Feb. 12, 1942.

Cody, Louisa Frederici, in collaboration with Courtney Ryley Cooper. *Memories of Buffalo Bill.* New York: D. Appleton & Co., 1919.

Cody, William F. *Life and Adventures of Buffalo Bill.* [Incorporating the original autobiography published in 1879, and extending it to 1888.] Chicago: John R. Stanton Co., 1917.

——. *The Life of the Honorable William F. Cody, Known as Buffalo Bill, the Famous Hunter, Scout and Guide.* Hartford, Conn.: F. E. Bliss, 1879.

——. *The Story of the Wild West and Camp-fire Chats.* Philadelphia: Historical Publishing Co., 1888.

——. *True Tales of The Plains.* New York: Cupples & Leon Co., 1908.

Cole, Redmond S. "History of the Opening of the Cherokee Strip." *Pawnee Courier-Dispatch and Times-Democrat,* Sept. 28, 1923.

Connelley, William Elsey. *The Life of Preston B. Plumb, 1837-1891.* Chicago: Browne & Howell Co., 1913.

——. *Wild Bill and His Era. The Life and Adventures of James Butler Hickok.* New York: Press of the Pioneers, 1933.

Cooke, Louis E. "The Wild West. Its Origin, Scope and Usefulness as an Education Exhibition." *The Billboard,* Oct. 2, 1915.

Cooper, Courtney Ryley. *Annie Oakley, Woman at Arms.* New York: Duffield & Co., 1927.

Crane, R. C. "King of Them All." *Amarillo Sunday News and Globe,* Golden Anniv. Ed., 1938.

———. "Then the Hunters Finished the Buffalo." *Amarillo Sunday News and Globe,* Golden Anniv. Ed., 1938.

Croft-Cooke, Rupert, and Meadmore, W. S. *Buffalo Bill. The Legend, the Man of Action, the Showman.* London: Sidgwick & Jackson, Ltd., 1952.

Custer, General George A. *My Life on the Plains, or, Personal Experiences with Indians.* New York: Sheldon & Co., 1874.

Daily Oklahoman, April 22, 1906, Dec. 18, 1910, Nov. 7, 1926, Aug. 30, 1936, April 23, 1939, Feb. 11, 1940, Feb. 4-6, 1942.

Daily Oklahoma State Capital (Guthrie), July 29, 1894, Feb. 13, 1906.

Dale, Edward Everett. "The Cheyenne-Arapaho Country." *Chronicles of Oklahoma,* Vol. XX, No. 4, Dec. 1942.

Davenport Daily Times (Iowa), June 12, 1907.

Davenport Democrat and Leader (Iowa), Sept. 29, 1929.

DeLysle, Jack. "Life of Pawnee Bill, Last of the Old Western Figures." *International Highways Magazine,* Vol. 1, No. 1, July 1935.

———. "Major Gordon W. Lillie (Pawnee Bill)." *Pony Express Courier,* Vol. II, No. 6, Nov. 1935.

Densmore, Frances. *Pawnee Music.* (Smithsonian Institution, Bureau of American Ethnology, Bulletin No. 93.) Washington: Govt. Printing Office, 1929.

Denver Post, Feb.–Sept. 1913.

Detroit Evening News, Aug. 8, 1890.

DeWolff, J. H. *Pawnee Bill (Major Gordon W. Lillie), His Experience and Adventures on the Western Plains; or, From the Saddle of a "Cowboy and Ranger" to the Chair of a "Bank President."* Pawnee Bill's Historic Wild West Co., 1902.

Dorsey, George A. *The Pawnee Mythology.* (Pub. No. 59.) Washington: Carnegie Institution, 1906.

Dubuque Times-Journal (Iowa), June 13, 1907.

Dunbar, John Brown. "The Pawnee Indians. Sketches: Their History and Ethnology, Their Habits and Customs." *Magazine of American History,* Vol. 4, No. 4; Vol. 5, No. 5, 1880-82.

El Reno Daily Tribune (Okla.), May 2, 1937.

Finney, Frank F. "William Pollock: Pawnee Indian, Artist and Rough Rider." *Chronicles of Oklahoma,* Vol. XXXIII, No. 4, Winter, 1955-56.

Fletcher, Alice C. *The Hako: a Pawnee Ceremony.* (Smithsonian Institution, Bureau of American Ethnology, 22d Ann. Rep., 1900-01.) Washington: Govt. Printing Office, 1904.

Foreman, Grant. *A History of Oklahoma.* Norman: Univ. of Oklahoma Press, 1942.

Forshey, Guy. "Diamond Dick Rounds Up His Old Pals: Dime Novel and Pioneer Heroes Come to Life at Norfolk, Nebraska, in One Last Celebration." *St. Louis Post-Dispatch,* Sunday Mag., July 10, 1927.

————. "He Killed 30,000 Buffaloes: Doc Carver, the 'Evil Spirit of the Plains,' Now Dead at the Age of 87, Was the Most Famous Pistol and Rifle Shot Who Ever Lived." *St. Louis Post-Dispatch,* Sunday Mag., Oct. 2, 1927.

Frank Leslie's Popular Monthly, July 1889.

Freeman, G. D. *Midnight and Noonday, or, the Incidental History of Southern Kansas and the Indian Territory.* [Incidents happening in and around Caldwell, Kans., 1871-90.] Caldwell: privately printed, 1892.

Garretson, Martin S. *The American Bison. The Story of Its Extermination as a Wild Species and Its Restoration under Federal Protection.* New York: New York Zoological Society, 1938.

Garrett, Virginia. "Number One Oklahoman." *Ponca City Profiles, a Miscellany,* May 1937.

Gentry, Bill. "Pawnee Bill—Farmer-Stockman—Raises White-Face Hogs and Buffalo." *Pawnee Courier-Dispatch,* June 29, 1916.

Gittinger, Roy. *The Formation of the State of Oklahoma, 1803-1906.* (Univ. of California Publications in History, Vol. VI.) Berkeley: Univ. of California Press, 1917.

Gloucester Advertiser (N. J.), July–Aug. 1888.

"Gordon W. Lillie—Pawnee Bill." *The Log of Long Bell,* Vol. VIII, No. 8, Aug. 1926.

Grinnell, George Bird. *The Fighting Cheyennes.* New York: Charles Scribner's Sons, 1915.

————. *Pawnee Hero Stories and Folk-Tales, with Notes on the Origin, Customs and Character of the Pawnee People.* New York: Forest & Stream Publishing Co., 1889.

————. *Two Great Scouts and Their Pawnee Battalion. The Experiences of Frank J. North and Luther H. North, Pioneers in the Great West, 1856-1882, and Their Defense of the Building of the Union Pacific Railroad.* Cleveland: Arthur H. Clark Co., 1928.

Guie, Heister Dean. "Buffalo Beef Industry Developed in Northwest by Yakima Man." *Portland Sunday Oregonian,* Dec. 11, 1932.

Hale, James H. "Brief History of Pawnee County." *Pawnee Courier-Dispatch and Times-Democrat*, Feb. 20, 1919.

Hamner, Laura V. "Stupidity of Plains Buffalo Was Partly Responsible for Its Rapid Extinction." *Amarillo Sunday News and Globe*, Golden Anniv. Ed., 1938.

Harlow, Victor E. *Oklahoma, Its Origins and Development*. Oklahoma City: Harlow Publishing Co., 1935.

Havighurst, Walter. *Annie Oakley of the Wild West*. New York: Macmillan Co., 1954.

Heizer, Chester C. "Pawnee Bill, Last of the Old West, Was Waiter in Caldwell Cafe When Town Was New." *Caldwell Messenger* (Kans.), Border Queen Ed., April 1956.

Hill, Luther B. *A History of the State of Oklahoma*. (2 vols.) Chicago: Lewis Historical Publishing Co., 1908.

Hornaday, William T. "The Extermination of the American Bison, with a Sketch of Its Discovery and Life History." *U. S. National Museum Report*, Part II. Washington, 1887.

Hornbeck, Lewis N. "When Oklahoma Was a Hunter's Dream." *Sturm's Oklahoma Magazine*, Vol. 5, No. 3, Nov. 1907.

Houston Chronicle, Nov. 27, 1938.

Houston Post, Aug. 1936, July 1937.

"How Pawnee Bill Rode In." *New York World*, May 5, 1889.

Hudson, John. "*Wichita Eagle* Was Real Founder of Oklahoma." *Wichita Eagle*, Nov. 29, 1931.

Hyde, George E. *The Pawnee Indians*. (Old West Series, No. 4.) Denver: J. Van Male, 1934.

———. *Pawnee Indians*. Denver: Univ. of Denver Press, 1951.

Indianapolis Journal, June 13, 1888.

Indian-Pioneer History (Foreman Collection). Indian Archives, Oklahoma Historical Society, Oklahoma City. Vols. 4, 32, 34, 38, 42, 44, 47, 51, 66, 76, 78, 93, 101, 104, 105, 106, 108, 112.

Jackson, A. P., and Cole, E. C. *Oklahoma! Politically and Topographically Described. History and Guide to the Indian Territory. Biographical Sketches of Capt. D. L. Payne, W. L. Couch, W. H. Osborn, and Others*. Kansas City, Mo.: Ramsey, Millet & Hudson, 1885.

Jenness, Captain George B. "Fight of Payne and the Boomers." *Sturm's Oklahoma Magazine*, Vol. 8, No. 2, April 1909.

Johnson, John C. "Versatile and Resourceful." *Safety Mutual News* (Tulsa), Vol. I, No. 8, Jan. 1937.

Johnson, W. Fletcher. *Life of Sitting Bull and History of the Indian War of 1890-91*. Edgewood Publishing Co., 1891.

Joliet Herald (Ill.), June 1907.

Joplin Herald (Mo.), Jan. 1911.

Kansas City News, June 1888.

Kansas City Star, June 1927.

Kansas City Times, June 1888.

Kennedy, Paul. "When the Noose Was Tightened." *Daily Oklahoman*, July 15, 1934.

Lake, Stuart N. *Wyatt Earp, Frontier Marshal*. Boston: Houghton Mifflin Co., 1931.

Lands in the Indian Territory. Senate Exec. Doc. No. 109, 48th Congress, 1st session.

Lawton Constitution (Okla.), March 13, 1929.

Leonard, Elizabeth Jane, and Goodman, Julia Cody. *Buffalo Bill: King of the Old West*. New York: Library Publishers, 1955.

Letter Press Copy Books, Kiowa Agency. (Feb. 27–Sept. 20, 1882.) Indian Archives, Oklahoma Historical Society, Oklahoma City.

Letter Press Copy Books, Pawnee Agency. Vol. 4 (May 25, 1881–April 1, 1885), Vol. 8 (Nov. 10, 1890–Feb. 17, 1892), Vol. 9 (Feb. 17, 1892–Sept. 1, 1893). Indian Archives, Oklahoma Historical Society, Oklahoma City.

Letter Press Copy Books, Ponca Agency. (Oct. 1–Dec. 17, 1889.) Indian Archives, Oklahoma Historical Society, Oklahoma City.

Lillie, Major Gordon William. "Cimarron County, Oklahoma, and U. S. Highway No. 64." *The Western Empire*, July 1930.

———. *Life Story of Pawnee Bill. Thrilling Stories of the Wild West. (By Himself.)* Topeka: T. O. Warfield, 1916.

———. *Major Gordon W. Lillie's Own Story*. [Unpublished ms. written in Kansas City about 1937.]

———. "Restoring the Bison to the Western Plains." *Cosmopolitan Magazine*, 1904.

Linton, Ralph. *Annual Ceremony of the Pawnee Medicine Men*. (Dept. of Anthropology, Leaflet No. 8.) Chicago: Field Museum of Natural History, 1923.

———. *Purification of the Sacred Bundles, a Ceremony of the Pawnee*. (Dept. of Anthropology, Leaflet No. 7.) Chicago: Field Museum of Natural History, 1923.

———. *The Sacrifice to the Morning Star by the Skidi Pawnee*. (Dept. of Anthropology, Leaflet No. 6.) Chicago: Field Museum of Natural History, 1922.

———. *The Thunder Ceremony of the Pawnee*. (Dept. of Anthropology, Leaflet No. 5.) Chicago: Field Museum of Natural History, 1922.

Logan, Herschel C. *Buckskin and Satin.* Harrisburg, Pa.: Stackpole Co., 1954.

Longview News-Journal (Tex.), Oct. 29, 1933.

Los Angeles Examiner, Oct. 1926, July 1939.

Lynn, Ernest. *The Blazing Horizon. The True Story of Pawnee Bill and the Oklahoma Boomers.* Chicago: White House, 1929.

Marble, A. D. "Oklahoma Boomers' Trials and Troubles." *Sturm's Oklahoma Magazine*, Vol. 6, No. 5, July 1908.

Mead, James Richard. "The Pawnees as I Knew Them." *Kansas State Historical Society Transactions*, 1907-08, Vol. X.

Memphis Commercial Appeal, May 1907.

Minneapolis News, June 17, 1907.

Minneapolis Tribune, June 1907.

Monaghan, Jay. *The Great Rascal. The Life and Adventures of Ned Buntline.* Boston: Little, Brown & Co., 1952.

Montreal Herald, Aug. 21, 1890.

Moore, Guy Rowley. "Pawnee Traditions and Customs." *Chronicles of Oklahoma*, Vol. XVII, No. 2, June 1939.

Mootz, Herman Edwin. *Pawnee Bill. A Romance of Oklahoma.* Los Angeles: Excelsior Publishing Co., 1928.

Morris, Lerona Rosamond. *Oklahoma, Land of Opportunity.* Guthrie, Okla.: Co-Operative Publishing Co., 1934.

———. *Oklahoma, Yesterday—Today—Tomorrow.* Guthrie, Okla.: Co-Operative Publishing Co., 1930.

Moulton, Robert H. "Giving the Bison a Chance To Come Back." *Illustrated World*, Vol. XXXVII, No. 5, July 1922.

Murphy, Thomas F. *The Hearts of the West.* Boston: Christopher Publishing House, 1928.

Muskogee Phoenix (Okla.), Sept. 1936, Jan. 1937.

The Nation's Highways (Oklahoma City), Vol. 8, No. 6, June 1928.

New Orleans Item, Dec. 18, 1910.

New York Standard, Jan. 7, 1911.

New York World, Dec. 24, 1910, Oct. 31, 1926.

Occupation of Indian Territory by White Settlers. Senate Exec. Doc. No. 20, 46th Congress, 1st session.

Oehler, Gottlieb F., and Smith, David Z. *Description of a Journey and Visit to the Pawnee Indians, Who Live on the Platte River, a Tributary of the Missouri, 70 Miles from Its Mouth, April 22–May 18, 1851, to Which Is Added a Description of the Manners and Customs of the Pawnee Indians.* (Repr. from *Moravian Church Miscellany*, 1851-52.) New York, 1914.

Oelwein American (Iowa), June 1907.

Oklahoma, a Guide to the Sooner State. (Compiled by workers of the Writers' Program, Work Projects Administration, Oklahoma.) Norman: Univ. of Oklahoma Press, 1941.

"Oklahoma Buffalo's Friend in Need." *Daily Oklahoman*, March 16, 1934.

Oklahoma News, Nov. 8, 1928.

Oklahoma War Chief, May–Aug. 1884.

Omaha Herald, Sept. 29, 1926.

Paducah News-Democrat (Ky.), April 1907.

Pawhuska News (Okla.), March 1929.

"Pawnee Bill, Famous Scout, Tells of Stirring Life of the Early Border." *Boston American*, Aug. 9, 1908.

"Pawnee Bill Gives Camp Site in Oklahoma to Boy Scouts." *Bulletin of Boy Scout Activities*, Nov. 8, 1930.

"Pawnee Bill Is Savior of the Buffalo." *Wichita Eagle*, March 9, 1924.

"Pawnee Bill Recalls His Part in the Cherokee Run." *Ponca City News*, Nov. 24, 1932.

"Pawnee Bill Recalls Sacrifice of a Territorial Thanksgiving." *Muskogee Daily Phoenix*, Nov. 26, 1931.

"Pawnee Bill Relates How and Why He Led Boomers into Oklahoma." *Daily Oklahoman*, April 18, 1926.

"Pawnee Bill's Wife. She Manages the Biggest Buffalo Ranch in the World." *Utica Saturday Globe* (N. Y.), Feb. 28, 1914.

Pawnee County Outlook, Nov. 14-21, 1907.

Pawnee Courier, Sept. 1936.

Pawnee Courier-Dispatch, Sept. 1905, Nov. 1907, Sept. 1908, July, 1909, April, Dec. 1910, Aug. 1913, Sept.–Dec. 1915, June–Nov. 1916, Jan.–July 1917, May 1918, March, Aug.–Dec. 1929, Jan.–March, May–June 1930, Feb.–April 1931, Oct. 1933.

Pawnee Courier-Dispatch and Times-Democrat, Jan.–Dec. 1921, May–Dec. 1922, Jan.–Oct. 1923, May–Nov. 1926, March–Nov. 1927, Feb.–Nov. 1928, Feb.–July 1929.

Pawnee Dispatch, Dec. 1895.

"Pawnee Indian School." *The Mirror* (Wichita, Kans.), Vol. 12, No. 26, March 20, 1897.

"Pawnee Indians Once Powerful." *Pawnee Courier-Dispatch and Times-Democrat*, Jan. 26, 1922.

Pawnee Naming Ceremonial. [Pawnee, Okla., Armistice Day, Nov. 11, 1932.] New York: privately published, 1933.

Pawnee Times, Jan. 1894.

Pawnee Times-Democrat, Aug. 1894 (Special Ed.), Jan. 1895, Oct.–Nov. 1907.

Peery, Dan William. "Captain David L. Payne." *Chronicles of Oklahoma*, Vol. XIII, No. 4, Dec. 1935.

———. "Colonel Crocker and the Boomer Movement." *Chronicles of Oklahoma*, Vol. XII, No. 3, Sept. 1935.

Philadelphia Dispatch, Aug. 12, 1888.

Philadelphia News, Aug. 19, 1888.

Philadelphia Press, Aug. 19, 1888, Jan. 8, 1911.

Philadelphia Public Ledger, Aug. 3, 1888.

Philadelphia Record, Aug. 30, 1936.

Philadelphia Sunday Republic, Aug. 12, 1888.

Philadelphia Times, July 20-23, Aug. 19-20, 1888.

"Pioneer Village Constructed by Pawnee Bill Is Reproduction of Old West." *Tulsa Tribune*, July 6, 1930.

Pittsburgh Sun (Pa.), Dec. 16, 1910.

Platt, Mrs. E. G. "Some Experiences as a Teacher among the Pawnees." *Kansas State Historical Society Transactions*, 1915-18, Vol. XIV.

Ponca City News (Okla.), March 1929, Feb. 1942.

Portrait and Biographical Record of Oklahoma. (Commemorating the Achievements of Citizens Who Have Contributed to the Progress of Oklahoma and the Development of Its Resources.) Chicago: Chapman Publishing Co., 1901.

Randolph, N. F. "Pawnee—in an Agricultural Paradise." *Sturm's Oklahoma Magazine*, Vol. 8, No. 3, May 1909.

Records, Department of Interior, United States Indian Service. (Oct. 1901–Feb. 1915.) [In re Chief Blue Hawk.]

Records of the Pawnee Indian Agency. (1880-1907.) Indian Archives, Oklahoma Historical Society, Oklahoma City.

Rister, Carl Coke. *Land Hunger: David L. Payne and the Oklahoma Boomers.* Norman: Univ. of Oklahoma Press, 1942.

Rogers Daily News (Ark.), Oct. 14, 1935.

Rucker, Alvin. "The Last of the Boomers." *Daily Oklahoman*, Dec. 16, 1928.

———. "Payne's Boomer Camp Fading." *Daily Oklahoman*, Jan. 22, 1928.

St. Joseph Daily Gazette (Mo.), May 25, 1888, Jan. 2, 1911.

St. Louis Post-Dispatch, May–June 1907.

Salt Lake Tribune, Oct. 23, 1926.

San Francisco Call-Post, Oct. 20-26, 1926.

Sarchet, Corb. "Because Pawnee Bill Went Broke with Show, He Made Run of 1889." *Ponca City News*, Nov. 27, 1932.

Sell, Henry Blackman, and Weybright, Victor. *Buffalo Bill and the Wild West*. New York: Oxford Univ. Press, 1955.

Shirley, Glenn. *Six-gun and Silver Star*. Albuquerque: Univ. of New Mexico Press, 1955.

———. *Toughest of Them All*. Albuquerque: Univ. of New Mexico Press, 1953.

"Short Route U. S. 64, from East to West, Owes Existence to Mason, Pawnee Bill, Gordon W. Lillie, the White Chief of the Pawnee Tribe of Indians." *The Masonic News*, Feb. 1934.

Shultz, Gladys Denny. "At Home on the Range." *The Home Desirable*, Vol. 6, No. 9, Sept. 1938.

Sorrenson, Alfred. "Life of Major Frank North, the Famous Pawnee Scout." *Columbus Times* (Nebr.), May 9, 1886–Jan. 30, 1887. [Serialized.]

Southwest American (Fort Smith, Ark.), June 1934.

Southwest Times-Record (Fort Smith, Ark.), April–June 1934.

Stevens, Jason. "To Pawnee Bill, Last Living Boomer Chief, the Run Was Good Showmanship." *Daily Oklahoman*, April 23, 1939.

Streeter, Floyd Benjamin. *The Kaw: the Heart of a Nation*. New York: Farrar & Rinehart, Inc., 1941.

———. *Prairie Trails and Cowtowns*. Boston: Chapman & Grimes, Mount Vernon Press, 1936.

Superior News Tribune (Wisc.), Jan. 12, 1911.

Sutton, Fred E. "The Big Five—Men Who Opened Oklahoma." *Daily Oklahoman*, April 21, 1929.

Taos Review (N.M.), July–Sept. 1936.

Terre Haute Post (Ind.), April 29, 1907.

Terril, I. N. "The Boomers' Last Raid." *Sturm's Oklahoma Magazine*, Vol. 8, No. 2, April 1909.

Thoburn, Joseph B. *A Standard History of Oklahoma*. (5 vols.) Chicago: American Historical Society, 1916.

Thoburn, Joseph B., and Wright, Muriel H. *Oklahoma, a History of the State and Its People*. (4 vols.) New York: Lewis Historical Publishing Co., 1929.

Tomblin, Marion N. "Pawnee—Echo of the Heroic Past." *This Week in Tulsa*, Souvenir Ed., Fourth Year, No. 23, June 10-14, 1929.

Treat, John Irving. *Indian Sketches, Taken During an Expedition to the Pawnee Tribes, 1833*. (Edited and annotated by John Francis McDermott.) Norman: Univ. of Oklahoma Press, 1955.

Trenton Advertiser (N.J.), Jan. 1911.

Trenton True American (N.J.), Feb. 1911.

"True Life of Major Gordon W. Lillie, 'Pawnee Bill.' " *Philadelphia Dispatch*, March 16, 1890.

Tulsa Tribune, Sept. 1928, Sept. 1936, Feb. 1942.

Tulsa World, April 1928, Jan.–Feb. 1937, Feb. 1942.

Tushkahomman, the Red Warrior. (A General Newspaper, Independent and Indianesque, Published in the Interest of 350,000 Indians in the United States.) Stroud, Okla., April 2, 1935. [Issue devoted to the Pawnee, Otoe, Ponca, Kaw and Tonkawa tribes, and to the home of Pawnee Bill.]

The United States Biographical Dictionary. (Kansas Vol. Containing Accurately Compiled Biographical Sketches, into Which Is Woven the History of the State and Its Leading Interests.) Kansas City: S. Lewis & Co., 1879.

Visscher, William Lightfoot. *Buffalo Bill's Own Story of His Life and Deeds.* (Memorial Ed.) Copyright by John R. Stanton, 1917.

Walsh, Richard J., in collaboration with Milton S. Salsbury. *The Making of Buffalo Bill.* Indianapolis: Bobbs-Merrill Co., 1928.

Wellington News (Kans.), Nov. 1884.

Wellman, Paul I. "Pawnee Bill Thinks of the 'Kids' in Last Act of Colorful Career." *Kansas City Star*, July 31, 1939.

Wetmore, Helen Cody. *Last of the Great Scouts. The Life Story of Col. William F. Cody, "Buffalo Bill."* Duluth: Duluth Press Printing Co., 1899.

Wheeler, Colonel Homer W. *Buffalo Days.* Indianapolis: Bobbs-Merrill Co., 1925.

White, Owen P. *Lead and Likker.* New York: Minton, Balch & Co., 1932.

Whittaker, Frederick. *A Complete Life of Gen. George A. Custer.* New York: Sheldon & Co., 1876.

Wichita Eagle, May–July 1874, June 1933.

Wild Life on the Plains and Horrors of Indian Warfare. (By a Corps of Competent Authors and Artists.) St. Louis: Royal Publishing Co., 1891.

Wilkinson, John W. "The World's Greatest Buffalo Ranch." *Oklahoma Farmer*, Vol. 23, No. 16, Dec. 15, 1913.

Winch, Frank. *Thrilling Lives of Buffalo Bill (Colonel Wm. F. Cody, Last of the Great Scouts) and Pawnee Bill (Major Gordon W. Lillie, White Chief of the Pawnees).* New York: S. L. Parsons & Co., 1911.

Winget, Dan. *Anecdotes of Buffalo Bill That Have Never Appeared in Print*. Chicago: Historical Publishing Co., 1927.

Wisconsin News (Milwaukee), Oct. 18, 1926.

Wood, Samuel N. *The Boomer. The True Story of Oklahoma, or the "Beautiful Land."* Topeka: Bond & Neill, 1885.

FICTION ABOUT PAWNEE BILL

BEADLE'S HALF DIME LIBRARY, Beadle & Adams, New York.

Ingraham, Colonel Prentiss. *Pawnee Bill, the Prairie Shadower; or, The Gold Queen's Secret*. 1888.

———. *The Buckskin Avenger; or, Pawnee Bill's Pledge*. 1888.

———. *Pawnee Bill's Pledge; or, The Cowboy Kidnapper's Doom*. 1890.

———. *Daring Dick, Pawnee Bill's Pard; or, The Red Cavalry Raid*. 1890.

WIDE AWAKE LIBRARY, Frank Tousey, Publisher, New York.

Braddon, Paul. *Pawnee Bill Doomed; or, The Great Scout in No Man's Land*. 1890.

———. *Pawnee Bill's Oath; or, The Oklahoma Scout's Lost Gold Cache*. 1890.

———. *Pawnee Bill's Shadow; or, May Lillie, the Girl Dead Shot*. 1891.

———. *Pawnee Bill's Double; or, The Great Scout's Best Trail*. 1891.

———. *Pawnee Bill's Gold Hunt; or, The Lost Treasure Train*. 1891.

———. *Pawnee Bill's Boys; or, The Young Boomers of Oklahoma*. 1893.

———. *Pawnee Bill; or, The White Chief's First War Trail*. 1897.

DIAMOND DICK LIBRARY, Street & Smith, New York.

Wheeler, E. W. *Pawnee Bill's Great Fight; or, May Lillie, the Rifle Queen*. 1896.

———. *Pawnee Bill and Jesse James; or, The Kansas Rangers*. 1896.

———. *Pawnee Bill at Work for Uncle Sam; or, On the Trail with Spotted Tail*. 1896.

NEW BUFFALO BILL WEEKLY, Street & Smith, New York.

Buffalo Bill and the Boomers; or, Pawnee Bill's Strike at Kingfisher. No. 242, April 28, 1917.

Buffalo Bill Calls a Halt; or, Pawnee Bill's Texas Tangle. No. 243, May 5, 1917.

Buffalo Bill and the Ke-Week Totem; or, Pawnee Bill's Blacksnake Magic. No. 244, May 12, 1917.

Buffalo Bill's Thunderbolt; or, Pawnee Bill and the Buffalo Killers. No. 287, March 9, 1918.

Buffalo Bill's Sioux Circus; or, Pawnee Bill, Prince of the Plains. No. 288, March 16, 1918.

Buffalo Bill's Medicine Trail; or, Pawnee Bill, King of the Rope. No. 291, April 6, 1918.

Buffalo Bill and the Red Bedouins; or, Pawnee Bill on the Great Staked Plains. No. 293, April 20, 1918.

Buffalo Bill and the Prairie Corsairs; or, Pawnee Bill's Red Razzle-Dazzle. No. 294, April 27, 1918.

Buffalo Bill's Scarlet Pick-up; or, Pawnee Bill's Comanche Capture. No. 295, May 4, 1918.

Buffalo Bill's Conquest; or, Pawnee Bill and the Gem. No. 298, May 25, 1918.

Buffalo Bill and the Klan of Kan; or, Pawnee Bill and Old Porcupine. No. 302, June 22, 1918.

Buffalo Bill and the Gambler; or, Pawnee Bill's Wonderful Discovery. No. 309, Aug. 10, 1918.

Buffalo Bill and the Toll Takers; or, Pawnee Bill at Hallelujah City. No. 311, Aug. 24, 1918.

Buffalo Bill and the Blue Masks; or, Pawnee Bill's Queer Pard. No. 312, Aug. 31, 1918.

Buffalo Bill and the Valley Terrors; or, Pawnee Bill's Great Round-up. No. 313, Sept. 7, 1918.

Buffalo Bill and the Affair of Honor; or, Pawnee Bill's Mexican Comrades. No. 315, Sept. 21, 1918.

Buffalo Bill and the Mysterious Ranchero; or, Pawnee Bill on the Twin Brother's Trail. No. 323, Nov. 16, 1918.

Buffalo Bill and the Silk Lasso; or, Pawnee Bill's Masquerade. No. 330, Jan. 4, 1919.

Buffalo Bill in Lost Valley; or, Pawnee Bill's Heroic Deeds. No. 332, Jan. 18, 1919.

Buffalo Bill's Outlaw Allies; or, Pawnee Bill's Danger Trail. No. 335, Feb. 8, 1919.

Buffalo Bill's Hard Chase; or, Pawnee Bill and the Saddle Knight. No. 342, March 29, 1919.

Buffalo Bill and the Amazon; or, Pawnee Bill and the Timber Thieves. No. 350, May 24, 1919.

Buffalo Bill's Escape; or, Pawnee Bill and the Running Fight. No. 351, May 31, 1919.

Buffalo Bill's Canyon Cache; or, Pawnee Bill at the End of the Game. No. 353, June 14, 1919.

Buffalo Bill's Government Mission; or, Pawnee Bill and the Night Alarm. No. 355, June 28, 1919.

WESTERN STORY MAGAZINE (formerly NEW BUFFALO BILL WEEKLY), Street & Smith, New York.

Buffalo Bill's Fiercest Fight; or, Drawing Lots with Pawnee Bill. No. 359, July 26, 1919.

Buffalo Bill's Navaho Ally; or, Pawnee Bill and the Cave Dwellers. No. 360, Aug. 2, 1919.

PLUCK AND LUCK, COMPLETE STORIES OF ADVENTURE, Harry E. Wolff, Publisher, New York.

Pawnee Bill in Oklahoma; or, Fighting with the White Chief. By an Old Scout. No. 1226, Nov. 30, 1921.

The Boyhood Days of "Pawnee Bill"; or, From the Schoolroom to the Frontier. By an Old Scout. No. 1356, May 28, 1924.